"The training offered by this book should be a staple in every school. Not only does it provide a breadth of understanding about students' emotions, but it discusses teachers' own emotions, their sources, and their role in professional identity and well-being, as well. This could allow an entire staff to learn the emotional competencies necessary to recognize and respond to students' emotions in a positive manner while teaching emotional skills. As a professor of future school leaders, I intend to use the work in this book to prepare administrators with critical tools to lead emotionally healthy schools."

–**Maureen Marshall**, Ph.D., *Assistant Professor of Education Leadership in the College of Education and Human Development at George Mason University, USA*

"This essential book identifies an unspoken truth: most, if not all, educators feel minimally prepared to address the majority of the challenges related to the emotions of children in classrooms. Pre-service training lays a foundation that must be further developed in order for educators to possess the efficacy required to respond rather than react to the emotions of children. By systematically addressing emotions in all necessary contexts, the authors have filled a void of attention within classroom management to issues of student engagement and success. This should be required reading for all educators and child-welfare professionals invested in educating the whole child."

–**Adam Cahuantzi**, M.Ed., *Program Manager of Multi-Agency Services at Fairfax County Public Schools, USA*

"Essential and applicable, this book is great for understanding the myriad of factors that contribute to a student's underlying emotional functioning and behaviors observed in the classroom. The examples provided are relevant and highlight the important interplay between emotional intelligence in teachers and emotional development and regulation in students. There are a variety of self-reflection and group activities to help teachers appreciate the concepts of emotional intelligence and learn self-care skills. I highly recommend this book for educators as well as mental health professionals, as it is an ideal resource for teacher in-service and professional development trainings."

–**Danielle Budash**, Psy.D., *Licensed Psychologist and Certified Trauma & Resilience Practitioner at Milton Hershey School, USA*

"This is an essential book for any teacher focused on social emotional learning in their classrooms. The small group activities and reflection opportunities in these chapters can truly expand teachers' responses to students as well as their understanding of what our students may be trying to tell us."

—**Shauna E.-v.d.M. Gilbert**, Psy.D., *Director of Special Education at Cardiff School District, USA*

Training Teachers in Emotional Intelligence

Training Teachers in Emotional Intelligence provides pre- and in-service teachers with foundational knowledge and skills regarding their own and their students' emotions. Teachers are increasingly charged with providing social-emotional learning, responding to emotional situations in the classroom, and managing their own stress, all of which have real consequences for their retention and student achievement. Focused on the primary/elementary level, this book is an accessible review of children's emotional development, the role of emotions in learning, teaching, and teachers' professional identity. The book provides strategies for teachers to foster their emotional awareness, use emotions to promote learning and relationships, foster emotional competencies in students, and stay emotionally healthy.

Elena Savina is a professor in the Department of Graduate Psychology at James Madison University, USA.

Caroline Fulton is a psychologist at Northwestern Medicine, USA.

Christina Beaton is a doctoral student in the Combined-Integrated Doctoral Program in Clinical and School Psychology at James Madison University, USA.

Training Teachers in Emotional Intelligence

A Transactional Model For Elementary Education

*Elena Savina,
Caroline Fulton, and
Christina Beaton*

NEW YORK AND LONDON

First published 2022
by Routledge
605 Third Avenue, New York, NY 10158

and by Routledge
2 Park Square, Milton Park, Abingdon, Oxon, OX14 4RN

Routledge is an imprint of the Taylor & Francis Group, an informa business

© 2022 Elena Savina, Caroline Fulton, and Christina Beaton

The right of Elena Savina, Caroline Fulton, and Christina Beaton to be identified as authors of this work has been asserted by them in accordance with sections 77 and 78 of the Copyright, Designs and Patents Act 1988.

All rights reserved. No part of this book may be reprinted or reproduced or utilised in any form or by any electronic, mechanical, or other means, now known or hereafter invented, including photocopying and recording, or in any information storage or retrieval system, without permission in writing from the publishers.

Trademark notice: Product or corporate names may be trademarks or registered trademarks, and are used only for identification and explanation without intent to infringe.

Library of Congress Cataloging-in-Publication Data
A catalog record for this title has been requested

ISBN: 9780367678371 (hbk)
ISBN: 9781032114064 (pbk)
ISBN: 9781003219774 (ebk)

DOI: 10.4324/9781003219774

Typeset in Bembo
by Apex CoVantage, LLC

Contents

About the Authors   xiii

1 Introduction   1

   Emotional Intelligence 3
   What to Expect From and How to Use This Book 4
      Chapter Summary 5
      Self-Reflective Activities 5
      Small Group Activities 5
      Self-Care Tool Kit 8

2 Features of Emotions   10

   Emotions Are Multidimensional 10
   Emotions Are Functional 11
   Emotions Are Informative 12
   Emotions Lead to Actions 13
   Emotions Are Contextual 13
   Emotions Are the Result of Appraisal 14
      Chapter Summary 16
      Self-Reflective Activities 16
      Small Group Activities 16
      Self-Care Tool Kit 18

3 Negative Emotions   21

   Anxiety 21
   Anger 23

  Sadness 24
  Shame and Guilt 25
   Chapter Summary 27
   Self-Reflective Activities 27
   Small Group Activities 28
   Self-Care Tool Kit 30

4 Positive Emotions   33

  Pride 34
  Gratitude 35
  Love 37
  Humor and Laughter 38
   Chapter Summary 40
   Self-Reflective Activities 40
   Small Group Activities 41
   Self-Care Tool Kit 41

5 Awareness, Expression, and Regulation of Emotions   43

  Emotional Awareness 43
  Emotional Expression 45
  Emotion Regulation 47
  Emotion Regulation Strategies 49
   Chapter Summary 51
   Self-Reflective Activities 51
   Small Group Activities 52
   Self-Care Tool Kit 55

6 Emotional Development of Children   58

  Attachment as a Foundation for Emotional Development 58
  Emotional Development in Early Childhood 60
  Temperament and Emotional Development 62
  Socialization of Emotions in Families 64
  Emotions in Children With Special Needs 65
   Chapter Summary 66
   Self-Reflective Activities 66
   Small Group Activities 67
   Self-Care Tool Kit 68

7 Emotions and Culture   72

   What Is Culture? 73
   Cultural Orientations 74
   Culture and Emotions 75
   Cultural Models of Ideal Affect 76
   Cultural Models of Parenting and Child Emotional
      Development 77
   Socialization of Emotions in Schools 77
   Emotions and Emotion Regulation in Different Cultural
      Groups 78
   Emotional Life of Immigrant Children 80
      Chapter Summary 81
      Self-Reflective Activities 82
      Small Group Activities 82
      Self-Care Tool Kit 84

8 Students' Emotions in the Classroom   88

   Sources of Emotions in the Classroom 89
      Emotions Directly Linked to Learning 89
      Teachers' Instruction and Behavior 90
      Emotional Contagion 90
      Peer Relationships 90
   Anxiety 91
      How to Reduce Anxiety in the Classroom 92
   Boredom 94
      How to Mitigate Boredom 95
   Curiosity 96
      Chapter Summary 97
      Self-Reflective Activities 97
      Small Group Activities 97
      Self-Care Tool Kit 98

9 How to Understand and Respond to Children's Emotions   101

   Placing a Child's Emotional Behavior
      in Context 102
   Emotions Signal a Child's Needs 103
   Awareness of Your Own Emotional Experiences and
      Reactions 104

Empathetic Attunement 104
Emotional Coaching 106
*What to Do When the Emotional Connection Is
   Broken* 107
   Chapter Summary 108
   Self-Reflective Activities 109
   Small Group Activities 109
   Self-Care Tool Kit 112

10 Dealing With Difficult Emotions in the Classroom   115

*Understanding the Emotions of Children With Insecure
   Attachment* 116
*Emotions and Emotion Regulation in
   Children With Trauma* 118
Tantrum in the Classroom 121
   What Can Cause a Temper Tantrum? 122
   Phases of a Tantrum 122
   *Emotions During a Tantrum and How to Respond to
      Them* 123
*Teacher Emotions When Responding to an Emotionally
   Dysregulated Child* 125
   Chapter Summary 126
   Self-Reflective Activities 127
   Small Group Activities 128
   Self-Care Tool Kit 131

11 Creating an Emotionally Positive Classroom   133

*Why Positive Teacher-Student Relationships Are
   Important* 134
Dimensions of Teacher-Student Relationships 134
Student Needs and Relationships 135
   Need for Relatedness 135
   Need for Competence 136
   Need for Autonomy 136
How to Infuse Positive Emotions into the Classroom 137
   *Have High Expectations and Confidence in Your
      Students* 137
   Make Students Proud of Their Achievements 138

Discipline With Care 139
What Can Undermine Positive Relationships in the Classroom? 140
Chapter Summary 141
Self-Reflective Activities 142
Small Group Activities 143
Self-Care Tool Kit 143

12 How to Foster Children's Emotional Competencies 145

Teaching Children Emotional Awareness Skills 145
How to Foster Emotion Regulation in Students 147
Teaching Student Emotion Regulation Self-Talk 148
Strategies to Reduce Emotional Arousal 149
  Deep Breathing 149
  Visualization 150
Teaching Children to Express Their Emotions 150
Strategies to Teach Emotional Vocabulary 151
Teaching Students to Understand Others' Emotions 152
  Chapter Summary 154
  Self-Reflective Activities 154
  Small Group Activities 155
  Self-Care Toolbox 157

13 Teacher Emotions in the Classroom 161

Sources of Teacher Emotions in the Classroom 162
  Students' Performance 162
  Student Classroom Behavior 163
  Changes in the Educational Setting 163
  Relational Context 164
  Teacher Self-Efficacy 164
Anger and Guilt in Teachers 164
Emotional Labor and Burnout 165
Teacher Emotion Regulation 167
  Chapter Summary 167
  Self-Reflective Activity 168
  Small Group Activities 168
  Self-Care Tool Kit 170

14 Teacher Identity and Emotional Well-Being — 174

   Teacher Professional Identity and Emotions 174
   Teacher Emotional Well-Being 176
     Be Aware of Your Goals and Values 176
     Develop Self-Efficacy 177
     Maintain Separation Between Professional and Personal Identities 178
     Focus on Positive Emotional Experiences 178
     Find Joy in Teaching 179
     Understand Things You Can and Cannot Control 179
     Find a Sense of Purpose and Meaning 180
     Strive to Build a Social Support System 180
     Create a Self-Care Routine 181
   Chapter Summary 182
   Self-Reflective Activity 183
   Small Group Activities 183

Index — 187

About the Authors

Christina Beaton received a master of science in counseling and human development degree from Radford University, with a specialty in school counseling. She was a middle school counselor for four years prior to pursuing her doctorate. Currently, she is a doctoral student in the Combined-Integrated Doctoral Program in Clinical and School Psychology at James Madison University. Mrs. Beaton's professional interests include developing social-emotional learning curriculums for PK–12 schools, training emotional competencies of educators, and integrating yoga and mindfulness practices into therapy.

Caroline Fulton attained her Psy.D. in clinical and school psychology at James Madison University. Prior to her doctorate, she worked for four years as a school psychologist, providing services for students and teachers. Currently, Dr. Fulton is a psychologist at Northwestern Medicine. Her professional interests include teacher emotional competence, parent and teacher training, and development of self-regulation in children.

Elena Savina received a Ph.D. in developmental and educational psychology from Moscow State Pedagogical University, Russia, and a Ph.D. in school psychology from the University of Central Arkansas, USA. Presently, she is a professor at the Department of Graduate Psychology at James Madison University. Throughout her career, Dr. Savina has also provided mental health services to children and adolescents, parent education, and teacher training. Dr. Savina is the author of books and articles on children's self-regulation and socioemotional development and learning.

CHAPTER 1

Introduction

Teaching and learning are both saturated with emotions. Students experience a wide range of emotions in the classroom. Some emotions result directly from learning. For instance, students might feel joy and pride when mastering a difficult task, but they might also feel anxious about making mistakes. Other emotions arise in a relational context. Some students might feel lonely when their friend is sick and does not come to school, and some might feel angry when they are not invited to play a game. Emotions have a powerful effect on learning: Positive emotions can ignite students' engagement and support the acquisition of academic skills, whereas negative emotions can distract students from learning. Moreover, when experiencing anxiety and boredom in the classroom, students perceive school as a place where they have to go every day but not a place they really want to be. Teachers also experience a wide range of emotions in the classroom. They may feel pride when a student who struggled with spelling does well on a spelling test. They also may feel anxious about an upcoming observation by the assistant principal or become angry when a student refuses to do an assignment.

The classroom represents a very complex social context where the teacher and students constantly interact with each other and respond to each other's behaviors. Furthermore, both teachers and students bring their expectations, beliefs, and goals to these interactions. Emotions arise at the intersection of teachers' and students' relational histories and events in the classroom. For example, a child whose parents do not provide him with enough attention may seek attention from his teacher. This child might feel upset or even angry if the teacher does not give him the desired attention. Quite often, teachers become affected by students' emotions and their life stories. Some students may not have breakfast in the morning, and some witness domestic violence. As a teacher, you need to be empathetic and caring. At the same time, you need to manage your own emotional reactions well so you will not become emotionally overwhelmed and distressed.

Teachers often have questions about emotions in the classroom: What emotions are appropriate to show to students? Can I show anger to my students? What are the best ways to handle my frustration? Teachers believe that mastery of the "right" emotions indicates professionalism (Zembylas, 2002). Some teachers think that they should be emotionally authentic with their students in order to build relationships in the classroom. Others may be reluctant to show their true emotions because they believe that emotions are private, or they may distract students from learning. Through reading this book, you will gain a better understanding of the nature of emotions and their role in teachers' professional lives.

As a teacher, you will have a great impact on the classroom's emotional climate and students' emotions. Schoolteacher and child psychologist Haim G. Ginott wrote in his book *Teacher and Child: A Book for Parents and Teachers*, "I have come to the frightening conclusion that I am the decisive element. It is my personal approach that creates the climate. It is my daily mood that makes the weather. I possess tremendous power to make life miserable or joyous" (p. 15). Teachers play a pivotal role in creating a positive emotional classroom environment, a key factor in effective teaching and learning (Pianta & La Paro, 2003).

You will need to understand your students' emotions. At first glance, it can seem simple and straightforward. For example, if Johnny is pushed by another student, it is reasonable to assume that Johnny feels angry. However, Johnny might also feel anxious or sad. Understanding why a person feels a particular emotion is not always easy. Have you noticed that the same situation might evoke very different emotional reactions in different people? Why is that? Because our emotional reactions are affected by many factors, including family, school, and culture at large. Through reading this book, you will learn how each of these factors influences our emotions and their expression.

Another important point is that teaching is a very demanding profession. Often, teachers have to manage many things in the classroom simultaneously. "Creating and sustaining a dynamic, engaging lesson . . . requires hard emotional work, investment, or labor. So too does remaining calm and unruffled when confronted by threatening student behavior" (Hargreaves, 2000, p. 814). Additionally, teachers have to build relationships with students, respond to their needs, and manage students' emotional reactions. As a teacher, you can be pulled in different directions and begin to question your role: Am I a teacher, a parent, or a therapist? To stay emotionally healthy and prevent emotional burnout, you need to learn how to understand and manage your own emotions.

EMOTIONAL INTELLIGENCE

Given the centrality of emotions for learning and teaching, it is important for teachers to be emotionally intelligent. What does it mean to be emotionally intelligent? Emotional intelligence is a set of competencies or skills that make people effective in social interactions and help them to understand their own emotions and the emotions of others (Bar-On, 2006; Mayer, Caruso, & Salovey, 2016). Emotionally intelligent people can use so-called affective forecasting, that is, to predict their own emotions and the emotions of others. This makes them better prepared to handle many situations. They can also manage their own emotions, reduce stress, and generate positive emotions (Bar-On, 2006; Mayer et al., 2016).

Research informs us that emotionally intelligent teachers are more effective in their instruction and behavior management in the classroom. They use emotions to promote engagement and learning. For example, they know how to reduce boredom and fuel curiosity. They use proactive and preventative classroom management strategies rather than reactive and punitive responses (Jennings & Greenberg, 2009). They are also more successful in managing classroom conflicts and creating a positive classroom environment (Valente & Lourenço, 2020; Valente, Monteiro, & Lourenço, 2019). Emotionally intelligent teachers help students to develop their cognitive and emotional skills (Jennings & Greenberg, 2009; Zinsser, Denham, Curby, & Shewark, 2015). Furthermore, they are less reactive in emotionally charged situations in the classroom (Perry & Ball, 2007). Emotionally intelligent teachers are attuned and responsive to students' emotional and academic needs. They can cultivate a positive classroom environment to promote student learning and warm, cooperative relationships. Having strong emotional skills protects teachers from burnout and helps them to stay emotionally healthy (Fernández-Berrocal, Gutiérrez-Cobo, Rodriguez-Corrales, & Cabello, 2017; Mérida-López & Extremera, 2017). Finally, they can successfully implement social-emotional learning curriculum in the classroom and promote students' emotional competencies.

WHAT TO EXPECT FROM AND HOW TO USE THIS BOOK

This book will provide you with knowledge about emotions, their sources, and their regulation. It will review children's emotional development and contextual factors, including culture and family, that can influence emotion socialization in children. It will further focus on students' emotions in the classroom, their sources, and their impacts on learning. Finally, it will discuss teachers' own emotions, their sources, and their role in professional identity and well-being. You will learn the emotional competencies necessary for you to recognize and respond to students' emotions, create emotionally positive classrooms, teach students emotional skills, and promote your own emotional well-being.

The book is based on a transactional, process-based training model. The transactional aspect of the model emphasizes that emotions emerge as a result of interpersonal transactions in the classroom informed by teachers' and students' personal histories and experiences. The process-oriented aspect highlights that teachers need experiential training to promote the awareness of their own and others' emotional experiences. The training model will further help you to build your sense of self-efficacy as an emotionally competent educator.

You will be asked to do several activities. In a self-reflection journal, you will reflect on your emotional experiences and your professional identity. Emotional reflection is an essential tool for understanding the emotional nature of teaching. For self-reflection activities, you will need to set aside about 30 minutes when you will not be interrupted by other commitments. You will also need a quiet place to complete the exercises.

In class, you will be involved in small group discussions and activities. You will work on vignettes depicting various emotional situations in the classroom. The vignettes will help you to understand students' and teachers' emotional experiences and how to manage these experiences. You will explore your beliefs about emotions and how they might influence your emotional behavior. You will also participate in role-plays to practice your emotional competencies.

Finally, you will learn several mindfulness and stress-reduction strategies as part of a self-care tool kit. It is recommended to practice these strategies every day. Like with a self-reflection journal, you will need a quiet place to practice self-care strategies.

Chapter Summary

- The educational experience is full of emotions, both positive and negative. Emotions affect students and teachers, the learning process, and social experiences.
- Emotions in the classroom depend on students' and teachers' relational histories and the appraisals they make in each situation.
- Teachers have a powerful influence on emotions in the classroom. Emotions also have powerful impacts on teachers and their professional lives.
- Emotional intelligence skills help teachers to be effective in social interactions and understand emotions in themselves and others. Emotionally intelligent teachers are more effective in their instruction and behavior management in the classroom.

Self-Reflective Activities

Part 1. Think about one of your favorite teachers and recall how you felt when you were with this teacher. Write down in your self-reflection journal why this person was your favorite teacher.

Think about one of your least favorite teachers and recall how you felt when you were with this teacher. Write down why this person was your least favorite teacher.

Part 2. Imagine yourself five years from now. Envision in great detail what you are doing, your classroom, and your students. What do you enjoy the most? What is challenging to you? What strengths, skills, or resources help you to do your job? Write down what comes to mind.

Small Group Activities

Activity 1. Beliefs About Emotions

In small groups, explore your beliefs about emotions using the following statements. Discuss why you agree or disagree with those statements.

- It is OK to let students know that you are angry.
- Teachers should show only positive emotions to their students.

- Teachers have to constantly control their emotions in the classroom.
- If you are upset, you do not need to show it to your students.
- Good teachers are those who know how students feel.
- Dealing with students' emotions requires a lot of energy.

Activity 2. Emotions in the Classroom

- List students' emotions in the classroom. Pick the three most frequently experienced emotions and discuss when (in which situations) students might experience those emotions and why they experience them.
- List teachers' emotions in the classroom. Choose the three most frequently experienced emotions and discuss when (in which situations) they might experience those emotions and why they experience them.

Activity 3. Emotional Charades

Have each group act out the scenario without any words. Use only gestures and facial expressions. Make sure to depict emotions. Ask other participants to guess what is being depicted.

SCENARIO 1

You are sailing on a sailboat. You are working together to hoist and man the sail to help steer the boat. As the boat sails out onto the ocean, a storm begins to brew. Suddenly, the ropes tying down the sail are unwound by the wind and the sail begins flapping aimlessly in the wind. The boat is tipping from side to side, and everyone on the boat becomes very scared. Just as suddenly as the storm blew in, the waters begin to calm, and the sun begins to come back out. The sail flutters back down so you are easily able to place the ropes in their rightful place, and you can pull the anchor back up so you can smoothly sail back home.

SCENARIO 2

Family members are in the kitchen preparing your Thanksgiving meal. One by one, people begin to notice a smell and search where it is coming from. One of you gasps as you open the oven to reveal billowing smoke. Someone grabs the oven mitts and pulls out the burned ham, a staple in your family's traditional Thanksgiving meal. One of you then realizes that you have another ham in the refrigerator and rushes to get it in the oven so that it is prepared in time. Everyone feels relieved and is able to go back to their tasks calmly while laughing at the mess the first ham made.

SCENARIO 3

A teacher team has been tasked with making the grade-level hallway bulletin board. You all convene in the hallway and begin taking down the previous bulletin board. As you do so, you also begin to show your different ideas for your bulletin board. You begin to argue in dyads (in pairs) or trios about the ideas you have. The argument morphs into a whole group argument, and you can see tensions running high. One person eventually says it must stop. Another person quickly makes a sketch of the bulletin board, and another grabs the cutouts. Holding up the sketch and the cutouts, everyone starts to see how it could form a nice bulletin board and begins to smile and laugh with one another.

SCENARIO 4

You are preparing to go on a vacation. Everyone is packing suitcases and putting them in the trunk of the car. You begin your road trip. Suddenly the car comes to an abrupt halt. The driver and passengers pile out of the car to see what the issue is and find one tire is flat. Someone goes to the back of the car to check for a spare tire and discovers there is no spare. Everyone gets upset about their vacation being ruined. Suddenly, you see a service station. It is about a quarter-mile down the road, so everyone would need to work together to push the car that far. Even though it is hard work, everyone is back to joking and having fun as they push the car toward the station.

SCENARIO 5

Children are playing outside. They are having fun and laughing. One mom comes outside to tell them to come inside to wash their hands, as dinner is almost ready. They all ignore her and pretend they did not hear. She asks them a little louder, and they continue to ignore her. Finally, she yells at them. The children ask for 15 more minutes. She stands her ground and says no. The children continue playing. The mother walks toward them and gives them "the look." The children drag their feet, heads hanging low, as they slowly approach the house.

Self-Care Tool Kit

Deep Breathing

Deep breathing is an effective strategy to reduce stress and anxiety. By breathing deep into your diaphragm, you decrease feelings of anxiety and frustration. It's important to practice deep breathing in situations when you are not experiencing negative emotions in order to master this skill and increase your ability to apply it in more challenging situations. It would be good to practice deep breathing for five minutes every morning and night to create the habit in a neutral situation, so it comes naturally when you are in a stressful situation. Here are the basic steps of deep breathing:

1. Sit or stand with good posture.
2. Breathe in slowly through your nose (about four seconds). You can count to enhance your awareness of how long you inhale.
3. As you inhale, take your breath into your lower belly.
4. Hold your breath for a few seconds.
5. Exhale slowly through your mouth (about four seconds). Try to exhale at the same count or slower than your inhale.

REFERENCES

Bar-On, R. (2006). The Bar-On model of emotional-social intelligence (ESI). *Psicothema*, *18*, 13–25. Retrieved from www.researchgate.net/publication/6509274_The_Bar-On_Model_of_Emotional-Social_Intelligence

Fernández-Berrocal, P., Gutiérrez-Cobo, M. J., Rodriguez-Corrales, J., & Cabello, R. (2017). Teachers' affective well-being and teaching experience: The protective role of perceived emotional intelligence. *Frontiers in Psychology*, *8*, 1–8. https://doi.org/10.3389/fpsyg.2017.02227

Hargreaves, A. (2000). Mixed emotions: Teacher's perceptions of their interactions with students. *Teaching and Teacher Education*, *16*, 811–826. https://doi.org/10.1016/S0742-051X(00)00028-7

Jennings, P. A., & Greenberg, M. T. (2009). The prosocial classroom: Teacher social and emotional competence in relation to student and classroom outcomes. *Review of Educational Research*, *79*(1), 491–525. https://doi.org/10.3102/0034654308325693

Mayer, J. D., Caruso, D. R., & Salovey, P. (2016). The ability model of emotional intelligence: Principles and updates. *Emotion Review*, *8*(4), 290–300. https://doi.org/10.1177/1754073916639667

Mérida-López, S., & Extremera, N. (2017). Emotional intelligence and teacher burnout: A systematic review. *International Journal of Educational Research*, *85*, 121–130. https://doi.org/10.1016/j.ijer.2017.07.006

Perry, C., & Ball, I. (2007). Dealing constructively with negatively evaluated emotional situations: The key to understanding the different reactions of teachers with high and low levels of emotional intelligence. *Social Psychology of Education*, *10*, 443–454. https://doi.org/10.1007/s11218-007-9025-z

Pianta, R. C., & La Paro, K. (2003). Improving early school success. *Educational Leadership*, *60*(7), 24–29. Retrieved from https://eric.ed.gov/?id=EJ666024

Valente, S., & Lourenço, A. A. (2020). Conflict in the classroom: How teachers' emotional intelligence influences conflict management. *Frontiers in Education*, *5*. https://doi.org/10.3389/feduc.2020.00005

Valente, S., Monteiro, A. P., & Lourenço, A. A. (2019). The relationship between teachers' emotional intelligence and classroom discipline management. *Psychology in the Schools*, *56*, 741–750. https://doi.org/10.1002/pits.22218

Zembylas, M. (2002). Structures of feeling in curriculum and teaching: Theorizing the emotional rules. *Educational Theory*, *52*(2), 187–208. https://doi.org/10.1111/j.1741-5446.2002.00187.x

Zinsser, K. M., Denham, S. A., Curby, T. W., & Shewark, E. A. (2015). "Practice what you preach": Teachers' perceptions of emotional competence and emotionally supportive classroom practices. *Early Education and Development*, *26*(7), 899–919. https://doi.org/10.1080/10409289.2015.1009320

CHAPTER 2

Features of Emotions

EMOTIONS ARE MULTIDIMENSIONAL

What are emotions? Many people would probably say that emotions are what they feel. This answer is correct but incomplete. Think about a situation when you felt anxious about an upcoming test. In addition to the feeling of apprehension, you likely experienced physiological reactions such as sweaty palms and a racing heart. You may also have had some thoughts about not doing well on the test. Your friends might see tension on your face, "telling" them that you are anxious. This example demonstrates that emotions are complex phenomena that have several dimensions: physiological, experiential, cognitive, and expressive. Let's take a closer look at each dimension.

Emotions are associated with bodily changes such as heart rate, sweating, muscle tension, or "butterflies" in the stomach. These reactions can be quite specific for different emotions. For example, when we feel angry, our finger temperature increases, but this does not happen when we feel fear. Our heart rate increases when we feel anger and sadness, but not disgust (Keltner, Oatley, & Jenkins, 2018). At the same time, smiling can reduce stress-induced heart rate.

Emotions also have an expressive dimension. This dimension makes emotions visible to others. The expression of emotions is important for telling others how we feel and also for understanding how other people feel (Scarantino, 2019). There are many ways to express our emotions, including facial expressions, posture, voice, gestures, and words. Keep in mind that facial expression of emotions can be ambiguous. For instance, a smile might mean happiness but it might also indicate embarrassment

(Keltner et al., 2018). In order to accurately decode the facial expression of an emotion, we need to know the context. For example, a student who smiles and avoids eye contact when caught doing something wrong likely feels embarrassed.

Emotions also involve subjective experiences, which are called "feelings." Broadly speaking, emotions can be experienced as pleasant and unpleasant. Interestingly, negative emotions are usually more intense, arise more rapidly, and are more difficult to regulate (Keltner et al., 2018). Such differences have an evolutionary explanation: Negative emotions might signal us about a threat to our survival. Therefore, delaying emotional reactions to potentially dangerous situations could cost people their lives.

Finally, emotions are associated with thoughts and beliefs. As you will learn later, emotions often arise as a result of appraisals people make about the personal meaning of situations or events (Lazarus, 2006). For instance, simply thinking about not doing well on a test can cause significant anxiety. Understanding that emotions arise as a result of appraisals is important for emotion regulation, as quite often we need to change our thoughts about the situation to change the way we feel. For example, changing a negative thought, "I will fail the test," to a positive one, "I will try my best," may reduce anxiety.

EMOTIONS ARE FUNCTIONAL

Some people may believe that emotions can derail our thoughts and make us irrational (Cole & Hall, 2008). Yet another belief is that we need to avoid negative emotions. These beliefs are not accurate. Emotions serve a very important function: They signal to us that something important is happening around us and prepare us for action (Cole & Hall, 2008). For instance, anxiety might signal that you want to do really well on an upcoming test but may not be sufficiently prepared. Therefore, emotions do not compromise our ability to engage in reasonable actions; instead, they help us adapt to changes in the environment (Cole & Hall, 2008). Ignoring or suppressing our emotions is not helpful, as it can limit our ability to adjust our behavior in accordance with changes in the environment.

Another function of emotions is to enable us to form and maintain relationships with others (Fisher & Manstead, 2008). Sharing emotional experiences with other people promotes intimacy. Emotions may also distance us from others when we feel anger, contempt, or fear. Emotions are contagious, as we tend to synchronize our emotions with the emotions of others (Anders, Heinzle, Weiskopf, Ethofer, & Haynes, 2011). We can do this because we have specialized brain cells called mirror neurons. When we observe the emotions of other people, we fire the same neurons as the person displaying those emotions. This is very important for our relationships with others. Essentially, it is the brain mechanism underlying our ability to understand others' emotions. Even when we imagine doing something, we activate the same neurons as if we were actually doing it. This has important implications for the classroom. When children see their teacher smile, they will likely smile also. However, if a student has an emotional meltdown, other students and the teacher may become emotionally aroused as well.

EMOTIONS ARE INFORMATIVE

When we see other people's emotions, we can use this information to make decisions about how we should respond. The facial expression of emotions is essential for our relationships with others. Not only does it signal to others how one feels, but it can also indicate his or her intentions (Barrett & Nelson-Goens, 1997). Therefore, facial expressions help us to decide whether we should approach or avoid another person. For instance, if someone smiles at you, you will likely interact with that person, while you would likely avoid a person with an angry face. The expression of emotions informs others about what we need. If you have a sad face, it tells others that you need emotional support.

Take a couple of moments to remember a time when you felt sad. What did your sadness say about what your needs were? You probably felt that you needed comfort and support from others. Emotions are important because they tell us about our psychological needs. Needs drive our behavior. That is why by attending to your own emotions and the emotions of students, you can better understand your own needs and the needs of others. For example, anger may signal a need for power, while anxiety may signal a need for control (Keltner et al., 2018).

Students' expression of emotions provides teachers with information about how they are doing on task. For example, students' anxiety might indicate that you set very high expectations that students cannot meet. Students' boredom, on the other hand, tells you that the topic is not interesting, or your presentation is not very engaging. Therefore, you need to modify your teaching and make it more interesting for the students.

EMOTIONS LEAD TO ACTIONS

Emotions prepare us for actions (Keltner et al., 2018). When we feel happy, we want to continue what we are doing. Anger might motivate us to try harder, while sadness might lead us to give up. Emotions have a motivational power and lead to actions (Izard et al., 2011). If we want to understand students' behavior, we need to look at the emotions that underlie their behavior. Furthermore, if you know how emotions work, you can use them to facilitate learning and positive classroom behaviors, as well as to prevent negative behaviors. For instance, curiosity leads to learning, and compassion leads to helping behavior. Therefore, by evoking curiosity and compassion in your students, you can facilitate positive behavior. We also know that anxiety often leads to avoidant behavior. Let's say that you have a student who asks for permission to go to the bathroom every time you give an independent math assignment. It is reasonable to assume that he may be experiencing anxiety associated with math performance. By addressing the student's anxiety, you can prevent avoidant behavior that leads to missed opportunities for learning. Anger, on the other hand, often fuels aggression. Therefore, diffusing anger in your students can prevent aggressive behavior.

EMOTIONS ARE CONTEXTUAL

Emotions are always affected by proximate and distal contexts – there are no emotions without context (Saarni, 2008). We bring our emotional expectations and experiences into communication with others. Distal contexts involve some events or experiences that happened in the past but might be triggered in the current context and affect how we respond. For example, a student who acts out in the classroom may be responding to something negative that happened at home. Teachers are in a similar situation. If you had several negative classroom incidents in the past, you may have doubts about your ability to manage difficult situations in the classroom. As a result, you might feel anxious if a student refuses to do his or her work. You may choose not to approach this student, thus leaving the problem unresolved. On the other hand, if you have been successful in managing challenging behaviors in the past, you would address refusal behavior with confidence.

Proximal contexts, on the other hand, involve events or experiences which happened in close proximity to a current situation. For example, students who were involved in a fight right before class started might react with anger toward you when you ask them to stop talking during your lesson. Keep in mind that your emotional behavior might also be impacted by some proximal event. If you just had a stressful conversation with a parent, you would likely have difficulty showing warm feelings to your students right away.

School creates another context for emotions. Each school has unwritten rules and values regarding emotions, such as which emotions are appropriate, and which are not. Some schools may discourage teachers from showing negative emotions and instead expect them to always look happy and positive. Schools are embedded in a larger culture that defines which emotions are appropriate, with whom, and when (Rothbaum & Rusk, 2011). Cultural studies show that mainstream American culture promotes high-intensity positive emotions because they signal to others, "I am well and successful!" In East Asian cultures, like China or Japan, people prefer not to show strong emotions because these emotions can damage good relationships with others. Later you will learn more about the impact of different contexts, including culture, on emotional experiences.

EMOTIONS ARE THE RESULT OF APPRAISAL

Emotions arise as a result of appraisal of a situation or event (Lazarus, 2006). "Appraising makes it possible to construct relational meanings, which refer to the significance for the individual of what is happening in the person-environment relationship, the most important aspect of which is interpersonal" (Lazarus, 2006, p. 12). In order to understand emotions, we need to place them in a context that includes the personality of individuals involved in the event, their goals, and their relational histories.

The classroom represents a unique intersection of the teacher's and students' goals and personal histories, which all contribute to emotional episodes and experiences. For example, you set high standards for yourself because your parents always expected the best from you. You prepare a lesson plan in advance and expect that things will go well. However, when delivering your lesson Friday afternoon, you observe tired and disengaged students who are not doing what you expected. It is reasonable to assume that you would feel disappointed or even angry. In this case, your expectations lead to negative emotions.

Emotions may also be evoked as a result of an inaccurate appraisal of a situation. For example, one of your students refused to do an assignment. You think that he does not want to do it because he does not like you as a teacher. As a result, you feel sad and defeated. Later, this student comes to you and shares that his father was deported from the United States, and he feels very sad. He apologizes that he did not do the assignment. Apparently, your appraisal was wrong! However, you experienced very real negative emotions based on your erroneous appraisal.

You probably wonder why we make inaccurate appraisals. We appraise a situation based on emotional schemas stored in our memories (Izard et al., 2011). These schema are developed through repeated experiences, and many schemas emerge early in life. Quite often, we are not aware of these schemas, but they have a powerful impact on how we understand social situations. For example, if parents repeatedly do not attend to their child's feelings, the child might develop a schema, "No one really cares about my feelings." The child may then choose not to show his true feelings, which, as you will learn later, is unhealthy. Similarly, if parents often criticize a child, he or she might develop a schema, "I am good for nothing." When a child has a task to complete, he might become apprehensive about the task and his ability to complete it. Hence, it is important for you to understand that your emotions and the emotions of your students might be rooted in schemas developed long before the current situation. An accurate appraisal of emotion-eliciting events will likely lead to successful regulation of emotions and appropriate use of emotional arousal to motivate actions (Izard, Stark, Trentacosta, & Schultz, 2008). Maladaptive emotion information processing makes emotion regulation more problematic.

Keep in mind that not all situations will lead to emotions, only those that have personal significance to us. When we have an important goal at stake, we likely have emotions that will signal to us about how we are doing in achieving that goal (Lazarus, 2006). The more important the goal is, the stronger our emotional reaction when the goal is accomplished or blocked. Recall a time when you finished a project you spent a lot of quality time on. How did you feel when you accomplished your goal? Very likely you felt happy. On the other hand, when we are unable to attain our goal, we feel sad. For example, you tried very hard but could not establish a good relationship with one of your students. So you gave up. The resulting emotion in this case would be sadness. Further, encountering obstacles to goal attainment often leads to frustration and anger. For example, you worked very hard to teach math skills to your students. However, students with significant behavioral problems derailed your efforts. Instead of teaching, you had to devote significant time to classroom management. These circumstances prevented you from attaining your goal and made you feel frustrated or even angry.

Chapter Summary

- Emotions include physiological sensations, subjective internal experiences, our thoughts, and the expressions we display.
- Not all emotions feel good, but all emotions have an important purpose. Emotions tell us about what is happening around us, provide us with information about ourselves and others, guide our actions, inform us of our needs, and help us to manage and maintain relationships with others.
- Emotions inform what we do and how we act. Depending on what we feel, we might be motivated to continue an action, do something differently, or move toward something else.
- The emotions we feel in a situation are influenced by prior experiences that occur around the time of the event (proximal) or even a long time ago (distal). Because we each have unique experiences and histories, the emotions that arise in the same situation can be very different across individuals.
- The meaning we make of a situation, called an appraisal, affects the emotion that results. Our appraisals are influenced by our history, what we think is important, our goals, and the role we see others as playing in a situation.

Self-Reflective Activities

Over the past week, recall at least two events or situations that made you feel happy or joyful. Reflect on those events and the feelings associated with them in your self-reflection journal.

Small Group Activities

Activity 1. Sharing About Your Most and Least Favorite Teacher

Share with your group your thoughts and feelings associated with your most favorite and least favorite teachers. Take turns in sharing. Observe the facial expressions and body language of your peers when they are talking about their most versus least favorite teachers. Summarize your ideas in the group. Be ready to present them to the whole group.

Activity 2. Dimensions of Emotions

Recall a situation when you felt happy or saw other people being happy. Recall your own physiological reactions, feelings, and thoughts. Then, recall a situation when you felt angry. Recall your physiological reactions, feelings, and thoughts. Complete Table 2.1.

Table 2.1

Emotion	Body Reactions	Feelings	Facial Expression/ Body Language	Thoughts
Happiness				
Anger				

Activity 3. Emotions and Appraisal

Read the following vignette and answer the questions at the end of the vignette.

> *Yesterday during her planning period, Mrs. Jones could not prepare an introductory lesson for a new math unit because she was busy substituting for a colleague at a special education meeting. When Mrs. Jones delivers the lesson the following day, students are silly and off task. Mrs. Jones's heart rate is increasing, and she feels herself beginning to sweat. She snaps at the students to "focus." When a student calls out, she quickly tells him that he has had enough reminders and is to go to the office.*

It is fair to think that Mrs. Jones is experiencing anger and anxiety. Her goal of preparing an effective lesson has not been achieved. As she watches the students struggle, she is experiencing a threat to her efficacy as a teacher. Her attributions and appraisals might take the following forms:

- "I hate this school; the administration has no respect for teacher time. When the kids fail the state tests this spring, they better not blame me." What emotions might be evoked from this appraisal? What actions could Mrs. Jones take based on that appraisal?
- "This group of kids is so low academically, why did I get assigned the low kids again? They never get anything. It feels like they're not even trying; how am I supposed to teach when they don't even listen to me?" What emotions might be evoked from this appraisal? What actions could Mrs. Jones take based on that appraisal?
- "It's so unfortunate that my planning was interrupted, I had envisioned this going very differently. It doesn't seem like they're getting it. How can I slow this down for today and adjust going forward? Maybe we'll just focus on two shapes today instead of five." What emotions might be evoked from this appraisal? What actions could Mrs. Jones take based on that appraisal?

Activity 4. Beliefs and Emotions

Consider a student who has arrived late to the first-period class. Teacher A becomes angry, thinking that the student is old enough to manage getting himself to class on time. Teacher B feels sad, thinking that the student missed the chance to have the school-issued breakfast he relies on. Teacher C feels anxious, anticipating the disruption to the lesson as the student settles into his seat.

Discuss in your group potential reasons why these teachers had different reactions. How might the teachers' beliefs and personal histories influence their emotional reactions?

Self-Care Tool Kit

Centering

Centering is a way that we can bring ourselves to the present moment and focus our attention on what is happening right now. This allows us to slow down and find moments of peace. Often, our minds are drawn to think about the past or future. This means that we do not focus on the present. Having a centering practice allows you to focus on the here and now. The following is a short centering practice that you can use to refocus your attention when you need it.

Begin wherever you are – sitting, standing, or laying down. Bring your attention to your body and give yourself permission to settle into it. You may stand a little taller, sit back into your chair, or let your body be supported by the ground. Now, lower or close your eyes and begin to focus your attention on your breath. Notice where you feel the most sensation as you breathe. You may notice a cool or hot sensation as you breathe out of your nose. Your breath may draw your attention to your abdomen as it moves in and out with your inhale and exhale. You may feel that your shoulders move up and down. Whatever you notice, focus your attention there. Pay close attention to the rhythm of your breath. Don't change it, simply notice if it is short or long, if you take long pauses or short pauses between breaths. Maybe your breath catches at some place in your body that you have never noticed before. Again, whatever you notice, focus your attention there. Now, bring your attention to a full breath cycle and notice what it feels like. Put your hand to your belly. On your inhale, notice what it feels like coming into your nose, moving down your throat, and filling your lungs. Notice your belly and your hand rise with it. Pause at the top. Do this for ten breaths. If you notice your attention is moving to something else, bring it back, focusing on your breath. When you are ready, begin to bring your awareness back to your seat or whatever is supporting you. You may want to move around for a second and notice if you feel any sensations throughout your body.

REFERENCES

Anders, S., Heinzle, J., Weiskopf, N., Ethofer, T., & Haynes, J. D. (2011). Flow of affective information between communicating brains. *NeuroImage*, *54*(1), 439–446. https://doi.org/10.1016/j.neuroimage.2010.07.004

Barrett, K. C., & Nelson-Goens, G. C. (1997). Emotion communication and the development of the social emotions. *New Directions for Child Development*, 77, 69–88.

Cole, P. M., & Hall, S. E. (2008). Emotion dysregulation as a risk factor for psychopathology. In T. P. Beauchaine & S. P. Hinshaw (Eds.), *Child and adolescent psychopathology* (pp. 265–298). John Wiley & Sons Inc.

Fisher, A. H., & Manstead, A. S. R. (2008). Social function of emotion. In M. Lewis, J. M. Habiland-Jones, & L. F. Barret (Eds.), *Handbook of emotions* (pp. 456–468). Guilford Press.

Izard, C., Stark, K., Trentacosta, C., & Schultz, D. (2008). Beyond emotion regulation: Emotion utilization and adaptive functioning. *Child Development Perspectives*, 2(3), 156–163. https://doi.org/10.1111/j.1750-8606.2008.00058.x

Izard, C. E., Woodburn, E. M., Finlon, K. J., Krauthamer-Ewing, E. S., Grossman, S. R., & Seidenfeld, A. (2011). Emotion knowledge, emotion utilization, and emotion regulation. *Emotion Review*, 3(1), 44–52. http://dx.doi.org/10.1177/1754073910380972

Keltner, D., Oatley, K., & Jenkins, J. M. (2018). *Understanding emotions* (4th ed.). Wiley-Blackwell.

Lazarus, R. S. (2006). Emotions and interpersonal relationships: Toward a person-centered conceptualization of emotions and coping. *Journal of Personality*, 74(1), 9–46. https://doi.org/10.1111/j.1467-6494.2005.00368.x

Rothbaum, F., & Rusk, N. (2011). Pathways to emotion regulation: Cultural differences in internalization. In X. Chen & K. H. Rubin (Eds.), *Socioemotional development in cultural context* (pp. 99–127). Guilford Press.

Saarni, C. (2008). The interface of emotional development with social context. In M. Lewis, J. M. Haviland-Jones, & L. F. Barrett (Eds.), *Handbook of emotions* (pp. 332–347). Guilford Press.

Scarantino, A. (2019). Affective pragmatics extended: From natural to overt expressions of emotions. In U. Hess & S. Hareli (Eds.), *The social nature of emotion expression* (pp. 49–81). Springer. https://doi.org/10.1007/978-3-030-32968-6_4

CHAPTER 3
Negative Emotions

ANXIETY

Think about a recent situation when you felt anxious. What prompted your anxiety? How did your body feel when you were anxious? What thoughts did you have? What actions did you want to take when you felt anxious?

Anxiety is a negative emotional state associated with a real or perceived threat (Rachman, 2019). These threats can be physical, emotional, or a threat to self-esteem, also called ego-threat. An example of a physical threat is a natural disaster. When hearing a tornado-warning siren, we often become anxious. In this case, there is a real and imminent threat to physical safety that makes us anxious. Another type of threat is emotional threat associated with the fear of not being loved. Children who have experienced emotional rejection from their parents often have heightened anxiety reactions in interpersonal situations where they perceive potential rejection. Ego-threat is activated when we are being evaluated. In this case, anxiety results from the fear that we do not meet certain standards, or we are not good enough. Ego-threat is especially relevant to classroom settings where students are being evaluated on a regular basis. If a student failed multiple spelling tests, he or she may have heightened anxiety when a teacher announces the next test. Students with low self-esteem are especially anxious in evaluative situations. And students are not the only ones who face evaluation at school. Teachers might also feel anxiety when their performance is being evaluated by the school administration.

Anxiety involves the apprehensive anticipation that something bad is going to happen and is often associated with anxious thoughts. For example, "I am going to fail this test," or "I will not get a good job." Anxious people often focus either on past or future events. They think of things like, "I wish I did not say that to my friend," or "I am going to fail this exam." Negative thoughts about past events are often associated with feelings of guilt, regret, or shame, while negative thoughts about the future fuel anxiety (Semple & Lee, 2008).

Quite often, it is not the situation but our appraisal of the situation that makes us anxious (Rachman, 2019). For example, you may interpret your shortness of breath as resulting from running or misinterpret it as a sign of an impending heart attack. If you appraise your shortness of breath as a sign of a heart attack, your anxiety will skyrocket. Since anxiety is an unpleasant emotion, people often try to reduce it (Rachman, 2019). The most common reaction to anxiety is to avoid anxiety-provoking situations. For instance, a student who has not been doing well in science might tell his mother that he is too sick to go to school on the day of the science test. A teacher might delay returning a call from a parent who indicated in her voicemail that the teacher is not doing enough to help her child perform well in math.

People who are vulnerable to anxiety often enter novel and intimidating situations with negative expectations (Rachman, 2019). These expectations make them hypervigilant to any potentially threatening stimuli. Furthermore, their attention narrows and focuses on potential threat signals but disregards other stimuli. This is called negative attentional bias. As a result, people may downplay positive events and miss joy in their lives. For example, a student who is anxious about being called on might be so focused on watching for a sign that the teacher is going to call on her that she cannot pay attention to the lesson or that other children are volunteering to answer. People who are prone to anxiety become self-focused and preoccupied with their worries (Wells, 2010). Worries may be triggered by intrusive thoughts that take the form of "what if" questions. For example, "What if something bad happens with the car when we drive to my parents' house?" "What if I do not have time to prepare for my exam?" Such worries take up a lot of mental resources and leave few resources left for performing tasks or other productive activities.

There are several anxiety-provoking situations at school for teachers, including performance evaluations, observations by administrators, telling parents that their child is not performing at grade level, receiving parent feedback, being questioned about instructional methods, having lesson plans scrutinized, or having unexpected adults visiting their classroom. For students, anxiety-provoking situations might include exams, being rejected by peers, teacher disapproval, reading aloud, being called on, having to work in groups, worrying about "what other people think about me," and getting into trouble.

ANGER

Now, think about a recent situation when you felt angry. What caused you to feel angry? How did your body feel when you were angry? What was going on in your mind? What actions did you want to take because of your anger?

Anger is associated with the blockage of a goal: "I want something, but I cannot get it." Anger can be adaptive because it helps us to attain difficult goals and overcome obstacles (Lemerise & Dodge, 2008; Williams, 2017). It also facilitates showing assertiveness and power. Regulated anger can help students persist with school tasks, as it motivates them to overcome difficulties. Empathetic anger makes us stand up for a victim (Hoffman, 2008). On the other hand, poorly regulated anger can fuel aggression, relationship problems, property destruction, and other behavioral problems.

You will probably be surprised to learn that anger can make people anxious, and this anxiety can make the anger worse! Why is this? For one, many children are taught not to show anger and may feel worried about the idea of acting angry. This may have some merit since anger in children often leads to aggression. We are also afraid that expressing anger can damage our relationships with others or that we would upset others. Unfortunately, when anger is not expressed, it goes inside us (Esposito, 2016). Unexpressed anger does not disappear; instead, it accumulates and becomes increasingly difficult to contain. That is why children whose anger is pent up often explode seemingly without reason.

Children who are prone to aggression often have what is called attributional bias. They erroneously perceive others as doing "mean" things to them intentionally. As a result, they make mistakes regarding people's intentions and behavior (Hudley, 2008; Schultz, Izard, & Ackerman, 2000). For example, a child may blame a peer who accidentally bumped into him in the hallway for doing it on purpose. It is not surprising that if the child interprets the action as purposeful, he or she would react with aggression. In another situation, when you raise your voice to calm down a class, the child with an anger attribution bias might mistakenly perceive you as being angry. Consequently, he might react with anger. Children may learn an anger attribution bias from their families. For instance, mothers of aggressive children often perceive their children's negative behaviors as intentional and respond with harsh punishment (Hudley, 2008). Aggressive children are likely to be rejected by peers which leads to more attributional bias and aggression (Dodge et al., 2003).

SADNESS

Now, think about a recent situation when you felt sad. What precipitated your sadness? How did your body feel when you felt sad? What thoughts did you have? What did you want to do when you felt sad?

Sad feelings emerge when we experience a loss of someone or something significant or perceive that we are no longer positively viewed by another (Karnaze & Levine, 2018). Sadness may also be a result of loss of meaning. Situations that usually evoke sadness include bereavement, separation from caregivers or significant others, social exclusion, ending of romantic relationships, or job loss. Missed opportunities to participate in pleasurable activities, lack of power or control, and goal failure may also elicit sadness.

We often want to avoid sadness – just think of how often we say to children, "Don't be sad. You will be fine." However, sadness can be adaptive and bring us benefits (Firestone, 2015). When we feel sad, our body and mind calm down, giving us time to reflect inward or revise our goals in order to compensate for a perceived loss (Bonanno, Goorin, & Coifman, 2008). The facial expression of sadness evokes feelings of empathy in others, connectedness, and a desire to provide social support. That is why "hiding" your sad feelings might not be a good idea because you might lose an opportunity to receive support from others. Sadness prompts cognitive change, including revision of one's goals, expectations, and beliefs (Karnaze & Levine, 2018). It further helps us to process loss, disengage from a goal that we cannot attain, and adjust our expectations. Such revisions contribute to our well-being, as we can invest ourselves in something more tangible that can lead to potential success.

While brief episodes of sadness have benefits, a longer depressive state is less helpful as it might lead to a feeling of powerlessness or helplessness (Lazarus, 1991). The problem is that people often confuse sadness with depression. While depression is a non-adaptive reaction to a painful event, sadness is a normal part of life. Sadness reminds us of what is important and what gives us meaning. Therefore, it is important to be in touch with your sad feelings and not push them away. While sad feelings are uncomfortable, they serve a purpose and will pass or diminish with time.

SHAME AND GUILT

Negative self-conscious emotions, shame and guilt, are elicited through self-evaluations of our own actions. They are also called "self-critical emotions," as they arise from the negative appraisal of one's self or actions (Miceli & Castelfranchi, 2018). We feel shame when we do something that may make others view us as "bad." Shame is an unpleasant emotion, and we try to avoid it. Therefore, it helps us to regulate our behavior and to avoid doing things that would make us feel bad. As such, shame helps us to maintain respect for ourselves. Shame is often experienced as a sense of being small, worthless, powerless, or exposed (Tangney, Stuewig, & Mashek, 2007). People who feel shamed may react with defensiveness or even anger. For example, a student caught salvaging food from the trash can to bring home may chase down the person who walked into the room, screaming for them to "get out." A teacher whose class performs worst in the grade level on state exams may angrily rant that she was given the lowest-performing students this year and fume that she was not given enough resources.

Guilt is also an uncomfortable self-conscious emotion. Like shame, it arises from self-reflection and self-evaluation (Miceli & Castelfranchi, 2018). Guilt signals to us that our behavior did not meet the standards we set for ourselves or that others set for us. Guilt has a regulatory function, as it makes us follow a social contract and behave in a prosocial manner. When we feel guilt, we try to repair what we have done. For example, a teacher who notices something missing from her desk and accuses her students of taking it would feel guilty when she later realized she had actually left the item at home. She would potentially repair her action by apologizing to the class for her hasty accusation.

If shame and guilt are unpleasant feelings, why would we have them? Recall that all emotions are functional and adaptive. Guilt and shame are no different. They give us feedback about our behaviors and inform us if we have done something wrong. In a sense, they serve as an emotional moral barometer that tells us if we are acting in socially and morally acceptable ways (Tangney et al., 2007). Shame and guilt also help us to maintain our standing in a group. If we did not have these emotions, we could act in our own interests without consideration of how we impact others. Lacking such feedback would lead people to engage more readily in negative behaviors like lying, cheating, or stealing. Those who engaged in these types of behaviors would be abandoned by their group. When people feel shame or guilt, they are less likely to repeat the behaviors that evoke those feelings in the future, thus protecting their ability to maintain a connection with others.

Keep in mind that too much guilt and shame have negative consequences for our well-being. Shame-prone people experience more emotional problems (e.g., anxiety and depression) than those less prone to shame reactions (Tangney et al., 2007). Those who feel shame frequently may develop so-called shame traits, including a pervasive sense of feeling less than others, hopeless, and powerless (Velotti, Garofalo, Bottazzi, & Caretti, 2017). People who often experience guilt may feel fatigued by their frequent attempts to please others. They may also have difficulty keeping healthy boundaries.

The emotions of shame and guilt share many characteristics and are often used interchangeably. However, there are important differences between them. Shame may lead to feelings of inferiority and inadequacy. In addition, it often causes us to retreat. Guilt is more likely to lead to a change in behavior. Consider a student who cheats on a test. If that person afterward thinks, "I cheated. I'm a terrible person," he or she is likely experiencing shame. If the same person reflects on the situation and thinks, "I cheated. I did a terrible thing," the feeling of guilt is more probable. The first evaluation (shame) is global and focused on the self, while the second (guilt) is more specific to the action and specific occurrence. This distinction often makes shame a more painful experience. When we feel ashamed, we are negatively evaluating ourselves, while guilt provides some separation between who we are and what we did.

Like all feelings, shame and guilt affect our behavior. Shame threatens our core self and motivates us to deny the shameful thing, hide, or get away from a situation that brings shame (Tangney et al., 2007). It is associated with a desire to escape (Terrizzi & Shook, 2020). Additionally, shame makes us self-focused and limits our ability to think empathically about others and to take reparative actions (Terrizzi & Shook, 2020). When shame threatens our sense of self, we want to protect ourselves by blaming others or external circumstances, and we might engage in hostile behaviors toward others (Tangney et al., 2007). In contrast, guilt leads us to think more about how our actions affect others. Because guilt is more about the things we did, there is a motivation to fix them by apologizing, telling the truth, or otherwise making reparations for the actions. In this way, guilt brings more action-oriented strategies where a person seeks to remedy his or her behaviors.

Keep in mind that the meaning of shame may be different across different cultures (Mascolo, Fisher, & Li, 2003). In the United States, shame has a stigmatizing connotation and, therefore, should be avoided. In China, shame plays a central role in moral education. Because shame is closely associated with obligations to others, it is not a threat to self-esteem and helps to build social relationships with others. Experiencing shame opens opportunities for self-improvement and restoring honor to others by fixing the situation. Interestingly, while in American culture shame and guilt are clearly differentiated, Chinese culture does not make a clear distinction between them.

Chapter Summary

- Negative emotions mean "unpleasant" but not "bad" emotions. All emotions have important functions and should not be avoided.
- Anxiety arises from a real or perceived threat of physical or emotional harm or harm to self-esteem. Our appraisal of a situation and the information we pay attention to affect how much anxiety is felt.
- Anger arises from not being able to reach a goal. Cultural beliefs about anger can lead to anxiety and feelings of uncertainty about how to express anger. Some people try not to feel anger, which can lead to unexpected outbursts later.
- Sadness is an adaptive reaction to loss. It helps us to get support and to develop new goals. Sadness is different than depression, which is a less adaptive experience.
- Shame and guilt are negative self-conscious emotions. They have important functions in regulating behaviors and social relationships.

Self-Reflective Activities

Part 1. Imagine you are a teacher in a classroom. What situations might make you anxious, angry, and sad? Write about them in detail. Reflect and write down how your emotions (anxiety, anger, and sadness) can affect your students.

Part 2. Recall one event or situation that made you feel ashamed. This could be a recent situation or a situation in the past. Who was involved in that situation? What made you feel ashamed? What did you want to do when you felt ashamed? Write down your experiences associated with shame. Recall another event or situation that made you feel guilty. This could be a recent situation or situation in the past. Who was involved in that situation? What made you feel guilty? What did you want to do when you felt guilty? Write down your experiences associated with guilt.

Small Group Activities

Activity 1. Beliefs About Emotions

Discuss your beliefs about emotions using the following questions:

- Is it OK to feel anxious? How might it be helpful? When would anxiety get in the way?
- Is it OK to feel angry? How might it be helpful? What kind of responses might anger evoke?
- Is it OK to feel sad? How might it be helpful? When would sad feelings get in the way?
- Do we always need to feel happy?

Activity 2. Vignettes

Discuss each vignette and answer follow-up questions.

> **Bennett**
>
> *Bennett, his friend Seth, and other children are playing "Truth or Dare" on the playground. They play rock-paper-scissors to determine who goes first. Bennett loses and Seth turns to him and says, "Truth or Dare." Bennett chooses Truth, as it seems to be the less risky of the two options. Seth says, "Bennett, tell us your deepest darkest secret." Bennett hesitates and thinks. He knows what his deepest secret is, but his parents have told him not to say a word to anyone. He tries to think of an alternative, but Seth catches him as he's trying to figure out what to say. "Bennett! You have to tell the truth, you picked it."*

Bennett can't think of anything else to say, so he blurts out, "We can't pay the electric bill this month so we're just going to live in the dark at home on peanut butter sandwiches." As soon as Bennett realizes what he said, he quickly covers his face with his hands and runs away.

- How does Bennett feel?
- Why do you think he feels this way?
- How would you address this situation if you were there?

Rachael

Rachael and Sabrina have been best friends since second grade. One day, Sabrina texts Rachael before school starts and asks her to take notes for her in math. Sabrina has been really struggling with the content but has to miss school to take care of her younger sister who is sick. Rachael promises she'll take great notes in class and will even help Sabrina after school to help her get caught up. As the day goes on, Rachael notices Sabrina is missing, but completely forgets about her promise. The math lesson seems easy, so she just listens and does not write anything down. At the end of the school day, she suddenly realizes what she did, and her face becomes hot.

- How does Rachael feel?
- Why do you think she feels this way?
- How would you address this situation if you were there?

Faculty Meeting

All the teachers are gathered for their monthly faculty meeting. The room is abuzz with talk about academic data and what the teachers have been doing in their classrooms to help the school meet accreditation standards. The principal walks in and everyone goes silent, as the look on her face is not pleasant. The principal pulls up a PowerPoint slide that displays the discipline data for the last month, divided by grades. Everyone gasps.

"Thank you for coming to our meeting this afternoon. I know you are all tired, but I wanted to bring your attention to something. As you can see, first and fifth grade are putting in a lot of work to make sure their students are behaving well. Their office referrals are down, the hallways are peaceful, and the students are really showing respect to adults and other students. I credit this to the hard work the teachers are doing to curb negative behavior. However, as you can see by this red column in the center, the

third-grade classes have more referrals than I have ever seen."

- How do the third-grade teachers feel?
- Why are they feeling this way?
- What thoughts are running through their heads?
- What can they do to make themselves feel better?

Mr. Gammon

Last year, Mr. Gammon was the elementary school teacher of the year, and everyone wanted to be just like him. He cares for his students very much, as shown by his willingness to stay after school to offer extra help and how much his students adore him. He tries hard to connect with all of them individually. One day, Mr. Gammon is letting students tell stories or show items they brought with them to class. He calls on each student one by one, always calling on the hand he sees raised. After he feels like all the students have had a chance to speak, he switches gears and begins a math lesson. All of a sudden, one of his students, Tyler, bursts into tears and runs out of the classroom. Puzzled, Mr. Gammon walks over to his desk and notices a little toy stuffed dog on his desk with a note attached to the collar from Tyler's grandfather who recently passed away. Mr. Gammon realizes he forgot to call on Tyler for show-and-tell.

- How does Mr. Gammon feel?
- Why does he feel this way?
- What thoughts are running through his head?
- What can he do to repair this situation?

Self-Care Tool Kit

Mindful Walking

Mindful walking helps us to be present. To begin this activity, find a space that allows you to walk. As you get used to it, you can incorporate this activity wherever you are – in the hallway, in the classroom, or at home. Begin by bringing your attention to your breath and taking a few breaths steadily in and out. Now, we will add some movement. First, begin to walk slowly, just noticing your breath with your steps, not changing anything, just slowly walking and breathing. As you are walking, notice any sensations you may feel throughout your body.

You may feel the ground beneath you as hard or soft, and you feel the temperature of the air on you. As you breathe in and out, notice how your breath is in rhythm with your steps. If it is not, try to synchronize your steps and your breath together, inhale step, exhale step. Begin to bring your attention to your feet as you walk. Notice when your heel touches the ground. Notice whether you feel the arch of your foot on the ground or in your shoe. Then notice the ball of your foot as you finish your step and move to the next one. Focus on the cadence of your walk – heel, arch, ball, heel, arch, ball, and repeat. Continue the pattern and notice any sensations you feel in your body that may not be your feet. You may notice your knees or your hips. You may pay attention to your arms swinging from side to side. Whatever you notice, be present there. Walking mindfully and being present.

The benefit of mindful walking is you can do it for however long or however short you need to. It can just be a couple of steps down the hallway to remind yourself to come back to the present, or it can be on a hike up and down a mountain to really focus on the present while you are in nature. In truth, it is a reminder that wherever you are and wherever you go, it is important to be there. You can continue this activity or finish wherever you would like.

REFERENCES

Bonanno, G. A., Goorin, L., & Coifman, K. G. (2008). Sadness and grief. In M. Lewis, J. M. Haviland-Jones, & L. F. Barrett (Eds.), *Handbook of emotions* (pp. 797–810). Guilford Press.

Dodge, K. A., Lansford, J. E., Burks, V. S., Bates, J. E., Pettit, G. S., Fontaine, R., & Price, J. M. (2003). Peer rejection and social information-processing factors in the development of aggressive behavior problems in children. *Child Development*, 74(2), 374–393. https://doi.org/10.1111/1467-8624.7402004

Esposito, L. (2016). The surprising emotion behind anxiety. *Psychology Today*. Retrieved from www.psychologytoday.com/us/blog/anxiety-zen/201607/the-surprising-emotion-behind-anxiety

Firestone, L. (2015). Compassion matters. *Psychology Today*. Retrieved from www.psychologytoday.com/us/blog/compassion-matters/201507/the-value-sadness

Hoffman, M. L. (2008). Empathy and prosocial behavior. In M. Lewis, J. M. Haviland-Jones, & L. E. Barrett (Eds.), *Handbook of emotions* (pp. 440–455). Guilford Press.

Hudley, C. (2008). *You did that on purpose: Understanding and changing children's aggression*. Yale University Press. Retrieved from www.jstor.org/stable/j.ctt1np78r

Karnaze, M. M., & Levine, L. J. (2018). Sadness, the architect of cognitive change. In H. C. Lench (Ed.), *The function of emotions: When and why emotions help us* (pp. 45–58). Springer International Publishing. https://doi.org/10.1007/978-3-319-77619-4_4

Lazarus, R. S. (1991). *Emotion and adaptation*. Oxford University Press.

Lemerise, E. A., & Dodge, K. A. (2008). The development of anger and hostile interactions. In M. Lewis, J. M. Haviland-Jones, & L. F. Barrett (Eds.), *Handbook of emotions* (pp. 730–741). Guilford Press.

Mascolo, M. J., Fisher, K. W., & Li, J. (2003). Dynamic development of component systems of emotions: Pride, shame, and guilt in China and the United States. In R. J. Davidson, K. Shrerer, & H. H. Goldsmith (Eds.), *Handbook of affective science* (pp. 375–408). Oxford University Press.

Miceli, M., & Castelfranchi, C. (2018). Reconsidering the differences between shame and guilt. *Europe's Journal of Psychology, 14*(3), 710–733. https://doi.org/10.5964/ejop.v14i3.1564

Rachman, S. (2019). *Anxiety* (4th ed.). Taylor & Francis Group. https://doi.org/10.4324/9780429458958

Schultz, D., Izard, C. E., & Ackerman, B. P. (2000). Children's anger attribution bias: Relations to family environment and social adjustment. *Social Development, 9*(3), 284–301. http://doi.org/10.1111/1467-9507.00126.

Semple, R., & Lee, J. (2008). Treating anxiety with mindfulness: Mindfulness-based cognitive therapy for children. In L. A. Greco & S. C. Hayes (Eds.), *Acceptance and mindfulness treatments for children and adolescents* (pp. 63–88). New Harbinger.

Tangney, J. P., Stuewig, J., & Mashek, D. J. (2007). Moral emotions and moral behavior. *Annual Review of Psychology, 58*, 345–372. https://doi.org/10.1146/annurev.psych.56.091103.070145

Terrizzi, J. A., Jr, & Shook, N. J. (2020). On the origin of shame: Does shame emerge from an evolved disease-avoidance architecture? *Frontiers in Behavioral Neuroscience, 14*, 19. https://doi.org/10.3389/fnbeh.2020.00019

Velotti, P., Garofalo, C., Bottazzi, F., & Caretti, V. (2017). Faces of shame: Implications for self-esteem, emotion regulation, aggression, and well-being. *The Journal of Psychology, 151*(2), 171–184. https://doi.org/10.1080/00223980.2016.1248809

Wells, A. (2010). Metacognitive theory and therapy for worry and generalized anxiety disorder: Review and status. *Journal of Experimental Psychopathology, 1*(1), 133–145. https://doi.org/10.5127/jep.007910

Williams, R. (2017). Anger as a basic emotion and its role in personality building and pathological growth: The neuroscientific, developmental and clinical perspectives. *Frontiers in Psychology, 8*. https://doi.org/10.3389/fpsyg.2017.01950

CHAPTER 4

Positive Emotions

Think about a recent situation when you felt happy. What precipitated your happiness? What was happening in your body and mind when you felt happy?

Research evidence strongly supports that people who experience positive emotions tend to have better relationships with others, cope better with stress, and are healthier and more resilient (Le Nguyen & Fredrickson, 2018). Your own experiences probably tell you that positive emotions feel good, but what is it that makes them so beneficial for us? A psychologist, Barbara Fredrickson (2013), has spent much of her career exploring how positive emotions work. Her broaden-and-build theory posits that positive emotions broaden our experiences and desire to learn and be creative. They also widen the scope of our attention and propel interest in exploring new things. Positive emotions can offset some of the impacts of negative emotions. During times when we experience positive emotions, we accumulate personal resources that we can use later when we experience distress. This accumulation is important because negative emotions will decrease those resources. Furthermore, when a situation elicits negative emotions, positive emotions help us to place a situation in a broader context, offering perspective and making the situation seem better. The experience of positive emotions can help to undo negative emotions (Fredrickson, 2013). For instance, experiencing negative emotions leads to an increase in cardiovascular activity, and subsequently increased heart rate and blood pressure. However, when we experience positive emotions right after negative emotions, the cardiovascular system returns more quickly to a normal state, thereby "undoing" the effects of the negative emotion. This finding is

DOI: 10.4324/9781003219774-4

very important for the classroom. After a stressful task or event, providing children with emotionally positive experiences can help them to recover more effectively from negative emotions.

There are many types of positive emotions, including, among others, joy, gratitude, love, and humor (Fredrickson, 2013). Positive emotions share a positive valence, meaning they are all subjectively experienced as pleasant or enjoyable. They vary in their focus and degree of intensity. For example, joy is associated with great pleasure and happiness, while serenity is a feeling that what we have is how we want it to be. Interest is an emotion related to new and potentially pleasant experiences. It propels learning and engages us with others or with a task. Amusement, on the other hand, is associated with experiencing something funny. Inspiration is a positive emotion that arises when we see something that impresses us and motivates us to improve. Hope is associated with anticipation of the possibility of something joyful. It often emerges in difficult circumstances, such as in the wake of a disappointment or when we think that something bad might occur. Hope may inspire us to take action. For example, a student who is repeatedly left out by his peers may hope that someone will invite him to play. He may then take steps to make friends with others.

Let's take a closer look at the positive emotions of pride, gratitude, love, and humor.

PRIDE

Pride is a self-conscious positive emotion. It is often elicited by attaining a desired status, overcoming a challenge, or when a positive outcome results from our efforts (Fredrickson, 2013; Keltner, Oatley, & Jenkins, 2018). Pride serves to enhance our self-worth. It motivates us to work hard or achieve in order to reach a social standard of worth or merit. Most often pride arises in scholastic, occupational, or athletic contexts, but it can also be tied to our moral behavior by meeting high moral standards. In the school context, a teacher may feel pride when she works hard on her lessons, and her students score well on the unit assessment. Students may feel pride when they read a chapter book alone for the first time or when they receive a high mark on a difficult test.

Pride has social and motivational functions as well. Showing pride communicates status and suggests that the individual should be respected as someone with power or influence (Bolló, Bőthe, Tóth-Király, & Orosz,

2018). Pride also offers feedback that an individual is well-regarded or that their behavior has increased their position within the group. Pride also feels good to the person who is experiencing it, making him or her more likely to repeat the behaviors that led them to feel that way. This can perpetuate social or leadership behaviors and support group functioning.

Pride can be divided into two types, each of which functions differently in social groups. In *authentic pride*, pride stems from internal and controllable causes (Bolló et al., 2018). For instance, if a person assessed that he or she had used his or her motivation to study hard for a test, authentic pride would arise from receiving a high mark. Those who frequently experience authentic pride are often well-accepted socially and feel true self-worth and self-esteem. As a result, the people around them respect them, trust them to share their resources, and perceive them as knowledgeable. This allows them to use constructive strategies, such as listening to others, maintaining an open stance, projecting confidence, and capitalizing on their achievements to maintain their social standing and influence (Bolló et al., 2018).

In contrast to authentic pride, *hubristic pride* is experienced as a result of external and uncontrollable forces. Consider, as an example, the pride a student feels when he makes the varsity football team only after his parents donate to the athletic department. Those who experience hubristic pride tend to engage in less prosocial behaviors and display more aggressive behaviors. Hubristic pride is associated with a tendency to be disagreeable, experiencing high levels of negative emotions, and having an inflated sense of self. Hubristic pride fosters a sense of arrogance and superiority. These can lead to relational difficulties and poor mental health. Those who experience hubristic pride tend to maintain their social standing through dominance strategies, such as threatening others, aggressive behavior, and excessive and disingenuous portrayals of self (Bolló et al., 2018).

GRATITUDE

Another positive emotion, gratitude, inspires us to be kind or to share our good fortune with others (Fredrickson, 2013). A teacher may feel grateful when school administrators take away her bus duty so that she can have more planning time. Students may feel grateful when their teacher provides them with extra help to prepare for an important exam.

As these examples show, gratitude is a positive emotion that arises from recognition that another person's actions were beneficial to us (Lomas, Froh, Emmons, Mishra, & Bono, 2014). Feelings of gratitude contribute to the give-and-take relationships with others.

Gratitude is a powerful emotion that has physical, psychological, and relational benefits (Lomas et al., 2014). Those who feel gratitude more frequently tend to have better overall well-being than those who do not. This is in part because gratitude fosters better relational interactions and social acceptance. Gratitude is also associated with empathy and forgiveness. Grateful people are more likely to behave kindly toward others, including helping or offering emotional support. People who experience more gratitude also have better sleep and get more exercise. Gratitude is an especially important emotional experience for teachers, as it can help protect against feelings of burnout and emotional exhaustion.

Since gratitude is beneficial to our psychological well-being, let's consider several strategies to promote grateful feelings. We can increase our experience of gratitude through noticing, recording, and reflecting. Here are some more specific ideas for how you might increase gratitude in your own life (Lomas et al., 2014):

- Build gratitude into a daily routine. Identify a time of day that you can spend time reflecting on your day and identifying one to two things you feel grateful for. This might be while driving home from work or just before sleep.
- Using a gratitude journal, you can spend time each week reflecting on the past week and writing down five things you feel grateful for. Consider when someone helped, went out of their way to make something easier for you, or offered you a small kindness.
- Replay moments that made you feel grateful. Visualize the event and the actions of the other person who helped you.
- Begin to notice how gratitude feels. Where do you feel it in your body? What is the sensation of gratitude like for you?
- Identify someone who has contributed to your professional path in some way. What did they do that helped you or shaped your professional interests? Write down why you are grateful to them in a letter.
- Notice and keep track of grateful moments you experience as they happen. Keep a piece of paper in your wallet or a file on your phone where you build a list of things you are grateful for as you notice them. Try revisiting your list when you are feeling low.

LOVE

Love is a powerful positive emotion felt in the context of connection to another person (Fredrickson, 2013). Students may feel love for their teacher, especially when they feel safe, respected, and understood. Teachers may also feel love for their students. The depth of this connection can be especially apparent as teachers prepare to say goodbye to their students at the end of a school year.

Love is characterized by positivity resonance, which describes a powerful, shared experience between individuals as their emotions sync and are reflected in one another (Fredrickson, 2016). Positivity resonance can happen between people who know each other well, like married couples, or between those who have only just met. There are several elements that foster positivity resonance. First, we share positive emotions with each other. Sharing emotions makes our positive feelings more powerful than when we experience them alone (Fredrickson, 2016). In fact, research has shown that sharing good news with others leads to increased positive feelings and makes events more memorable. Positivity resonance can also be achieved through mutual care and concern that make the other person feel important, worthwhile, or respected (Fredrickson, 2016). This mutual concern conveys that each person is cared for and creates an environment where it feels safe to share thoughts and ideas authentically. The last element of positivity resonance is called behavioral and biological synchrony. If you have observed two individuals engaged in warm and friendly conversation, you may have noticed how they mirror each other's postures and movements. During these interactions, the brain activity of both people synchronizes, aligning their internal pace and level of physiological arousal. The sensory connections between individuals are an important foundation for positivity resonance. Sensory connections include making similar eye contact, matching tone of voice, making physical contact (e.g., touching), mirroring facial expressions, and sharing body language. Research has indicated that these shared elements are important contributors to high-quality interpersonal relationships (Fredrickson, 2016).

Love is not an individual experience; instead, it is a connection that unfolds between and among people (Fredrickson, 2014). While love is an emotion experienced within your own body and brain, it triggers similar processes in the other person's body and brain. Love is rooted in connection, but you can still feel it when you are alone if you think about people you love or reflect on your past experiences of love. However, the physical presence of the other makes love very powerful. Unfortunately, we are often too busy to find time to truly connect with others and to enjoy these warm relational experiences. There seems to be ever-present pressure to achieve, complete chores, and respond to text messages or e-mails. As a result, many people lose their ability to slow down, be present, and be connected to others. Barbara Fredrickson (2014) encourages us to cultivate love every moment we can. This can be as simple as reaching out and hugging a loved one or sharing silly or inspiring ideas at the dinner table. These moments plant seeds of love and help us to stay emotionally connected to others. These seeds of love will ultimately bring fruits of positivity and optimism, which are very important for our well-being.

HUMOR AND LAUGHTER

Humor can help us to build relationships with others. It can also improve our performance by reducing anxiety and increasing motivation (Savage, Lujan, Thipparthi, & DiCarlo, 2017). Furthermore, it can decrease our levels of stress hormones and activate the brain reward system. Humor is beneficial if it is relevant to the situation and does not put others in a negative light. Humor can increase creative thinking and memory and is associated with life satisfaction (Martin & Ford, 2018). It can help us to save face when we feel embarrassed. Research studies evidence that a sense of humor is a desirable trait in friends and romantic partners (Martin & Ford, 2018). Humor allows shifting attention from negative elements of a situation to more positive ones. In the classroom, humor can reduce anxiety and boredom and make learning more enjoyable. When teachers use self-deprecating humor, it demonstrates to students that the teacher is a human being who can make mistakes and share this experience with others. It is important to avoid using humor at others' expense.

Laughter associated with humor is a form of communication when we express positive emotions but also evoke positive emotions in others. It helps us to bond with others and also synchronize and coordinate our interactions. Laughter is a universal and very powerful language that people share regardless of their birthplace or cultural identity (Savage et al., 2017). Laughing together builds a special connection between people. It is an especially important tool in the classroom where teachers might struggle to connect with students.

Furthermore, laughter can help us to reduce stress (Yim, 2016). Have you heard about laughter therapy? It is a kind of therapy aimed at increasing positive emotions and improving quality of life. Laughter decreases stress hormones, including cortisol and adrenaline, in the blood and as such can mitigate negative effects of stress. Furthermore, laughter can reduce depression and anxiety by increasing the activity of dopamine and serotonin, two neurotransmitters (brain chemicals) that affect our emotional states. Laughter is an easy remedy that can help you to recover from feeling down or anxious.

To increase humor and laughter, you can use these Seven Humor Habits (McGhee, 2010):

- *Surround yourself with humor.* Find the people you can share a good laugh with and seek them out. Model appropriate use of humor and you will find your students offering some back to you. In addition, be purposeful in seeking out amusing essays or audiobooks or saying yes to attending comedy shows or movies.
- *Cultivate a playful attitude.* It is easy to take things seriously. Make a purposeful effort to adopt a playful spirit and take this with you into your daily tasks.
- *Laugh more often and more heartily.* When something is funny (and not at someone else's expense), let yourself laugh. Relive funny moments by sharing funny stories with your teacher community and enjoy a wonderful, unrestrained laugh.
- *Create your own verbal humor.* Look for opportunities to bring jokes into your lessons or your social exchanges with your students. Banter with your friends.
- *Look for humor in everyday life.* You can be a professional teacher and still relish in the amusement around you. Both in and out of the classroom, be open to laughable moments.
- *Take yourself lightly: laugh at yourself.* Because you are human, you will inevitably mess things up along the way. Make a point to laugh at yourself and move forward.
- *Find humor in the midst of stress.* You will certainly find yourself at some point overwhelmed and thinking, "This is so bad, I could not have made it up." When life gets tough, relish the absurdity. Allow yourself to laugh even when things are stressful.

Chapter Summary

- Positive emotions have several important benefits. They promote exploration, generate interest, and allow us to attend to our broader environment. They can also help us to build our internal resources and offset some of the impacts of negative emotions.
- There are many types of positive emotions, including joy, hope, interest, amusement, gratitude, love, pride, and humor. All of these emotions share a pleasant or positive valence but vary in their intensity.
- Pride is a self-conscious emotion experienced in relation to overcoming a challenge or when desired results are achieved from our efforts. Authentic pride arises from internal, controllable causes and is associated with prosocial behaviors, good relational functioning, and constructive conflict resolution. Hubristic pride arises from external and uncontrollable forces and is associated with arrogance, superiority, and poor relational functioning.
- Gratitude is a type of positive emotion associated with physical, psychological, and relational benefits. You can generate grateful feelings by doing things like keeping a gratitude journal, replaying grateful moments, and taking time to purposefully thank others who have had a positive effect on you.
- Love is a powerful emotion rooted in connection with another. In exchanges with a loved other, there is sharing of positive emotions, mutual care and concern, emotional syncing, and sensory connections, like mirroring facial expressions. These make up *positivity resonance*, a special type of positive energy between individuals who love one another.
- Humor is another positive emotion with social, psychological, and physical benefits. Finding the humor in situations and laughing heartily can reduce stress, help overcome embarrassment, and promote connection with others.

Self-Reflective Activities

Think about a person or event that inspired you to be a teacher. What was it about this person or event that inspired you? What did it teach you about the value or importance of the teaching profession? How did you feel with this person or during the event? How did it change or inform your perspective of education? Reflect on this and write about it in your self-reflection journal.

Small Group Activities

Activity 1. My Favorite Place

Take a minute and think about your favorite place. Imagine that place in as much detail as possible. Share a story about your favorite place with the group. Tell what you like about it and how you feel when you are there. While listening to others' stories about their favorite place, observe their nonverbal behavior (e.g., facial expression, body postures, gestures, etc.). As a group, discuss the emotional experience of sharing and listening to the stories. Reflect on your level of positive emotions after this activity.

Activity 2. "Funny" Picture

As a group, pose yourself as a funny "picture" using your body postures and facial expressions. Take turns posing in your "picture" in front of the large group and make them laugh.

Activity 3. Gratitude Bouquet

To complete this activity, you will need to have markers, color paper, and poster paper. Make petal-shaped cutouts from colored paper. Have each group member write something that they are grateful for on each petal of the flower. Shape the petals into flowers to form a gratitude bouquet on the poster board. After finishing this activity, reflect on how you feel.

Self-Care Tool Kit

Basking

Savoring is a simple way to increase our positive emotions (Smith, Harrison, Kurtz, & Bryant, 2014). It might be feeling awe as you take in the beauty of a sunset, feeling grateful as you enjoy time with a friend, or slowly eating a delicious meal. Basking is a form of savoring. Basking is when we focus on a personal achievement or praise we have received. Take time now to write about a personal achievement. Include how you overcame obstacles to reach your achievement and consider the role of others in your personal achievement. When you complete your writing, reflect on how you feel.

REFERENCES

Bolló, H., Bőthe, B., Tóth-Király, I., & Orosz, G. (2018). Pride and social status. *Frontiers in Psychology, 9,* 1979. https://doi.org/10.3389/fpsyg.2018.01979

Fredrickson, B. L. (2013). Positive emotions broaden and build. *Advances in Experimental Social Psychology, 47,* 1–53. https://doi.org/10.1016/B978-0-12-407236-7.00001-2

Fredrickson, B. L. (2014, January–February). What is this thing called love? *Psychotherapy Networker.* Retrieved from www.psychotherapynetworker.org/blog/details/757/what-is-love

Fredrickson, B. L. (2016). Love: Positivity resonance as a fresh, evidence-based perspective on an age-old topic. In L. F. Barrett, M. Lewis, & J. M. Haviland (Eds.), *Handbook of emotions* (4th ed., pp. 847–858). New York: Guilford Press.

Keltner, D., Oatley, K., & Jenkins, J. M. (2018). *Understanding emotions* (4th ed.). Wiley-Blackwell.

Le Nguyen, K. D., & Fredrickson, B. L. (2018). Positive emotions and well-being. In D. S. Dunn (Ed.), *Frontiers of social psychology – Positive psychology: Established and emerging issues* (pp. 29–45). Routledge/Taylor & Francis Group.

Lomas, T., Froh, J. J., Emmons, R. A., Mishra, A., & Bono, G. (2014). Gratitude interventions: A review and future agenda. In A. C. Parks & S. M. Schueller (Eds.), *The Wiley Blackwell handbook of positive psychological interventions* (pp. 3–19). Wiley-Blackwell. https://doi.org/10.1002/9781118315927.ch1

Martin, R., & Ford, T. (2018). *The psychology of humor: An integrative approach.* Academic Press. https://doi.org/10.1016/C2016-0-03294-1

McGhee, P. E. (2010). *Humor as survival training for a stressed-out world: The 7 humor habits program.* Author House.

Savage, B. M., Lujan, H. K., Thipparthi, R. R., & DiCarlo, S. E. (2017). Humor, laughter, learning, and health! A brief review. *Advances in Physiology Education, 41*(3), 341–347. https://doi.org/10.1152/advan.00030.2017

Smith, J. L., Harrison, P. R., Kurtz, J. L., & Bryant, F. B. (2014). Nurturing the capacity to savor: Interventions to enhance the enjoyment of positive experiences. In A. C. Parks & S. M. Schueller (Eds.), *The Wiley Blackwell handbook of positive psychological interventions* (pp. 42–65). Wiley Blackwell. https://doi.org/10.1002/9781118315927.ch3

Yim, J. (2016). Therapeutic benefits of laughter in mental health: A theoretical review. *The Tohoku Journal of Experimental Medicine, 239*(3), 243–249. https://doi.org/10.1620/tjem.239.243

CHAPTER 5

Awareness, Expression, and Regulation of Emotions

EMOTIONAL AWARENESS

Take a moment and reflect on an emotion you feel right now. If you do not have any specific emotions, focus your attention on your body: Is it relaxed or tense? What can your body say about how you feel?

When we focus our attention on our emotional experiences, we are engaged in a process called emotional awareness. Emotional awareness is important because emotions provide us with cues to our needs and goals (Barrett, Mesquita, Ochsner, & Gross, 2007). For example, when we feel sad, it tells us that we need support from others, while when we are anxious, we need to regain control over a situation. People who have the ability to differentiate their own emotions also have better emotion regulation skills (Barrett & Gross, 2001). This is especially true for high-intensity negative emotions.

Having good emotional awareness is an important skill for teachers. When teachers attend to their own emotions, they are also more attentive to the emotions of their students and talk more about emotional experiences in the classroom (Ersay, 2007). One study showed that training pre-service teachers in emotional awareness improved their understanding of students' emotions and assisted them with emotion regulation (Perez, 2011). Teachers often experience more than one emotion at once in the classroom. Consider a teacher who is delivering a lesson that is going very well. She notices that her new student who recently emigrated from Ghana is wandering around and playing with materials on other students' desks. The teacher may feel pride in her lesson, frustration that she does not have enough resources to engage the new student, and anxiety that the student's performance on the upcoming state testing could negatively affect her performance evaluation. Being aware of mixed emotions in the classroom is important because it is easy for negative emotions to overshadow the positive ones.

Emotional awareness involves attention to several components of emotions. Attending to our body's signals helps us to understand how we feel (Price & Hooven, 2018). We can attend to physical sensations, such as feelings of tension, pain, or physical discomfort, as well as increased heart rate and respiration. Our energy level can also provide cues to our internal emotional states. For example, low energy may be associated with feeling down. Emotional self-awareness also requires the ability to recognize thoughts and attributions associated with emotions. Recall a recent situation when you felt anxious. Did you have anxious thoughts, for instance, "Something bad is going to happen," "I am going to fail this exam," or "My significant other is going to leave me"? It is important to be aware of thoughts associated with emotions because they can be the source of our emotions. We use emotion words to reflect on our emotional experiences. That is why having a rich emotional vocabulary is important for emotional awareness. Furthermore, putting feelings into words decreases the intensity of negative emotions through decreasing activity in the amygdala, the part of the brain that mediates emotional experiences (Lieberman et al., 2007).

It is important for teachers to be aware of their beliefs about emotions. Think about the following questions: Should we avoid negative emotions and only have positive ones? Can we change our emotions or not? Your answers to these questions may depend upon your beliefs. People who believe that negative emotions should be avoided often have anxiety and depression (Leahy, Wupperman, Edwards, Shivaji, & Molina, 2019). Beliefs about emotions are rooted in our personal experiences – for example, how emotions were expressed in one's family of origin. In addition, teachers acquire rules regarding emotional expression during their training. Importantly, ideas about emotional expression are embedded in a teacher's image of what it means to be a "good teacher" (Zembylas, 2002). Some teachers believe that "good" teachers have to hide their negative emotions from students.

Beliefs about emotions influence whether we accept our emotions or not. Emotional acceptance involves a nonjudgmental attitude toward emotions and a willingness to experience both negative and positive emotions (Chambers, Gullone, & Allen, 2009). This emotional skill is essential for our well-being and mental health. Clinical research has provided evidence that many emotional problems (e.g., depression and anxiety) result from people's inability to stay connected with their emotions. Sometimes we may experience an emotion about our emotion, called a secondary emotion. For example, you might feel angry with yourself that you were anxious during a job interview. Secondary emotions might interfere with our ability to fully experience and accept an emotion (Mitmansgruber, Beck, Höfer, & Schüssler, 2009). Teachers often believe that feeling anger, especially toward students, is not appropriate and may reflect that they are not "good teachers." As a result, teachers may experience guilt as a secondary emotion. This secondary emotion can hamper a teacher's ability to acknowledge the primary emotion, anger, but instead, deny or suppress it. While it might sound appealing to not feel anger, emotional suppression is not healthy. It leads to feeling more negative emotions and contributes to emotional burnout (Wang, Hall, & Taxer, 2019). Therefore, do not judge your emotions but accept them whether they are positive or negative.

It is important for you to understand proximal and distal factors that influence emotional experience. Teachers hold goals for the desired nature of relationships in the classroom, academic outcomes, and their performance (Frenzel, Goetz, Stephens, & Jacob, 2009). They also have attitudes about how students "should be" or what they "should do." These ideas influence the resulting emotional experience and behavior. That is why teachers should be aware of their professional goals and expectations. Additionally, you need to know triggers or circumstances that might elicit your emotional responses. For example, you might feel frustrated more often when teaching special education students if you do not have much experience working with them.

EMOTIONAL EXPRESSION

A teacher's emotional expression plays an important role in the emotional climate in the classroom and students' learning. Additionally, open expression of emotions promotes teacher well-being and reduces burnout (Oplatka, 2009). On the other hand, expressing emotions that one does not feel contributes to emotional exhaustion. For instance, teachers who fake their enthusiasm in the classroom often experience decreased well-being and lower job satisfaction (Taxer & Frenzel, 2015). Emotional expression is important for making others aware of our needs. For example, if you are able to say to the principal, "I feel frustrated and upset with my student's lack of progress," the principal may provide resources or offer needed validation for your ongoing efforts to support the student. However, if you decide to look "fine," you will not get the desired support.

There are many ways to express emotions. One way is to express emotions through words. Teachers need a good emotional vocabulary in order to do this. When using words to express your emotions, "I" statements are very effective. For example, you may say to your students, "I felt happy today because you worked so hard on your stories," or "I feel disappointed that we cannot go to the playground today." These types of statements teach students emotional words and model emotional expression. Teachers who engage in healthy emotional expression model to students that all emotions are acceptable and functional.

Another way to express emotions is through facial expressions and body language. In the classroom, teachers and students are involved in emotional communication where both parties send and receive emotion signals (Saarni, 2008). Teachers and students evoke and interpret each other's emotions and regulate each other's behaviors through the expression of emotions (Barrett & Nelson-Goens, 1997). Facial expression conveys information about one's emotional state and intentions. Teachers who display positive emotions send students a message that their behavior is desired and acceptable. On the other hand, the display of negative emotions, such as anger and disappointment, provides students with cues that they are not meeting expectations or are engaged in inappropriate behavior. Keep in mind that the overuse of negative emotional displays may elicit feelings of shame, hopelessness, and anger in students that would be counterproductive to changing the students' behavior.

Our relational histories and experiences influence how we appraise others' emotional expressions (Van Kleef, 2009). For example, when seeing a student with a sad face, Teacher A might think that the student needs comforting, while Teacher B could reason that she did something that made the student sad. It is easy to conclude that Teacher A is more confident in herself than Teacher B. Importantly, these two teachers would react differently based on their interpretation of the student's behavior: Teacher A would likely provide support to the student, while Teacher B might avoid approaching the student.

In the classroom, the teacher and students influence each other's emotions through emotional contagion. For example, a teacher who frequently feels down can unintentionally diminish positive emotions in her students. Similarly, a student who often looks sad might make the teacher feel sad as well. This emotional contagion means that the way teachers express and communicate their emotions in the classroom directly affects students. One study found that when teachers experience high stress, students' stress also goes up (Oberle & Schonert-Reichl, 2016). The good news is that teachers' and students' enjoyment is also reciprocally related: When teachers feel energized, students feel energized as well (Frenzel, Becker-Kurz, Pekrun, Goetz, & Lüdtke, 2018).

As you learned earlier, all emotions are acceptable and valid. It is *how* and *when* emotions are expressed that is important. Uncontrolled or explosive displays of emotion threaten students' sense of safety in the classroom. Skilled teachers can adjust the intensity of their emotions and present a genuine emotional expression without compromising a sense of security in students. Teachers' well-modulated emotional expression is especially important for children with a history of trauma. These children may feel threatened when witnessing an adult who is demonstrating strong emotions.

Finally, you have to be authentic in your emotional expression. If what you say and do does not match how you truly feel, it is disingenuous and potentially confusing to students. An example of this might be smiling while telling students that their grades were poor on a recent exam. This type of expression is problematic because students may become confused or infer that the exam was not important. Further, students are skilled in recognizing when adults are not being authentic.

EMOTION REGULATION

As you are learning from this book, all emotions are functional. However, when they become too intense and interfere with our activities, or they happen in the wrong context, we need to regulate them (Gross, 2015). Emotion regulation comprises the ability to accept one's own emotions, engage with emotional experiences that are desired, and disengage with negative emotions (Mayer, Caruso, & Salovey, 2016). The regulation of negative emotions is important for teachers, as it can impact the overall emotional climate of the classroom. Poorly managed emotions distract teachers from teaching as they become preoccupied with their emotional distress (Garner, 2010). Good emotion regulation helps teachers provide high-quality instruction and facilitates effective classroom management. Seeing a calm teacher who is in control provides students with a sense of security and a positive model for emotion regulation. Teachers with good emotion regulation skills are more flexible in responding to emotionally charged situations in the classroom and can diffuse situations with dysregulated students (Farb, Anderson, Irving, & Segal, 2014). On the contrary, teachers who have difficulty regulating their emotions in a stressful situation may react too quickly, causing a relational rift between them and their students, thus leading to an increased stress level in the classroom. Additionally, unregulated negative emotions contribute to teacher burnout (Fiorilli, Albanese, Gabola, & Pepe, 2017).

Our beliefs about emotions may significantly affect how we regulate them (Castella, Platow, Tamir, & Gross, 2018). Those who think that they have little control over their emotions and cannot change them tend to avoid their emotions and experience higher levels of distress. Think about your beliefs regarding emotions. If you think that you cannot change them, that can make emotion regulation more challenging. The good news is that you can learn effective emotion regulation strategies and adapt a growth mindset regarding your emotions.

It is important for teachers to differentiate their emotions and behavioral responses stemming from an emotion. For instance, "I can be angry, but I do not lash out at others." In other words, feeling an emotion does not necessarily mean that you must act immediately on that feeling. Response inhibition involves the ability to maintain control over emotions while responding to a situation. Teachers must be able to temporarily inhibit their emotional reactions and expression, even when they may be feeling intense emotions. It is important to note that response inhibition does not mean to suppress or deny an emotion. That would be unhealthy. Temporary inhibition simply means postponing a reaction. By lengthening the time between an emotional stimulus and response, the teacher can reflect on how he or she wants to respond and whether that response will contribute to a positive outcome.

Consider a teacher who has just witnessed one child kick another child in the classroom. The teacher may feel anger, as her classroom norms have been violated. She may also feel worried for the well-being of the victim and perhaps even concerned about possible repercussions from the child's parent. Her immediate urge may be to yell across the room to the offending student that his behavior is unacceptable. This urge can produce negative influences on the overall emotional climate of the room and the teacher's sense of self. A teacher who remains regulated makes more accurate appraisals and forms an adaptive response to the child's need and emotional experience.

EMOTION REGULATION STRATEGIES

Let's take a look at strategies we use to regulate our emotions (Gross, 2015). One strategy is *situation selection* when we enter into or avoid situations that can potentially evoke emotions. For example, we want to spend time with friends, as it promises positive emotional experiences. However, we may avoid going to a party where we may encounter a person with whom we have had a negative interpersonal experience. Situation selection can be adaptive and maladaptive. For example, when a child avoids aggressive peers so he or she does not get anxious about potential altercations, it is an adaptive response. However, if the child avoids peers or academic activities because of intense anxiety, this response is maladaptive. Similarly, when the class is rowdy, the teacher may feel anxious about students acting out. In order to reduce her anxiety, she refrains from giving students challenging tasks in an effort to keep them calm. This strategy may be adaptive if used occasionally. However, if avoidant behavior becomes a habit, the teacher will lose the opportunity to address students' behaviors, which creates more behavioral problems in the classroom.

Another emotion regulation strategy, *situation modification*, is aimed at changing the emotional impact of the situation (Gross, 2015). For example, when we feel sad, we may talk to someone to receive emotional support. There are times when even the best-planned lessons do not go as anticipated and you may find yourself feeling frustrated and upset. When this happens, it is good to have a backup plan to modify the situation. A good idea may be to assign something students can work on independently at their desks while you take time to recover. You can also change the classroom environment by turning on music or dimming the lights, which can improve your mood and the mood of your students. Further, allowing students to take a break can also help to regulate both teacher and student emotions. Movement breaks can either relax or energize students, depending on what you need. These breaks include allowing students to talk quietly with each other for two minutes, going on a short walk, playing a whole-class game, or engaging the class in guided imagery.

In addition to changing the situation, we can also change the focus of our attention in order to regulate our emotions. This strategy is called *attentional deployment* (Gross, 2015). Using this strategy, we can intentionally distract ourselves from unpleasant events or emotions and focus on pleasant ones instead. Attentional deployment can be an effective strategy. For example, when you worry about being evaluated, you can shift your attention to anticipating the relief you will feel when you are done with the evaluation. This can help to reduce arousal and save your mental resources for the task. However, distraction can be maladaptive when you are mentally "checking out" or daydreaming. If overused, these attempts to reduce negative emotions can prevent you from facing anxious thoughts and eventually reduce your drive to take action to solve a problem.

Another emotion regulation strategy, *cognitive change*, is aimed at the reappraisal of a situation in order to change its emotional significance (Gross, 2015). Cognitive change involves changing your thoughts about a situation or changing your thoughts about your ability to manage the situation. When you change your thoughts about a situation, you change what the situation means to you. This leads to a different emotional response. In addition, viewing the situation differently can reduce stress. One important reappraisal tactic is reminding yourself that you are working with children for whom school is not always a pleasant experience. When making reappraisals, it is helpful to consider why students might be responding in a particular way and what may be contributing to their behaviors. They may have learning difficulties or trouble controlling their behaviors, and they may struggle to get along with other students. Additionally, just as teachers do, students carry problems from home with them to the classroom. They may witness familial discord, have sick family members, or struggle with poverty. These situations significantly affect how students learn and how they behave in school, so keeping this in mind is helpful when dealing with students who may be frustrating.

Finally, in an attempt to regulate our emotions, we might directly alter our experiential, behavioral, and physiological responses associated with an emotion. This strategy is called *response modulation* (Gross, 2015). This strategy is adaptive when you are doing physical exercises or engaging in relaxation in order to reduce your negative emotions. An example of maladaptive use of this strategy is suppressing emotions or their expression. For instance, when you are upset with your significant other, you decide not to show your true emotions (i.e., suppress their expression) and try to look happy. While in the short run it might help, it may lead to negative consequences. Research informs us that people who often suppress their emotional expressions have worse memory and high blood pressure (Butler et al., 2003; Gross, 2015). They also have less intimate and satisfactory relationships with others because they do not show genuine emotions. Experiential suppression, on the other hand, involves the avoidance of one's emotional experience and the thoughts associated with it (Hayes-Skelton & Eustis, 2020). For example, a person might deny being anxious and behave as if he or she feels fine. In other words, a person becomes out of touch with his or her inner emotional experience. Frequent avoidance of emotional experiences maintains anxiety. That is why one of the objectives of therapy for people with high anxiety is to help them recognize and accept their anxiety.

Chapter Summary

- Emotional awareness involves attending to what we are feeling, ideally without judgment. Cues about our emotional state arise from our physical sensations, energy level, thoughts, and attributions.
- People hold beliefs and attitudes about emotions that develop from when they are young, as they receive implicit and explicit messages about what emotions are acceptable to feel and display.
- Emotions are expressed both verbally and nonverbally. Teachers and students influence each other's emotions in the classroom. While it might be tempting to not show certain emotions, emotional suppression is associated with feeling *more* negative emotions and leads to burnout. You can safely show your true emotions by modulating their expression.
- It is necessary to regulate your emotions if your emotions are too intense, as they can be distracting to you and interfere with teaching and learning. It is possible to learn to regulate your emotions.
- There are many different ways to regulate emotions. You can preemptively decide to engage or not engage with a situation, modify the situation to change its emotional impact, change your focus, change your thoughts about a situation, or change your experience.

Self-Reflective Activities

Recall a recent episode when you experienced an intense negative emotion. For example, you became angry with somebody, felt sad when you did not receive desired positive feedback, or felt anxious about a fast-approaching deadline. Record this episode in detail in your self-reflection journal. Using the strategies outlined by Gross (2015), reflect on how you managed that negative emotion. Is it your typical way to deal with negative emotions? What other strategies can you use to manage negative emotions?

Small Group Activities

Activity 1. Emotional Awareness

In a small group, complete Table 5.1. Recall episodes when you felt each of the emotions presented in the table. Replay the situation in your mind and reexperience the emotions in order to reflect on your physical experience of the emotion (e.g., heart rate, body tension), your subjective experience, how that emotion manifested in facial expression and body language, and thoughts likely associated with the emotion.

Table 5.1

Emotion	Body Reactions	Feelings	Facial Expression/ Body Language	Thoughts
Anxiety				
Sadness				
Joy				

Activity 2. Vignettes

Read the following vignettes and answer the questions after each one.

> **Emotions and Appraisal**
>
> *Mandy, a second-grade student, refused to work with other students on a math project. Instead, she took a book and started looking at the illustrations. The teacher's attempts to engage her in the group project were unsuccessful.*

Teacher A has the following thoughts in her mind: "She is old enough to be able to follow directions. Her parents clearly haven't punished her enough for this behavior; she's such a brat. They let her get away with everything."

- What emotions might result from these thoughts? How would the teacher react to Mandy's behavior?

Teacher B has the following thoughts in her mind: "I forgot what a hard time Mandy has with groups; she's probably feeling overwhelmed working with other students when her math skills are still so low."

- What emotions might result from these thoughts? How would the teacher react to Mandy's behavior?

Jack

It is the end of your animal unit in your kindergarten classroom, and your students are making masks to wear in the hallway parade later this week. The students are working well but need more support gluing things together than you initially anticipated. With only ten minutes until lunch, you let the class know that they can finish after recess. Most of the students follow your instruction to start cleaning up their areas, but you see that Jack is frantically gluing and cutting pieces. You remind him that he needs to start cleaning up and can work on his project later. He screams, "I want to finish it now!" and begins slamming materials on his desk. As you walk toward him to help calm him down, you see him grab a pair of scissors. As you rush over, you yell for him to put them down. Jack continues wailing and begins to throw the scissors toward another table of students.

- How would you feel in this situation?
- What would be your first reaction?
- What would you actually do?
- How would your feelings inform your action?
- What would you do with your feelings?

Annual Evaluation

Your formal observation for your annual evaluation is coming up, and you decide to have your principal visit during a review for a social studies test. After researching many ideas, you decide to craft a Jeopardy-style review game and spend several nights building it. As the day of your observation approaches, you carefully review the unit material. You spend extra time in class reviewing information with the students who seemed to be struggling. The students now appear to be well-prepared and are showing growth in their mastery of the information. Just before the observation starts, you discover that someone stepped on the board, and now it is covered in dirt smears, with a cracked corner and several missing question envelopes. The principal walks in as you are frantically attempting to repair the board and get the students situated. As you begin administering the questions from the game, you find your students are responding too quickly and most are giving incorrect answers. You see your principal scribbling notes in the corner.

- How would you feel in this situation?
- What would be your first reaction?
- What would you actually do?
- How would your feelings inform your action?
- What would you do with your feelings?

Mrs. Crenshaw

Mrs. Crenshaw is in a very noisy hallway trying to corral her students during class change. One student, Bradley, is running around making faces and animal noises. Mrs. Crenshaw tells him several times to stop but he continues. She loses her temper, yelling, "That's enough!" She takes Bradley's hand and marches him past the other students and back into the classroom.

Later that day, another teacher approaches Mrs. Crenshaw and tells her that Bradley was talking to other students about how Ms. Crenshaw is so mean and that she "dragged him" away from the other kids for no reason. He even said that he hated her. Mrs. Crenshaw became anxious and upset, as she and Bradley already had a rocky relationship, and his behavior has become increasingly difficult to manage. She is afraid this will only make matters worse. She also remembers that when they have these confrontations, Bradley tends to have angry outbursts when he is back in her classroom. Throughout the day, she notices that she is becoming more anxious and sadder, as she doesn't know how to handle the situation.

Discuss how Mrs. Crenshaw could regulate her emotions using the following strategies: situation selection, attentional deployment, cognitive change, and response modulation. Discuss each strategy and how her reactions might differ. Discuss the long-term and short-term consequences of each emotion regulation strategy.

Self-Care Tool Kit

Accept Your Emotions (Aguilar, 2018)

1. Take a moment to reflect on how you are feeling. You may feel more than one emotion. If that is the case, pick one to focus on. If you are unsure of how you are feeling, start by noticing the sensations in your body. Notice what thoughts are going through your mind.
2. Acknowledge your emotion and name it ("I am feeling . . ."). Explore your emotion. Do not judge it as good or bad. It is just the emotion you feel right now.
3. Envision your emotion as a shape or an object. Is it soft or hard? Smooth or rough? What color is this emotion? How big is it? Imagine yourself making this emotion using molding clay or other materials. What would it look like?
4. Imagine yourself holding your emotion in your hand and stretching out your arm, putting your emotion in a distance from you. Look at your emotion from a distance. Reflect how you feel.
5. Now bring your emotion inside of you. Say, "I accept that I am feeling . . ."
6. Reflect on how you feel after this activity.

REFERENCES

Aguilar, E. (2018). *The onward workbook: Daily activities to cultivate your emotional resilience and thrive.* John Wiley & Sons. https://doi.org/10.1002/9781119441779

Barrett, K. C., & Nelson-Goens, G. C. (1997). Emotion communication and the development of the social emotions. *New Directions for Child Development*, 77, 69–88. https://doi.org/10.1002/cd.23219977705

Barrett, L. F., & Gross, J. J. (2001). Emotional intelligence: A process model of emotion representation and regulation. In T. J. Mayne & G. A. Bonanno (Eds.), *Emotions and social behavior – Emotions: Current issues and future directions* (pp. 286–310). Guilford Press.

Barrett, L. F., Mesquita, B., Ochsner, K. N., & Gross, J. J. (2007). The experience of emotion. *Annual Review of Psychology*, 58, 373–403. https://doi.org/10.1146/annurev.psych.58.110405.085709

Butler, E. A., Egloff, B., Wlhelm, F. H., Smith, N. C., Erickson, E. A., & Gross, J. J. (2003). The social consequences of expressive suppression. *Emotion*, 3(1), 48–67. https://doi.org/10.1037/1528-3542.3.1.48

Castella, K. D., Platow, M. J., Tamir, M., & Gross, J. J. (2018). Beliefs about emotion: Implications for avoidance-based emotion regulation and psychological health. *Cognition and Emotion*, *32*(4), 773–795. https://doi.org/10.1080/02699931.2017.1353485

Chambers, R., Gullone, E., & Allen, N. B. (2009). Mindful emotion regulation: An integrative review. *Clinical Psychology Review*, *29*(6), 560–572. https://doi.org/10.1016/j.cpr.2009.06.005

Ersay, E. (2007). Preschool teachers' emotional experience traits, awareness of their own emotions and their emotional socialization practices. *Dissertation Abstracts International Section A: Humanities and Social Sciences*, *68*(5-A), 1806.

Farb, N. A. S., Anderson, A. K., Irving, J. A., & Segal, Z. V. (2014). Mindfulness interventions and emotion regulation. In J. J. Gross (Ed.), *Handbook of emotion regulation* (2nd ed., pp. 548–567). Guilford Press.

Fiorilli, C., Albanese, O., Gabola, P., & Pepe, A. (2017). Teachers' emotional competence and social support: Assessing the mediating role of teacher burnout. *Scandinavian Journal of Educational Research*, *61*(2), 127–138. https://doi.org/10.1080/ 00313831.2015.1119722

Frenzel, A. C., Becker-Kurz, B., Pekrun, R., Goetz, T., & Lüdtke, O. (2018). Emotion transmission in the classroom revisited: A reciprocal effects model of teacher and student enjoyment. *Journal of Educational Psychology*, *110*(5), 628–639. https://doi.org/10.1037/edu0000228

Frenzel, A. C., Goetz, T., Stephens, E. J., & Jacob, B. (2009). Antecedents and effects of teachers' emotional experiences: An integrative perspective and empirical test. In P. A. Schutz & M. Zembylas (Eds.), *Advances in teacher emotions research: The impact on teachers lives* (pp. 129–148). Springer.

Garner, P. W. (2010). Emotional competence and its influences on teaching and learning. *Educational Psychology Review*, *22*(3), 297–321. https://doi.org/10.1007/s10648-010-9129-4

Gross, J. J. (2015). Emotion regulation: Current status and future prospects. *Psychological Inquiry*, *26*(1), 1–26. https://doi.org/10.1080/1047840X.2014.94078

Hayes-Skelton, S. A., & Eustis, E. H. (2020). Experiential avoidance. In J. S. Abramowitz & S. M. Blakey (Eds.), *Clinical handbook of fear and anxiety: Maintenance processes and treatment mechanisms* (pp. 115–131). American Psychological Association. https://doi.org/10.1037/0000150-007

Leahy, R., Wupperman, P., Edwards, E., Shivaji, S., & Molina, N. (2019). Metacognition and emotional schemas: Effects on depression and anxiety. *International Journal of Cognitive Therapy*, *12*, 25–37. https://doi.org/10.1007/s41811-018-0035-8

Lieberman, M. D., Eisenberger, N. I., Crockett, M. J., Tom, S. M., Pfeifer, J. H., & Way, B. M. (2007). Putting feelings into words: Affect labeling disrupts amygdala activity in response to affective stimuli. *Psychological Science*, *18*(5), 421–428. https://doi.org/10.1111/j.1467-9280.2007.01916.x

Mayer, J. D., Caruso, D. R., & Salovey, P. (2016). The ability model of emotional intelligence: Principles and updates. *Emotion Review*, *8*(4), 290–300. https://doi.org/10.1177/1754073916639667

Mitmansgruber, H., Beck, T., Höfer, S., & Schüssler, G. (2009). When you don't like what you feel: Experiential avoidance, mindfulness, and meta-emotion in emotion regulation. *Personality and Individual Differences*, *46*, 448–453. https://doi.org/10.1016/j.paid.2008.11.013

Oberle, E., & Schonert-Reichl, K. A. (2016). Stress contagion in the classroom? The link between classroom teacher burnout and morning cortisol in elementary school students. *Social Science & Medicine*, *159*, 30–37. https://doi.org/10.1016/j.socscimed.2016.04.031

Oplatka, I. (2009). Emotion management and display in teaching: Some ethical and moral considerations in the era of marketization and commercialization. In P. A. Schutz & M. Zembylas (Eds.), *Advances in teacher emotion research* (pp. 55–71). New York, NY: Springer. https://doi.org/10.1007/978-1-4419-0564-2

Perez, L. (2011). Teaching emotional self-awareness through inquiry-based education. *Early Childhood Research and Practice*, *13*(2), 1–10.

Price, C. J., & Hooven, C. (2018). Interoceptive awareness skills for emotion regulation: Theory and approach of mindful awareness in body-oriented therapy (MABT). *Frontiers in Psychology*, *9*, 798. https://doi.org/10.3389/fpsyg.2018.00798

Saarni, C. (2008). The interface of emotional development with social context. In M. Lewis, J. M. Haviland-Jones, & L. F. Barrett (Eds.), *Handbook of emotions* (pp. 332–347). Guilford Press.

Taxer, J. L., & Frenzel, A. C. (2015). Facets of teachers' emotional lives: A quantitative investigation of teachers' genuine, faked, and hidden emotions. *Teaching and Teacher Education*, *49*, 78–88. https://doi.org/10.1016/j.tate.2015.03.003

Van Kleef, G. A. (2009). How emotions regulate social life: The emotions as social information (EASI) model. *Current Directions in Psychological Science*, *18*(3), 184–188. https://doi.org/10.1111/j.1467-8721.2009.01633.x

Wang, H., Hall, N. C., & Taxer, J. L. (2019). Antecedents and consequences of teachers' emotional labor: A systematic review and meta-analytic investigation. *Educational Psychology Review*, *31*, 663–698. https://doi.org/10.1007/s10648-019-09475-3

Zembylas, M. (2002). Structures of feeling in curriculum and teaching: Theorizing the emotional rules. *Educational Theory*, *52*(2), 187–208. https://doi.org/10.1111/j.1741-5446.2002.00187.x

CHAPTER 6

Emotional Development of Children

In order to understand children's emotions and the behaviors that result from those emotions, we need to know how children develop their emotional skills. At each developmental period, children acquire specific knowledge and skills related to emotions and their regulation. Some children master developmental tasks related to emotional competence successfully and some do not. When children fail to acquire developmentally appropriate emotional skills, they have difficulty dealing with emotionally laden situations in the classroom.

ATTACHMENT AS A FOUNDATION FOR EMOTIONAL DEVELOPMENT

During the first year of life, children form an attachment with their caregivers that serves as a template for future relationships and emotion regulation. Attachment is a specific type of relational connection between a child and caregiver associated with experiences of seeking safety, comfort, and security (Bowlby, 1988). Initially, babies emotionally respond to anyone in their social environment. However, around 7 months, they begin to show a definite preference for a particular person. This person is called the attachment figure. Usually, it is a parent or another adult who takes care of the child. While readily observed in early childhood, attachment behavior continues throughout the life span. Attachment relationships are internalized by the child and become an internal working model. A working model allows a child to predict how others will respond to his or her emotional bids, including whether they will support the child or not. Attachment relationships have important implications for a child's self-perception. For example, "I am worthy of love," or "I am not worthy of love" (Bowlby, 1988).

The way adults respond to a child's bids for engagement determines the type of attachment the child develops (Music, 2017). When parents are consistently present and responsive to children's emotional needs, they develop secure attachment. These children acquire a sense of safety and learn how to manage their negative emotions effectively. Securely attached children predict that their caregivers will respond to their emotional cues. When they cannot manage their emotions, they anticipate that others will help them. These children express their emotions openly, and this open and flexible expression of emotion promotes healthy relationships with others. The ability to regulate effectively their emotions allows children to be more resilient in response to failure and more resistant to the effects of stress. Furthermore, securely attached children use their caregivers as a secure base from which they can explore their environment. Without a doubt, their willingness to explore their environment and engage in new experiences propels their learning. Having a secure attachment also serves as a protective factor against emotional and behavioral problems (Music, 2017).

Children who do not experience attuned and consistent responses from their caregivers develop an insecure attachment (Music, 2017). These children tend to suppress or amplify their emotional expression. When a caregiver ignores a child's distress or responds with anger, the child may develop a strategy to avoid the caregiver when he or she is distressed. These children anticipate that an open expression of their emotions may threaten the relationship with the caregiver and lead to rejection. Experiences of rejection during times of high emotional need may lead the child to cope by suppressing emotions in order to reduce their dependence on the adult for comfort. They may suppress even positive displays of emotion, as the expression of happiness and joy may invite relational contact and engagement, and such connection puts them at risk for later rejection (Cassidy, Jones, & Shaver, 2013). These children are likely to present outwardly as more constrained than their securely attached peers when distressed; however, they show distress at the physiological level. Insecurely attached children tend not to seek help, which also limits their ability to learn new ways to cope (Cassidy et al., 2013).

When a caregiver responds in an unpredictable way or has poor timing with responding, some children may try to amplify negative emotions as a means of engaging the caregiver (Benoit, 2004; Cassidy et al., 2013). An extreme case of insecure attachment is called disorganized attachment. Disorganized attachment results from experiences of maltreatment or extremely insensitive caregiver behavior. In this case, the child does not develop a consistent or organized strategy for managing his or her distress but instead shows inconsistent and unpredictable emotional responses. At times, these children may shut down emotionally, while at other times, they may respond with temper tantrums and aggression. This type of attachment is the most problematic, as the child does not have a means for self-soothing when distressed. Children with disorganized attachment often develop significant emotional and behavioral problems and are at higher risks of serious psychopathology.

Knowing a child's attachment style is important for understanding his or her emotions and behavior in the classroom. Children with insecure attachment may present a significant challenge for teachers. They often become anxious in interpersonal situations and oversensitive to real or perceived threats to their relationships with others (Mikulincer, Shaver, & Pereg, 2003). As such, they become very attentive to any potential signs of disapproval, waning interest, or potential abandonment from adults. Finally, they consume a lot of mental energy in seeking a relationship with the teacher, which reduces the resources they have available for learning.

EMOTIONAL DEVELOPMENT IN EARLY CHILDHOOD

Let's take a look at how children develop emotional skills beyond infancy. Children as young as 18 months begin to understand some emotional words, such as happy or sad, and around 2 to 3 years of age use words to name their feelings (Ridgeway, Waters, & Kuczaj, 1985; Saarni, Campos, Camras, & Witherington, 2006). Their emotional vocabulary is limited and undifferentiated. Quite often, it is the words "good" or "bad" that describe their emotional experiences.

When toddlers begin to walk, they begin to explore their environment. Indeed, there are so many interesting things around that they can touch, use, or kick. Such exploratory behaviors often lead to the first parental prohibitions. Parents begin to impose limitations and set parameters for a child's activity (Cole & Hall, 2008). Some children resist these limitations and react with intense anger. This is an important opportunity for children to learn how to handle their anger. If parents respond to the child's anger with their own anger and irritation, the child cannot learn how to manage his or her own anger.

To understand children's emotional experiences, it is important to differentiate basic emotions, such as anger or sadness, from emotional schemas (Izard, Stark, Trentacosta, & Schultz, 2008). Basic emotions are an automatic response to events in a child's environment. As children become older, they begin to develop emotional schemas. Emotional schemas involve the integration of an emotion with the appraisal of the situation – that is, what the situation means for the child. Emotional schemas develop as a result of repeated experiences and are used to predict others' behavior. For example, a child whose emotional needs are not being met might develop a schema, "I do not deserve to be loved." This emotional schema affects how the child interprets his or her experiences. For example, when a child is not included in a game, the "I do not deserve to be loved" schema might be activated, resulting in feelings of rejection and low self-worth and leading the child to respond with anger. In contrast, a child with a positive emotional schema in the same situation might make different attributions and respond more adaptively.

The notion of emotional schema reminds us that we respond to a situation based on our interpretation of the situation rather than the situation itself. That is why you might be puzzled by a child who becomes very upset in a situation that appears not upsetting at all. The situation likely activated some emotional schemas of which you may not be aware.

During the preschool years, children show remarkable improvement in their ability to regulate their emotions (Izard, Fine, Mostow, Trentacosta, & Campbell, 2002). The rapid development of emotion vocabulary leads to making connections between feelings and words, which leads to an improved ability to regulate emotions. By age 6, children expand their emotional vocabulary and begin to understand emotion words such as "nervous," "embarrassed," "jealous," and even "miserable." Importantly, when parents use emotional words in their conversations with children, children are more likely to use emotional words themselves. Growth in the emotion lexicon allows children to seek support when feeling distressed, share their emotional experiences with others, and better understand emotions and their consequences (Saarni et al., 2006). Keep in mind that severely abused or traumatized children often have difficulty talking about their feelings.

In the preschool years, children are still learning how to deal with their anger. Some may react with intense anger when adults set limits, interrupt their activities, or discipline them (Izard et al., 2002). These children need special attention from adults to help them regulate their anger and frustration. Another common context for anger is play, when children need to coordinate their behavior with others (Lemerise & Dodge, 2008).

The preschool years are a crucial time for developing empathy and prosocial behavior (Izard et al., 2002). During this time, children need many opportunities to practice empathy, take the perspective of others, and act in a prosocial way. For example, if a child is hurt in the classroom, a teacher might narrate to the class ways to help others feel better, such as through affection or caring words. Furthermore, children need to learn emotion-based moral reasoning. Examples of such reasoning include, "We do not hurt others because it would make them feel sad or upset," and, "Helping others makes them feel better." Keep in mind that teaching empathy and emotion regulation should go hand in hand (Izard et al., 2002). When children observe others in distress (e.g., their friend is crying), they may become upset themselves. As a result, they may avoid providing support to a peer who is in distress. Helping a child manage his or her own response allows them to show empathy to others.

Preschool children already have the ability to separate their internal experience (how they feel) from their outward expression of emotion (what they show to others; Saarni et al., 2006). This ability is called "emotional disassembly." For example, children exaggerate their emotional expressions in order to get attention, such as when a child cries loudly in response to a small injury. Children disassemble emotions for several reasons (Saarni et al., 2006). First, they do it in order to avoid negative outcomes and protect their self-esteem. For example, boys might be reluctant to show fear so they will not be viewed as weak by their peers. Second, children disassemble emotions in order to maintain good relationships with peers. For instance, showing anger may not be the best thing to do if you want to keep your friendship. Finally, cultural norms may make children disassemble their emotions. In some cultures, showing anger to parents is not appropriate; therefore, children need to conceal this feeling.

TEMPERAMENT AND EMOTIONAL DEVELOPMENT

Imagine two children, Garrett and Ben. Garrett is very social, likes performing in front of his class, and often volunteers to take papers to the office. At the same time, he gets upset easily when he is told "no." Ben, on the other hand, is shy and likes playing by himself. He does not volunteer to take papers to the office and does not like to talk in front of the class. When the class becomes loud, Ben gets anxious quickly and puts his head down on the desk.

Why do these children have different behaviors? Because they have different temperaments. Temperament reflects biologically based differences that affect how children respond to their environment and regulate their emotions and behavior (Posner & Rothbart, 2007). Differences in temperament partially explain why children respond differently to the same situation and why some children adjust well to a new environment (like school) while others struggle.

Temperament is based on two systems: behavioral activation and behavioral inhibition (Blair, 2003). Children with a strong behavior activation system (like Garrett) are extroverted, like to take risks, and seek stimulation. They respond positively to rewards but might react with anger when a reward is taken away. Further, they do not like when someone puts limits on them. Therefore, they might present a challenge for the teacher if the teacher insists on doing things his or her way, which can cause a power struggle. Instead, finding opportunities for positive stimulation and independence might reduce the child's resistance to following the teacher's directions.

Children with a stronger behavioral inhibition system (like Ben) are introverted and shy. They often feel anxious in new situations and have difficulty expressing their emotions. These children are easily overstimulated and may react by shutting down. While these children might present as quiet and compliant, they often avoid challenging tasks so that they do not feel anxious. It is important for teachers to provide these children with gentle encouragement and support when introducing a new task.

Temperament also influences children's emotionality and makes some children more reactive and prone to negative emotions than others (Blair, 2003; Posner & Rothbart, 2007). Some children with negative emotionality become anxious and fearful very easily while some can be angry and irritable. These children present a challenge for the teacher in the classroom, as they may have difficulty regulating their negative emotions. They need to be provided with more positive emotional experiences to offset their tendency to feel negative emotions.

SOCIALIZATION OF EMOTIONS IN FAMILIES

A child's emotional development is influenced by how his or her parents explain emotions, react to the child's emotions, express their own emotions, and expose their children to emotionally charged situations (Barret & Campos, 1987; Morris, Criss, Silk, & Houltberg, 2017). Healthy emotional development is supported by warm, responsive, and accepting parenting. As children interact with various figures in their lives, they acquire beliefs about emotions and emotional expression. "Thus, even as we may observe emotional development *in the child*, those who interact with the child are communicating their own emotions *to the child*, often elicited by their evaluation of the child's emotional behavior" (Saarni, 1999, p. 57).

Parents have theories regarding emotions called metatheories (Gottman, Katz, & Hooven, 1997). These metatheories are a collection of beliefs regarding their emotions and their children's emotions. Parents who view negative emotions as a normal part of life coach their children in emotionally laden situations and help children to find constructive ways to manage their emotions. These parents have children with better emotion regulation skills (Gottman et al., 1997). On the other hand, parents who view negative emotions as unhealthy or harmful tend to dismiss or quickly alleviate negative emotions for the child (Lunkenheimer, Shields, & Cortina, 2007). For instance, when a child feels sad and starts crying, the parent may say, "You're fine, stop whining." By doing this, parents do not acknowledge the child's emotions and, as a result, miss an opportunity to teach the child to understand his or her emotional experiences.

The way parents express and regulate their own emotions has a significant impact on their children's emotional development. When parents frequently display anger, it is stressful for children, especially young ones (Cummings, Davies, & Campbell, 2000). In addition, it creates a negative model: Children learn that anger and hostility are common and acceptable. Angry parenting may lead children to develop an anger attribution bias, which we discussed earlier.

Parents who suffer from depression may also negatively influence a child's emotional development (Saarni et al., 2006). These parents are less likely to talk about and explain emotions to their children. When the children need emotional support, they are not available. As a result, the children have difficulty recognizing and dealing with their own emotions. They also often experience guilt and learn to suppress their emotions so that they do not distress their parents further. Depressed parents have higher levels of negative emotions and often criticize their children. As a result, children may feel anger toward their parents but displace it toward their teacher.

EMOTIONS IN CHILDREN WITH SPECIAL NEEDS

Children with special needs have unique ways to process emotional information and respond to emotionally charged situations. Children with attention deficit hyperactivity disorder (ADHD) might have difficulty processing emotionally laden stimuli, as they do not detect expression of emotions in faces and voices as quickly as children without ADHD (Shaw, Stringaris, Nigg, & Leibenluft, 2014). Difficulty with reading emotional cues might lead to misperceptions and responding in an inappropriate way. Children with ADHD also focus excessively on immediate rewards and have difficulty waiting. Coupled with heightened emotional arousal and lability, difficulty waiting often leads to impulsive responses. These children are also more irritable and have difficulty inhibiting their responses to emotionally charged situations.

Children with autism spectrum disorder experience lower levels of positive and higher levels of negative emotions than their typically developing peers (Hobson, 2005; Macari et al., 2018). This is especially noticeable in situations when they are engaged with others. In those situations, typically developing peers smile and share their feelings with others; for example, they laugh when others laugh. Children with autism have difficulty coordinating emotions in face-to-face interactions. Furthermore, they struggle to recognize emotions in others. Children with autism also may display unusual or ambiguous emotions, which make it difficult to understand how they feel (Hobson, 2005). They also may show more intense negative emotions in situations that elicit frustration or fear (Macari et al., 2018). Children with autism use fewer constructive emotion regulation strategies and have difficulty expressing experienced emotions to others (Zantinge, van Rijn, Stockmann, & Swaab, 2017).

Children with developmental language disorders may show emotions less congruent with emotions expressed by others (van den Bedem et al., 2018). They also demonstrate more inappropriate expressions of emotions and are less concerned about the impact of their emotions on others. Younger children with language disorders may have behavioral outbursts and difficulty regulating their emotions. Finally, they often experience depression, likely due to limitations in social communication.

Chapter Summary

- Emotional skills are developed across the life span. Some children develop these skills at expected times. Children who do not develop skills on time often struggle in emotionally laden situations in the classroom.
- Children develop a special connection with caregivers early in life called attachment. The way caregivers respond to a child's distress shapes the child's expectations regarding interactions with others.
- Children develop an emotion vocabulary and coping skills through experiences of early childhood. How adults respond to a child's emotions during this time influences how the child will use, experience, and regulate emotions later in life.
- Children are born with different emotional predispositions, called temperament. This is part of the reason why two children may respond differently in the same situation. Children can be inherently sensation seeking and extroverted or more introverted and shy.
- Family attitudes about emotions, emotional expression, and parental emotional displays, all influence children's emotional development. Children may have reactions to classroom events that stem from experiences at home.
- Children with special needs have unique ways of processing emotional information and responding to emotionally charged situations.

Self-Reflective Activities

In your self-reflection journal, reflect on the following questions:

- How were emotions expressed in your family?
- How did your parents respond to your negative emotions, such as anger or anxiety? Were there emotions that were acceptable or not acceptable to display?
- What did you learn about emotions and their expression from your childhood?
- How might your childhood emotional experience facilitate or impede your relationships with students?

Small Group Activities

Activity 1. Vignettes

In small groups, read the following vignettes and answer the follow-up questions.

Hannah

Hannah is in the third grade. Her parents often fight and yell at each other. They frequently yell at Hannah and her brother, especially if they forget to do their chores. One day at school, Hannah's teacher, Mr. Muñoz, begins a math lesson. While he is teaching, a couple of students at Hannah's table begin to talk to each other loudly. Mr. Muñoz then raises his voice to tell the students to quiet down. Hannah suddenly becomes upset and starts crying. Mr. Muñoz is confused and does not understand what he has done to make Hannah feel this way. He approaches Hannah and asks what happened. Hannah does not say anything. Mr. Muñoz shrugs his shoulders and continues teaching his lesson. At home later that evening, he remembers the episode and tries to understand what he said or did to make Hannah cry. He does not feel good about himself and the way he handled the situation.

- Why do you think Hannah reacted in this way?
- How might Mr. Muñoz make this situation better for Hannah?
- Predict how Hannah might respond to Mr. Muñoz's alternative response.

Carlos

Carlos was born to very young parents who struggled to care for him. He was ultimately removed from his home and placed in foster care before being placed in the care of his grandmother. When Carlos starts kindergarten, he is quite sullen and standoffish. He rarely talks to other children but becomes easily upset when they touch his things or move too close to him. His teacher makes a point to talk with him each day about things he enjoys and seats him with kind classmates who are respectful of his space. She notices that at first, Carlos seems to test limits by taking things from her desk but finds that as she continues to gently enforce the rules and shows that she cares for him, these behaviors completely stop. Carlos has a terrific kindergarten year and ends it with a small group of friends and very few behavior problems.

> When Carlos starts first grade with a new teacher, he has many arguments with his peers and shows many rule-breaking behaviors. His teacher rarely talks to him about anything that does not relate to school tasks. On two occasions when Carlos was very upset about his peers making fun of him, his teacher said in passing, "You will be OK." Carlos's behavior worsens, as he begins stealing from other children and lashing out at others physically. His teacher tries keeping him in from recess, sending him to the office, and sending notes home about his bad behavior, but nothing she is doing seems to make it get better.

- How do you think Carlos's early childhood experiences have affected his emotions, behaviors, and relationships?
- What do you think helped Carlos to succeed during kindergarten?
- What do you think is making it difficult for Carlos to be successful in first grade?
- What suggestions would you give to Carlos's first-grade teacher?

Sophia

> Sophia lives in a home where there is a high level of negative emotions. Her parents are easily angered and show their emotions by grumbling, shouting, and complaining. Even small things make them very upset. They are often preoccupied with their own problems and don't pay much attention to Sophia. In the classroom, Sophia also seems easily distressed by small events. When she drops her pencil during seat work, she loudly yells, "Oh my goshhhhh!" before dramatically retrieving it. When a task is challenging, she will call across the room, "Ms. Brown, I don't know how to do it!" She frequently seeks a teacher out during recess to complain of minor peer transgressions and small injuries. Other children seem annoyed by her behavior, and as a result, she is often excluded. Her behavior is especially disruptive when Ms. Brown is trying to support other children.

- What attachment experience may have contributed to Sophia's responses?
- How can Ms. Brown help Sophia in the classroom?

Self-Care Tool Kit

Positive Affirmations

Positive affirmations are statements that help to challenge negative thoughts, reduce anxiety, and increase positive emotions. From the following list, select affirmations that resonate with you. Use them when you experience stress or when you need to boost your confidence.

I deserve to live with ease.
Peace is within my reach.
Stress is not my friend.
Breathe and breathe again.
In every moment, peace is a choice.
Be here now.
One step at a time.
Smiling brings me joy.
I will stay calm and carry on.
The future is good.
I live in peace.
Let it be.
I can do hard things.

REFERENCES

Barrett, K. C., & Campos, J. J. (1987). Perspectives on emotional development II: A functionalist approach to emotions. In J. D. Osofsky (Ed.), *Wiley series on personality processes: Handbook of infant development* (pp. 555–578). John Wiley & Sons.

Benoit, D. (2004). Infant-parent attachment: Definition, types, antecedents, measurement and outcome. *Paediatrics & Child Health, 9*(8), 541–545. https://doi.org/10.1093/pch/9.8.541

Blair, C. (2003). Behavioral inhibition and behavioral activation in young children: Relations with self-regulation and adaptation to preschool in children attending Head Start. *Developmental Psychobiology, 42*(3), 301–311. https://doi.org/10.1002/dev.10103

Bowlby, J. (1988). *A secure base: Parent-child attachment and healthy human development*. Basic Books.

Cassidy, J., Jones, J. D., & Shaver, P. R. (2013). Contributions of attachment theory and research: A framework for future research, translation, and policy. *Development and Psychopathology, 25*(4 Pt 2), 1415–1434. https://doi.org/10.1017/S0954579413000692

Cole, P. M., & Hall, S. E. (2008). Emotion dysregulation as a risk factor for psychopathology. In T. P. Beauchaine & S. P. Hinshaw (Eds.), *Child and adolescent psychopathology* (pp. 265–298). John Wiley & Sons Inc.

Cummings, E. M., Davies, P. T., & Campbell, S. B. (2000). *Developmental psychopathology and family process: Theory, research, and clinical implications*. Guilford Press.

Gottman, J. M., Katz, L. F., & Hooven, C. (1997). *Meta-emotion: How families communicate emotionally*. Lawrence Erlbaum Associates, Inc.

Hobson, P. (2005). Autism and emotion. In F. R. Volkmar, R. Paul, A. Klin, & D. Cohen (Eds.), *Handbook of autism and pervasive developmental disorders: Diagnosis, development, neurobiology, and behavior* (pp. 406–422). John Wiley & Sons Inc.

Izard, C. E., Fine, S., Mostow, A., Trentacosta, C., & Campbell, J. (2002). Emotion processes in normal and abnormal development and preventive intervention. *Development and Psychopathology, 14*(4), 761–787. https://doi.org/10.1017/s0954579402004066

Izard, C. E., Stark, K., Trentacosta, C., & Schultz, D. (2008). Beyond emotion regulation: Emotion utilization and adaptive functioning. *Child Development Perspectives, 2*(3), 156–163. https://doi.org/10.1111/j.1750-8606.2008.00058.x

Lemerise, E. A., & Dodge, K. A. (2008). The development of anger and hostile interactions. In M. Lewis, J. M. Haviland-Jones, & L. F. Barrett (Eds.), *Handbook of emotions* (pp. 730–741). Guilford Press.

Lunkenheimer, E. S., Shields, A. M., & Cortina, K. S. (2007). Parental emotion coaching and dismissing in family interaction. *Social Development, 16*(2), 232–248. https://doi.org/10.1111/j.1467-9507.2007.00382.x

Macari, S., DiNicola, L., Kane-Grade, F., Prince, E., Vernetti, A., Powell, K. . . . Chawarska, K. (2018). Emotional expressivity in toddlers with Autism Spectrum Disorder. *Journal of the American Academy of Child and Adolescent Psychiatry, 57*(11), 828–836.e2. https://doi.org/10.1016/j.jaac.2018.07.872

Mikulincer, M., Shaver, P. R., & Pereg, D. (2003). Attachment theory and affect regulation: The dynamics, development, and cognitive consequences of attachment-related strategies. *Motivation and Emotion, 27*(2), 77–102. https://doi.org/10.1023/A:1024515519160

Morris, A. S., Criss, M. M., Silk, J. S., & Houltberg, B. J. (2017). The impact of parenting on emotion regulation during childhood and adolescence. *Child Development Perspectives, 11*(4), 233–238. https://doi.org/10.1111/cdep.12238

Music, G. (2017). *Nurturing natures: Attachment and children's emotional, sociocultural and brain development.* Routledge. https://doi.org/10.4324/9781315656939

Posner, M. I., & Rothbart, M. K. (2007). *Educating the human brain.* American Psychological Association.

Ridgeway, D., Waters, E., & Kuczaj, S. A. (1985). Acquisition of emotion-descriptive language: Receptive and productive vocabulary norms for ages 18 months to 6 years. *Developmental Psychology, 21*(5), 901–908. https://doi.org/10.1037/0012-1649.21.5.901

Saarni, C. (1999). *The development of emotional competence.* Guilford Press.

Saarni, C., Campos, J. J., Camras, L. A., & Witherington, D. (2006). Emotional development: Action, communication, and understanding. In N. Eisenberg, W. Damon, & R. M. Lerner (Eds.), *Handbook of child psychology: Social, emotional, and personality development* (pp. 226–299). John Wiley & Sons, Inc.

Shaw, P., Stringaris, A., Nigg, J., & Leibenluft, E. (2014). Emotion dysregulation in attention deficit hyperactivity disorder. *The American Journal of Psychiatry*, *171*(3), 276–293. https://doi.org/10.1176/appi.ajp.2013.13070966

van den Bedem, N. P., Dockrell, J. E., van Alphen, P. M., de Rooij, M., Samson, A. C., Harjunen, E. L., & Rieffe, C. (2018). Depressive symptoms and emotion regulation strategies in children with and without developmental language disorder: A longitudinal study. *International Journal of Language & Communication Disorders*, *53*(6), 1110–1123. https://doi.org/10.1111/1460-6984.12423

Zantinge, G., van Rijn, S., Stockmann, L., & Swaab, H. (2017). Physiological arousal and emotion regulation strategies in young children with Autism Spectrum Disorders. *Journal of Autism and Developmental Disorders*, *47*(9), 2648–2657. https://doi.org/10.1007/s10803-017-3181-6

CHAPTER 7

Emotions and Culture

As a teacher, you will work with students with diverse cultural, racial, and ethnic backgrounds. These students have different ways of expressing and regulating their emotions. Furthermore, their cultural background influences how they understand the events and situations in the classroom that give rise to different emotional experiences. For example, some students will eagerly follow your directions because respecting an authority figure is very important in their culture. At the same time, they might feel anxious when placed in a position where they are expected to speak for themselves.

Emotions play a central role in our interactions with others. Misreading the emotional behavior of people from different cultures may lead to misunderstandings and inappropriate responses (Tsai, 2021). For instance, a teacher may interpret the quiet and reserved behavior of a student of Chinese descent as disengagement or even boredom. However, in reality, the student could feel quite content. Students from East Asian cultures are often perceived as less friendly, as they do not show the high-intensity positive emotions that are common in mainstream American culture. As a result, they may not be invited to play with peers or have difficulties establishing friendships.

In order to create inclusive and welcoming classrooms, teachers must be culturally sensitive. Intercultural awareness is the ability to look at other cultures from the perspective of individuals within those cultures. This may require some effort because when encountering another culture, we often bring our own cultural frame of interpretation without being aware of it (Hofstede, Pedersen, & Hofstede, 2002). A good example took place in 1976 when the U.S. Department of Education

DOI: 10.4324/9781003219774-7

issued recommendations for teachers on how to teach Vietnamese students (Kraemer, 1978, cited by G. Hofstede, 1986). These recommendations stated that because of the existence of corporal punishment in Vietnam, children were afraid to speak freely. In reality, students were acting according to their cultural norm of respecting authority figures, such as teachers. "In any intercultural encounter, there is always a temptation to feel that the others have bad character or bad intentions, rather than realize that they are acting according to different rules" (Hofstede et al., 2002, p. 42). Therefore, it is best to avoid interpreting the behavior of people from different cultures until you have good knowledge of those cultures.

In addition to intercultural awareness, you also need to be aware of your own culture. Reflection on your own culture is not easy because cultural knowledge and practices are so integrated into our everyday life that they do not require reflection. "Much of the 'true face' of a culture, or an individual cultural competence lies deep underneath his/her level of consciousness and, as such, defies quick recognition by the person" (Wang, 2011, p. 3). Often, we are so embedded in our own culture, we do not even recognize some elements of our existence as being culturally specific.

WHAT IS CULTURE?

Culture can be defined as a "set of control mechanisms – plans, recipes, rules, and instructions" that we use to govern our behavior (Geertz, 1973, p. 44). As such, culture simultaneously constrains and enables our behaviors (Hays, 2000). Cultural psychologists believe that in any culture we can find specific cultural ideas, practices, and artifacts (Markus & Hamedani, 2007). Cultural ideas are reflected in the values, attitudes, and norms of a given culture. Knowing cultural values is critical for successful intercultural communication as, "meanings provide a basis for cultural exchange" (Bruner, 1996, p. 3).

In each culture, people are engaged in practices that include learning, teaching, parenting, playing, or working (Markus & Hamedani, 2007). While many cultures may have similar practices (e.g., teaching children), these practices are conducted in culture-specific ways because they are shaped by cultural beliefs and values. For example, in the United States, great value is placed on autonomy and self-expression. That is why in schools, students are given choices and receive frequent praise. In cultures that value conformity and adherence to cultural norms, schooling takes a different form. For example, in Asian countries, the teacher has higher authority and control in the classroom than in the United States; however, students do not perceive control imposed by teachers negatively. Furthermore, in China, children are trained to focus on self-improvement, and they might react to praise with embarrassment and doubt that they deserve high evaluation (Trommsdorff & Rothbaum, 2008).

Each culture also creates cultural products that reflect cultural values and meanings (Markus & Hamedani, 2007). For example, cultural products in American culture promote high self-esteem and self-enhancement. You have probably seen messages on bumper stickers or coffee mugs like, "Proud Parent of an Honor Student," "Refuse to be Average," "World's Best Dad, or "This Car Climbed Mt. Washington."

CULTURAL ORIENTATIONS

In order to understand better how culture impacts the way we behave, think, and feel, psychologists have identified two major cultural orientations: individualistic and collectivistic (Markus & Kitayama, 1991). Individualistic and collectivistic orientations correlate to different models of the self: independent and interdependent. These orientations lead us to view ourselves and others in a particular way and shape our emotions, motivation, and thinking (Markus & Kitayama, 1991). Individualistic cultures place emphasis on personal autonomy and achievement. For example, someone who grew up in an individualistic culture might work hard toward a promotion at her job, forgoing family functions in order to work late at night. In collectivistic cultures, it is very important to maintain good relationships with others. As a result, assertiveness and competition may not be desired (Markus & Kitayama, 1991; Rothbaum, Weisz, Pott, Miyake, & Morelli, 2000). Collectivistic cultures emphasize the importance of fulfilling social duties and expectations of others.

Individualistic cultures foster "standing out," while for collectivistic cultures, "fitting in" is more important (Markus & Kitayama, 1991). In one interesting study, Koreans and Americans were asked to choose a colored pen as a gift. American participants preferred the rarest color that reflected their desire for uniqueness, whereas Korean participants selected the most common color (Nisbett & Masuda, 2003). Furthermore, in American culture, talking about one's achievements is expected, while in other cultures (e.g., Japan, Russia, or China), modesty is a virtue. That is why in these cultures, talking about one's achievements might be considered bragging.

CULTURE AND EMOTIONS

Culture plays an important role in how we express and regulate our emotions. It informs us of which emotions are appropriate and which are not in particular situations. In different cultures, emotion regulation is aimed at achieving goals that reflect culture-specific ideas about self and relationships with others (Trommsdorff & Rothbaum, 2008). Members of individualistic cultures pursue so-called promotion goals, which are associated with enhancing one's self-esteem and sense of success. That is why they try to accentuate positive emotions, as a sign that they are doing well, and avoid negative emotions. In collectivistic cultures, people pursue prevention goals, which are associated with maintaining interpersonal harmony. For this reason, they prefer more reserved emotional expression, as intense emotions can be disrupting to interpersonal relationships (Trommsdorff & Rothbaum, 2008). One study arrived at interesting results: Americans rarely feel bad after positive events, while people in East Asia may experience both positive and negative emotions during positive events (Tsai, 2021). More specifically, they may feel bad that others were not included in the positive experiences. Members of East Asian cultures also have a more balanced view of emotions. Negative emotions (e.g., shame) motivate them to work harder to improve themselves (Miyamoto, Ma, & Wilken, 2017).

Cultural values regarding emotions are communicated through emotional language. Did you know that English has about 2,000 emotion-related words, but Taiwanese Chinese has 750 and Chewong language has only 7 (Russell, 1991)? Another interesting fact is that the Chinese words for emotions name the emotion and a body part. For example, the word *anger* literally translates to "to create energy within the body" (Yu, 2002). In the Russian language, emotion words often take a form of a verb, while in English they are often adjectives (Wierzbicka, 1999). This means that for Russians, emotions are more active and dynamic states than for English-speaking people. This might explain why Russians are emotionally expressive in interpersonal exchanges.

Culture also influences our attentional focus when we are observing others' emotions. In one study, when looking at cartoons,

Americans mostly focused on the emotions of the story's main character but paid less attention to the emotions of the surrounding characters (Masuda et al., 2008). The Japanese participants, however, focused on the emotional expressions of both the main character and the surrounding people.

CULTURAL MODELS OF IDEAL AFFECT

In each culture, some emotions are viewed as more desirable while others are less desirable. Desired emotions are called the ideal affect (Tsai, 2007). The ideal affect in the mainstream American culture is a high level of positive emotions, while in East Asian cultures emotional calmness is the ideal affect (Rothbaum & Rusk, 2011). One study looked at children's books as a potential vehicle to transmit cultural values regarding ideal affect. The study found that books in the United States portray more exciting facial expressions than those in Taiwan (Tsai, Louie, Chen, & Uchida, 2007). Interestingly, after reading books with more excited facial expressions, children in both cultures preferred more exciting activities. The cultural environment offers specific situations that can promote certain emotions. For example, in American culture, there are many situations that make one feel unique and happy. Think about end-of-year celebrations at school when students receive various awards. In Chinese culture, more emphasis is placed on opportunities for growth and self-improvement (Rothbaum & Rusk, 2011).

The emotion of pride also has cultural variations. Pride is valued in American culture, as it reflects personal achievement (Trommsdorff & Rothbaum, 2008). In East Asian cultures, however, pride is not a desirable emotion because it can be seen as a way to elevate one person over others and therefore distance one from others. Furthermore, shame is acceptable in East Asian or Russian cultures, and it is often used as a means for disciplining children (Mesquita & Leu, 2007). For example, parents might say, "You must feel shameful for what you have done." Children in East Asian cultures are more often exposed to shaming experiences compared to their peers in the United States, as it is regarded as means for teaching children self-regulation and self-improvement (Mascolo, Fisher, & Li, 2003). This is in contrast to American culture where shame is considered to be damaging to self-esteem and, therefore, should be avoided.

CULTURAL MODELS OF PARENTING AND CHILD EMOTIONAL DEVELOPMENT

Culture greatly influences parental goals and behavior (Bornstein, 2015). Parents have culture-specific theories (called ethnotheories) about how to raise a child. These theories are informed by individualistic and collectivistic cultural orientations. Parents from cultures that value independence (e.g., European American) promote assertiveness, verbal competence, and autonomy (Bornstein, 2015). For example, sleepovers or babysitting are common in American culture; however, these activities do not take place in other cultures (Rothbaum & Trommsdorff, 2007). Parental cultures that value interdependence (e.g., Japan, China) encourage self-control and emotional maturity. They further promote close and continuous contact with the child through co-sleeping and longer periods of holding the child than in independent cultures. This close physical contact between the caregiver and baby supports emotion regulation in young children in non-Western cultures, whereas babies in Western cultures are encouraged to self-soothe from a very early age (Trommsdorff & Rothbaun, 2008). One study found that Japanese parents responded to their child before the child expressed negative emotions, while German parents waited until the child expressed his negative emotions before they intervened (Rothbaum & Rusk, 2011). Teaching children how to regulate emotions is very important for parents from collectivistic cultures, while parents from individualistic cultures support open emotional expression in children. Cultural orientations also inform how parents discipline children. In one study, European American mothers used suggestions to change their child's behavior while mothers from Puerto Rico used more direct means, including commands (Bornstein, 2015).

SOCIALIZATION OF EMOTIONS IN SCHOOLS

School is an important emotion socialization context for children.

> *In schools . . . children learn not only the 'curriculum,' but also the ways of relating to each other and to adults that the structure of the institution embodies. By participating in the everyday formats and routines of cultural institutions and traditions, children engage in their underlying cultural assumptions.*
>
> (Rogoff, 2003, p. 234)

Teachers around the world have different ideas of how to support children's emotional development. Interestingly, teachers from different cultures have different beliefs about emotions and emotional learning in the classroom (Hyson & Lee, 1996). In one study, Korean early childhood education teachers believed that they have to protect children from emotionally upsetting events and the open expression of emotions should be avoided. American teachers, on the other hand, believed that teachers should be affectionate surrogate parents.

In Japan, schools promote a sense of responsibility, social connection, empathy, and cooperation with others (Hayashi, Karasawa, & Tobin, 2009). Interestingly, Japanese teachers often discuss a feeling of loneliness and sadness resulting from loneliness with their students. They believe that such a discussion is important to evoke *amae*, a feeling of empathy and close connection with others (Hayashi et al., 2009). Japanese teachers also believe that children need to learn how to deal with interpersonal situations without assistance from an adult (Rogoff, 2003; Hayashi et al., 2009). For this reason, they prefer large class sizes so that children have more opportunities to develop interpersonal and emotional skills. This is different from American schools where a small student-teacher ratio is preferred, likely stemming from a belief that students need individual attention and individualized instruction. The difference in schooling might explain why Japanese children have a better ability to regulate their emotions and show fewer aggressive responses than their North American peers (Zahn-Waxler, Friedman, Cole, Mizuta, & Hiruma, 1996).

In China, students are taught to show respect to teachers, comply with teachers' requests, and stay on task (Phelps, 2005). Moral education, rooted in Confucian traditions, is a significant part of the Chinese school curriculum that teaches students self-control and respect for others. Chinese students are regularly engaged in public evaluations in which they are assessed on school standards and areas for self-improvement are identified. In East Asian cultures, students feel both the positive emotions associated with their own success but may also feel bad for their classmates who did not perform well. American students, after receiving a good grade, rarely think about classmates who are less fortunate (Tsai, 2021).

EMOTIONS AND EMOTION REGULATION IN DIFFERENT CULTURAL GROUPS

In this section, you will learn about emotional behaviors in children from different cultural groups. This information will help you to understand better the emotional behavior of children from different cultural groups. While this information will provide you with broad themes from different cultures, it will be important for you to maintain a curious and open attitude to avoid making assumptions.

Members of Asian American culture highly value family interdependence and harmony with family members, including young ones (Cheah & Leung, 2014). They also put a strong emphasis on self-regulation and social responsibility. This may explain why Asian American children do not have a negative perception of strict parental discipline but instead see it as a way their parents express concern about children. Schooling is very important in Chinese culture as it brings honor to the child's family. That is why children want to perform well at school. Students of Chinese descent may feel that they are not good enough and there is room for them to improve. They may react to praise with embarrassment and doubt whether they deserve the praise (Trommsdorff & Rothbaum, 2008). They also attribute their success to effort as opposed to their ability.

Traditional African American culture places great value on family connectedness, oral communication, and emotional expressiveness. However, a history of oppression or discrimination may encourage behavioral and emotional control (Labella, 2018). Emotion regulation skills are essential to cope with racial discrimination. Some African American mothers may teach children, especially boys, to minimize the display of negative emotions. While such a practice may have a negative effect on European American children, in African American children, it is associated with better social relationships and less aggression. African American families teach children to express or hide their negative emotions depending on the situation (Dunbar, Leerkes, Coard, Supple, & Calkins, 2017). They may encourage boys to restrain expressions of anger so others will not perceive them as being aggressive (Labella, 2018). They also teach children to be flexible in emotional display and to express or suppress their emotions depending on the situation (Labella, 2018). Given that, African American children might not be willing to show their true feelings so they will not "get in trouble." Additionally, experiencing discrimination may heighten emotional reactivity and distress, which also can contribute to emotional problems in African American children (Dunbar et al., 2017).

Family is very important in Arab cultures (Haboush, 2007). Children are socialized to maintain family stability, honor, and collective good. They often seek solutions to their problems in the family rather than on their own. Children from Arab cultures might be very compliant with authority figures, including teachers, but have difficulty making their own decisions. Like in Chinese culture, shame is considered an important emotion for children's socialization. Children are discouraged from showing their emotions openly, except for anger in males. For this reason, teachers might have difficulty understanding how a child of Arabic descent feels. Teachers can use gentle probing ("How did you feel after playing with your friends at recess?") to help children share their emotional experiences.

EMOTIONAL LIFE OF IMMIGRANT CHILDREN

Immigration often creates many challenges for children and their families. Adapting to a new culture can be stressful, especially if families do not have sufficient resources and face language barriers. Immigrant children often encounter a cultural mismatch, meaning there are differences between home values and norms and those in school (Rogers-Sirin, Ryce, & Sirin, 2014). Such a mismatch can be experienced when interacting with both teachers and peers. Children face the stressful task of navigating relationships with peers when they have different norms for interpersonal behavior (Cheah & Leung, 2014). Such a mismatch can lead to misunderstandings of immigrant children by teachers and their peers. Negative emotions resulting from a cultural mismatch can fuel behavioral problems in the classroom, adding another layer of stress for immigrant children.

Children might have difficulty navigating two sets of cultural norms, especially if those norms are drastically different (Cheah & Leung, 2014). For example, after being exposed to the Western image of an affectionate parent, children of Chinese descent might question their parents' style, which might be less affectionate. Interestingly, when observing discrepancies between their own values and those of student's families, teachers perceive immigrant children as less capable and as having more behavioral problems (Rogers-Sirin et al., 2014). It is important to be aware of such a potential bias, as it may impact your relationships with immigrant children and their opportunities for learning.

Loneliness and sadness associated with separation from a familiar environment are common emotional experiences for immigrant children (Cheah & Leung, 2014). A loss of relatives, close friends, and familiar surroundings due to immigration often causes withdrawal behaviors. Importantly, negative emotions may last for an extended period of time after immigration. Children often become depressed if they were separated from their primary caregivers during migration. Such a separation may likely lead to problems with trusting their caregivers at the reunion. Very likely, these children will have difficulty developing trust with their teacher as well. Children who experience distress (especially young ones) often have behavioral problems, including acting out and disruptive behavior. It is important to understand that such behaviors are not intentional but likely result from limited coping skills.

A lack of English language proficiency is another potential cause of stress for immigrant children as it makes learning difficult and limits their opportunities to socialize with peers (Cheah & Leung, 2014). Furthermore, a lack of English language proficiency makes it difficult to express feelings and needs. As a result, these children may not receive the necessary help. Immigrant children also find themselves in the role of language brokers for their families. While it might facilitate their social maturation, it can also cause a feeling of burden, embarrassment, and sadness.

Chapter Summary

- Children's cultures influence how they understand the world and how they express and regulate their emotions. Teachers should be aware of their own culturally based expectations and beliefs and consider how culture may contribute to their students' behaviors and emotional reactions.
- While each culture is quite nuanced, there are two major cultural orientations: individualistic, based on an independent self who values standing out, and collectivistic, based on an interdependent self who values fitting in.
- Culture influences how we express our emotions. It also influences what emotions are considered "ideal" and in what situations certain emotions are desired or undesired.
- Parenting and schooling both have cultural influences. This includes how children are taught emotion regulation, what emotions and behaviors are expected, and how children relate to self and others.
- Immigration brings significant stressors for children, particularly in facing language barriers, acting as an interpreter for family, navigating different cultural norms across settings, and in social experiences.

Self-Reflective Activities

Imagine that you immigrated to another country. You know very little of the language and do not have any friends. What would your life be like in that country? What challenges would you experience living in that country? How would you feel? What strategies would you use to adapt to your new country? If you have ever traveled to another country, you may wish to use these experiences to inform your predictions. Write a one-page essay about your experiences as an immigrant in your self-reflection journal. Try to provide as many details as possible.

Small Group Activities

Activity 1. Discussion

- How does the information in the lesson inform you about emotions in your culture?
- What surprised you when you learned about emotions in different cultures?
- How can cultural differences in emotions inform your work with students and families from different cultures?

Activity 2. Sharing Essays

Share your essay about your imagined experiences as an immigrant with your group. After everybody is done sharing, discuss common emotional experiences depicted in the essays.

Activity 3. Vignettes

> **Chen**
>
> *Chen is a first-generation Chinese American immigrant in Mr. Walker's class. Mr. Walker has been impressed with Chen's hard work during third grade. She listens carefully to his teaching and is always quick to get to work. When Chen scores highest in the class on a math test, Mr. Walker thinks it is a great opportunity to celebrate Chen's performance. Before passing back the tests, he announces to the class, "This was a really hard test, and one of you did an especially good job! Chen, congratulations, you got a*

perfect score!" Mr. Walker is confused when Chen does not show a big smile.

- Why do you think Chen did not respond as he expected her to?
- What do you think Mr. Walker should do now?

Jorge

Jorge is a second-grade student in Mrs. Brady's classroom. Jorge was new to the school at the end of last year after moving to the United States with his father from El Salvador. After several months, Jorge still seems quite shy and keeps to himself throughout the day. He often appears distracted and is sometimes tearful. When Mrs. Brady tries to comfort him, he puts his head on his desk and ignores her. One day, Mrs. Brady sees Jorge take something out of another child's backpack. When he won't talk to her about it, she sighs and tells Jorge he will have to see the principal. Jorge's eyes go wide, and he looks terrified. Mrs. Brady later learns from the principal that Jorge's father was deported over the summer and that he has been living with his aunt.

- How do you think Jorge's father being deported affects his relationship with school staff and his sense of safety at school?
- What strategies would you use for helping Jorge to be more engaged in the classroom?

Aminata

Aminata is a fourth-grade student in Ms. Chapman's class. She is new to the school this year from Senegal and has not been exposed to any English before. Aminata carefully watches the other children at recess, but so far, no one has invited her to play with them. In the classroom, Ms. Chapman assigns partner work and finds Aminata sitting alone in the corner with her work. She has not been able to complete any of the work. Later that day, Ms. Chapman overhears some of the girls talking about Aminata's "weird clothes" and that the lunch food she brings "looks like dog food."

- What suggestions would you give Ms. Chapman for connecting with Aminata given her developing English?
- What do you think Ms. Chapman can do to help improve things for Aminata socially?

Self-Care Tool Kit

Mindfulness With Art

One way to reduce anxiety is to engage in mandala drawing. Mandala in Hinduism and Buddhism represents the universe. The mandala design shows the interconnected and harmonious nature of the universe. Drawing and coloring mandalas require following patterns, and this type of rhythmic activity helps to reduce anxiety and stress. You can download templates of mandala from the internet or buy a coloring mandala book. Engage in drawing or coloring a mandala for 10–15 minutes to enjoy a meditative state.

Om Meditation (Provided by Tara Rajagopal)

"Om" is regarded as a primordial sound in a variety of Indian-origin religions, including Hinduism and Buddhism. It is one of the most sacred and powerful sound vibrations, one that was present at the beginning of time, from which all other sounds and manifest reality emerge. Om is commonly chanted as part of meditation, yogic practices, and mantra chanting or prayer.

The sound "Om" or "Aum" is a combination of three syllables: aa (pronounced *aa* or *uh*), oo (pronounced *oo*), and mm (pronounced *mm*). These are the three sounds produced from the mouth without using the tongue, when it is in an open (*aa*) to slightly closed (*oo*) to closed (*mm*) position. Each of these syllables corresponds to a different part of our body, which can be experienced by saying them and observing where we feel the vibrations in our body. *Aa* relates to our lower abdomen, *oo* to our chest region, and *mm* to our head region. These three syllables are also considered symbolic of the body, mind, and spirit, the chanting of "Om" being the union of the body, mind, and spirit.

In the wisdom traditions, the sound "Om" is said to connect us to something fundamental in our nature and the nature of the universe, a process that in itself calms the mind and body and brings harmony between body, mind, and spirit.

To begin, sit comfortably in a quiet space. You may keep your eyes open or closed, and you can close them at any point during the meditation. Begin by taking a normal breath in and out. Then take a deep breath in, and on the exhale, chant "AAAA" for four counts. See if you can feel the sensations in your abdomen region. Breathe out completely and relax.

Breathe in again and on the exhale chant "OOOO" for four counts. You may feel vibrations in your chest and neck region. Exhale completely and relax. Next, inhale, and on the exhale, chant "MMMM" for four counts. You may feel the vibrations in your head region.

The three syllables will combine to form the "Aum" sound. Take a deep breath in. On the exhale, begin chanting "A-U-M," spending three-quarters of your exhale on the A-U sound and one-quarter on the M sound. Breathe out completely and relax. Breathe normally for a few breaths and observe the sensations in your body.

When you feel ready, take another deep breath in, and on the exhale, chant "A-U-M." Relax. Take your time in between the "A-U-M" chants and observe your body, breath, and mind. Inhale and on the exhale, repeat "A-U-M" one more time. You can do three rounds of Om, and if you'd like, you can do a few more. Once you're done, spend a few minutes sitting quietly and relax. You may observe your breath during this time, and you may also observe sensations in your body. Take a few normal deep breaths in and out.

REFERENCES

Bornstein, M. H. (2015). Culture, parenting, and zero-to-threes. *Zero to Three, 35*(4), 2–9. Retrieved from www.ncbi.nlm.nih.gov/pmc/articles/PMC5865595/

Bruner, J. (1996). *The culture of education*. Harvard University Press.

Cheah, C. S. L., & Leung, C. Y. Y. (2014). The social development of immigrant children: A focus on Asian and Hispanic children in the United States. In P. K. Smith & C. H. Hart (Eds.), *Wiley Blackwell handbooks of developmental psychology: The Wiley Blackwell handbook of childhood social development* (pp. 161–180). Wiley-Blackwell. https://doi.org/10.1002/9781444390933.ch9

Dunbar, A. S., Leerkes, E. M., Coard, S. I., Supple, A. J., & Calkins, S. (2017). An integrative conceptual model of parental racial/ethnic and emotion socialization and links to children's social-emotional development among African American families. *Child Development Perspectives, 11*(1), 16–22. https://doi.org/10.1111/cdep.12218

Geertz, C. (1973). *The interpretation of cultures*. Basic Books.

Haboush, K. L. (2007). Working with Arab American families: Culturally competent practice for school psychologists. *Psychology in the Schools, 44*(2), 183–198. https://doi.org/10.1002/pits.20215

Hayashi, A., Karasawa, M., & Tobin, J. (2009). The Japanese preschool pedagogy of feeling: Cultural strategies for supporting young children's emotional development. *Ethos, 37*(1), 32–49. https://doi.org/10.1111/j.5448-1352.2009.01030x

Hays, S. (2000). Constructing the centrality of culture and deconstructing sociology. *Contemporary Sociology, 29*, 594–602. https://doi.org/10.2307/2654560

Hofstede, G. (1986). Cultural difference in teaching and learning. *International Journal of Intercultural Relations, 10*, 301–320. https://doi.org/10.1016/0147-1767(86)90015-5

Hofstede, G. J., Pedersen, P. B., & Hofstede, G. (2002). *Exploring culture: Exercises, stories, and synthetic cultures.* Intercultural Press. Retrieved from www.jstor.org/stable/40212545

Hyson, M. C., & Lee, K.-M. (1996). Assessing early childhood teachers' beliefs about emotions: Content, contexts, and implications for practice. *Early Education and Development, 7*(1), 59–78. https://doi.org/10.1207/s15566935eed0701_5

Labella, M. H. (2018). The sociocultural context of emotion socialization in African American families. *Clinical Psychology Review, 59*, 1–15. https://doi.org/10.1016/j.cpr.2017.10.006

Markus, H. R., & Hamedani, M. G. (2007). Sociocultural psychology: The dynamic interdependence among self systems and social systems. In S. Kitayama & D. Cohen (Eds.), *Handbook of cultural psychology* (pp. 3–39). Guilford Press.

Markus, H. R., & Kitayama, S. (1991). Culture and the self: Implications for cognition, emotion, and motivation. *Psychological Review, 98*(2), 224–253. https://doi.org/10.1037/0033-295X.98.2.224

Mascolo, M. J., Fisher, K. W., & Li, J. (2003). Dynamic development of component systems of emotions: Pride, shame, and guilt in China and the United States. In R. J. Davidson, K. Shrerer, & H. H. Goldsmith (Eds.), *Handbook of affective science* (pp. 375–408). Oxford University Press.

Masuda, T., Ellsworth, P., Mesquita, B., Leu, J., Tanida, S., & Van de Veerdonk, E. (2008). Placing the face in context: Cultural differences in the perception of facial emotion. *Journal of Personality and Social Psychology, 94*, 365–381. https://doi.org/10.1037/pspa0000022

Mesquita, B., & Leu, J. (2007). The cultural psychology of emotion. In S. Kitayama & D. Cohen (Eds.), *The handbook of cultural psychology* (pp. 734–759). Guilford Press.

Miyamoto, Y., Ma, X., & Wilken, B. (2017). Cultural variation in pro-positive versus balanced systems of emotions. *Current Opinion in Behavioral Sciences, 15*, 27–32. https://doi.org/10.1016/j.cobeha.2017.05.014

Nisbett, R. E., & Masuda, T. (2003). Culture and point of view. *Proceedings of the National Academy of Science, 100*(19), 11163–11170. https://doi.org/10.1073/pnas.1934527100

Phelps, L. (2005). Academic achievement of children in China: The 2002 Fulbright experience. *Psychology in the Schools, 42*(3), 233–239. https://doi.org/10.1002/pits.20074

Rogers-Sirin, L., Ryce, P., & Sirin, S. R. (2014). Acculturation, acculturative stress, and cultural mismatch and their influences on immigrant children and adolescents' well-being. In R. Dimitrova, M. Bender, & F. van de Vijver (Eds.), *Advances in immigrant family research: Global perspectives on well-being in immigrant families* (pp. 11–30). Springer Science + Business Media. https://doi.org/10.1007/978-1-4614-9129-3_2

Rogoff, B. (2003). *The cultural nature of human development*. Oxford University Press.

Rothbaum, F., & Rusk, N. (2011). Pathways to emotion regulation: Cultural differences in internalization. In X. Chen & K. H. Rubin (Eds.), *Socioemotional development in cultural context* (pp. 99–127). Guilford Press.

Rothbaum, F., & Trommsdorff, G. (2007). Do roots and wings complement or oppose on another? The socialization of relatedness and autonomy in cultural context. In J. E. Grusec & P. Hastings (Eds.), *The handbook of socialization: Theory and research* (pp. 461–489). Guilford Press.

Rothbaum, F., Weisz, J., Pott, M., Miyake, K., & Morelli, G. (2000). Attachment and culture: Security in the United States and Japan. *American Psychologist, 55*(10), 1093–1104. https://doi.org/10.1037//0003-066x.55.10.1093

Russell, J. (1991). Culture and categorization of emotions. *Psychological Bulletin, 110*(3), 426–450. https://doi.org/10.1037/0033-2909.110.3.426

Trommsdorff, G., & Rothbaum, F. (2008). Development of emotion regulation in cultural context. In M. Vandekerckhove, C. von Scheve, S. Ismer, S. Jung, & S. Kronast (Eds.), *Regulating emotions: Culture, social necessity, and biological inheritance* (pp. 85–120). Blackwell.

Tsai, J. L. (2007). Ideal affect: Cultural causes and behavioral consequences. *Perspectives on Psychological Science, 19*, 242–259. https://doi.org/10.1111/j.1745-6916.2007.00043.x

Tsai, J. L. (2021). Culture and emotion. In R. Biswas-Diener & E. Diener (Eds.), *Noba textbook series: Psychology*. DEF Publishers. Retrieved from http://noba.to/gfqmxtyw

Tsai, J. L., Louie, J., Chen, E. E., & Uchida, Y. (2007). Learning what feelings to desire: Socialization of ideal affect through children's storybooks. *Personality and Social Psychology Bulletin, 33*, 17–30. https://doi.org/10.1177/0146167206292749

Wang, J. (2011). Communication and cultural competence: The acquisition of cultural knowledge and behavior. *Online Reading in Psychology and Culture, 7*(1). http://dx.doi.org/10.9707/2307-0919.1064

Wierzbicka, A. (1999). *Emotions across languages and cultures: Diversity and universals*. Cambridge University Press.

Yu, N. (2002). Body and emotion: Body parts in Chinese expression of emotion. *Pragmatics & Cognition, 10*(1), 341–367. https://doi.org/10.1075/pc.10.12.14yu

Zahn-Waxler, C., Friedman, R. J., Cole, P. M., Mizuta, I., & Hiruma, N. (1996). Japanese and United States preschool children's responses to conflict and distress. *Child Development, 67*, 2462–2477. https://doi.org/10.2307/1131634

CHAPTER 8

Students' Emotions in the Classroom

For many years, the role of emotions in learning was overlooked, and teachers mostly focused on teaching students academic skills. Today, we have mounting evidence that emotions are essential for learning (Immordino-Yang, 2016). Emotions impact students' ability to pay attention and process information. For example, when children feel anger or anxiety, they do not retain information well. Sadness, boredom, and hopelessness decrease learning motivation and task persistence (Pekrun & Stephens, 2012). Furthermore, when experiencing negative emotions, students have more behavioral problems that distract them from learning. They also have lower grades, regardless of their abilities (Gumora & Arsenio, 2002). The good news is that students experience many positive emotions in the classroom, such as happiness, curiosity, and pride. These emotions support learning. In addition, they fuel more positive emotions (Fredrickson, 2013). You learned earlier that positive emotions motivate us to explore and open our minds to new experiences. When students feel positive emotions, like interest and curiosity, they are more engaged in learning and approach learning tasks more readily.

Keep in mind that students' emotions can be both relevant and irrelevant to learning (Immordino-Yang, 2016). If students are excited when their teacher presents an interesting problem to solve or when they discover something new, their feeling of excitement is relevant to the task and, as such, promotes learning. Alternatively, if students are excited while anticipating a birthday party at the end of the school day, their excitement is not relevant to learning and likely distracts students from learning. Likewise, giving students extrinsic rewards for their learning efforts (e.g., tokens, food, preferred activity) may evoke positive emotions, but these emotions are not relevant to learning either. On the other hand, joy and pride associated with mastering a challenging task directly relate to learning and will sustain students' learning efforts.

SOURCES OF EMOTIONS IN THE CLASSROOM

As a teacher, you need to know potential sources of emotions in the classroom. This knowledge will help you to be strategic in shaping the classroom environment and instruction to increase positive emotions and decrease negative emotions in your students.

Emotions Directly Linked to Learning

Emotions arise as a result of control and value appraisals related to academic tasks (Pekrun & Stephens, 2012). These are called achievement emotions. *Control appraisal* is students' appraisal of their perceived control over the task ("Can I do this task?"), while *value appraisal* reflects the significance of the task for the student ("Is this task important to me?"). Tasks perceived as very important likely evoke strong emotions, while less important tasks elicit milder emotions. However, the valence of emotions, whether they are positive or negative, depends on the level of perceived control over outcomes. Very important but not achievable tasks trigger anxiety, while difficult but attainable tasks may make students feel joy and pride when they have completed the tasks. Additionally, students may experience shame when they fail a task and anger when they believe they did not have the ability to complete the task (Pekrun & Stephens, 2012).

The learning process itself elicits emotions (Pekrun & Stephens, 2012). These include joy when the student finds a solution to a learning problem or surprise when discovering something new and unexpected. Students also may experience confusion when learning new material that goes against their prior knowledge. For example, students may believe that one-eighth is greater than one-fourth. When a teacher explains that this is otherwise, they may feel confused. The learning content can also evoke emotions (Pekrun & Stephens, 2012). Students may feel guilt when learning that children in impoverished areas do not have basic necessities or angry that girls are not permitted to attend school in some countries. Their reactions vary depending on their unique life experiences. For instance, during a Martin Luther King presentation, a student may feel shame at racist ideas they have heard from family members.

Teachers' Instruction and Behavior

Teachers' instructional behaviors are another source of students' emotions. When teachers are perceived as cold, distant, unfriendly, or aloof, it evokes negative emotions in students (Mainhard, Oudman, Hornstra, Bosker, & Goetz, 2018). Teachers who are anxious or put a lot of pressure on students also elicit negative emotions. On the other hand, a teacher's warmth brings enjoyment and reduces anxiety in students. Several characteristics of teachers' behavior are associated with positive emotions in students (Goetz, Pekrun, Hall, & Haag, 2006; Mouratidis, Vansteenkiste, Michou, & Lens, 2013). They include giving clear instructions, enforcing clear rules, supporting students, and making them feel competent. Additionally, classroom management also affects students' emotional experiences. A predictable and well-organized classroom provides a sense of safety, while an unpredictable and poorly organized classroom environment may contribute to students' anxiety (Day, Connor, & McClelland, 2015).

Emotional Contagion

You already know about the contagious nature of emotions. Indeed, teachers' joy, anger, or anxiety influences students' emotions simply through emotional contagion. That is why you have to be mindful of what emotions you display in the classroom. This is not to say that you have to suppress or hide your negative emotions; to do so would be unhealthy and disingenuous. Furthermore, an occasional appropriate expression of negative emotions is not harmful. Instead, it shows your students that you are as human as they are. At the same time, if you often feel down or have difficulty managing your own anxiety, this may affect the emotional climate in the classroom. For this reason, your emotional health and the ability to regulate your own emotions are essential for your job.

Peer Relationships

Relationships with peers can significantly affect students' emotional experiences in the classroom. Good relationships with peers make students feel joy and happiness. However, when a student is rejected, teased, or coerced by others, it can fuel anger, shame, confusion, or sadness (Furrer, Skinner, & Pitzer, 2014). Negative peer relations are associated with depression and loneliness. Students who experience these emotions often have negative thoughts about themselves and school (Flook, Repetti, & Ullman, 2005).

Another route through which students can affect each other emotionally is social comparison (Steinbeis & Singer, 2013). Examples include when one student receives a high grade or praise while another does not or if a student is assigned to a lower-level reading group. These situations can evoke negative emotions. That is why you have to avoid comparing students with one another and creating competition among them. In order to help children grow, you can emphasize that each child's "best" is based on their previous performance and emphasize individual growth. A sense of mastery or accomplishment, even a small one, has a very positive effect on a child's motivation to learn.

Let's take a closer look at emotions that have significant implications for learning. These are anxiety, boredom, and curiosity.

ANXIETY

Anxiety is the most common negative emotion experienced in the classroom. About 10%–30% of children report test anxiety (Lobman, 2014). Anxiety is triggered when students believe that the demands of the task are greater than their capacities (Lohbeck, Nitkowski, & Petermann, 2016). Students with a low academic self-concept experience higher test anxiety. Test anxiety leads to lower grades, underachievement, reduced intrinsic motivation, lower confidence related to problem solving, and an increased risk of emotional problems (Lohbeck et al., 2016). The negative impact of test anxiety is even stronger for children from families with low socioeconomic status, non-native English speakers, and girls (McDonald, 2001). In addition, when students are praised for their ability ("You are smart") rather than for effort ("You worked very hard"), they perceive failure on tests as the result of their low ability. Equating grades with ability rather than effort makes children vulnerable to anxiety when they are not doing well academically (Lobman, 2014; McDonald, 2001).

Anxious students often have thoughts that take up space in their working memory. For example, "I am going to fail this test," "I worry that my father will be deported," or "I am afraid no one will sit with me at lunch." They also may experience intrusive thoughts about outcomes and the future, such as, "If I fail, I'm going to be held back," or "What if my mom doesn't get a job?" These anxious thoughts can compromise learning by reducing working memory resources allocated for learning (Pekrun & Stephens, 2012).

Keep in mind that anxiety can be linked to parental expectations (Ringeisen & Raufelder, 2015). Parents who have high performance expectations for their children may put their children at risk of becoming anxious, especially if the children believe their parents' love is contingent on how well they do at school. When this happens, children experience anxiety, alongside feelings of guilt or shame. As a coping mechanism, they may develop perfectionistic tendencies – they want to do everything very well. This can slow them down during academic tasks which then creates more anxiety.

It is important for you to identify anxious students in the classroom. These students worry frequently, can be clingy with adults, or have a hard time separating from their caregivers. They may also engage in nail-biting, hair twirling, leg bouncing, pencil tapping, and chewing on items, such as clothing or pens. Anxious students often have negative self-talk such as "I cannot do this task," "I am not good in math," "This is so difficult," or "I will fail the test." Keep in mind that anxiety in children may also manifest as anger or oppositional behavior. Furthermore, anxiety may cause inattentiveness and hyperactivity and be mistaken for ADHD.

It is important to remember the association between anxiety and avoidance. Students may develop patterns of asking to go to the nurse or the bathroom during difficult tasks or refuse to come to school altogether when their anxiety feels unmanageable. Misbehavior can also be a means of avoidance. For example, if a student throws a cup at math time, he may spend the block in a buddy classroom instead of doing math. In future difficult academic situations, he may use misbehavior to avoid the task and reduce his anxiety associated with low math competence. While safety is paramount, you need to be vigilant to these behaviors and not allow avoidance to become a pattern.

How to Reduce Anxiety in the Classroom

- ***Find ways to manage your own worries***. Children look to adults to learn how they need to react to situations. If you have difficulty managing your anxiety, you may struggle to be a good model for your students. It will be important for you to find ways to stay calm and promote confidence in your students.

- ***Help children understand what anxiety feels and sounds like.*** Provide developmentally appropriate explanations of how children may experience worry. This includes worried thoughts ("I'm scared," "This is too hard") and negative predictions ("I'm going to fail," "I can't do it."), worried sensations (tingling, tummy aches, headaches, dizziness, heart pounding), and a worried mood. Being able to identify worry is an important step for calming down.
- ***Give worry an image.*** Worry is an abstract thing, especially for young children. Help children to externalize their worries by drawing them, making them out of clay, or describing what they look and feel like. Students might even give their worries a name! This helps to move their worries outside of them rather than being an all-consuming, internal experience. This also allows students to interact differently with their worries. They can tell their worries to "go away" or that worries are "too loud," so they need to make worries quiet.
- ***Put the worry away.*** One way to move worries outside of oneself is through a "worry box." Choose a small box with a lid. Consider decorating it or allowing students to help decorate it. Give students paper and have them write or draw their worries on the paper. Then have them "put their worries away" by putting them in the box and closing it. For the same purpose, you can designate a "worry shelf."
- ***Teach stress-reduction techniques.*** Learning how to reduce stress and anxiety can help children calm themselves. Provide instruction about meditation, deep breathing, and visualization as tools that students can use during stressful situations. (You will learn more about these techniques in Chapter 12).
- ***Make children the experts.*** Tell students a story about a child who is worried and ask them to give the worried child ideas of what to do to feel better.
- ***Change the attitude.*** While your district may create a sense of angst about testing, you do not have to carry this into your classroom. Emphasize that testing is to allow students to show what they know and to help teachers know how they are doing at teaching students. Keep the focus on learning and growing and avoid focusing on performance.
- ***Normalize anxiety.*** Help children to understand that a little worry is helpful but having too much worry gets in the way. Give students a

chance to know that others are worried too. You can do this through anonymous means, like having students put their heads down and raise their hands to indicate if they are feeling anxious. You can do the same activity visually by asking students to stand in a circle and ask them to step forward in response to prompts like, "Step forward if you would rather pet a lion than take a test."

- ***Work together: Make it a team effort***. Working as a group to combat anxiety can have a positive effect. Make it a group effort to help everyone to manage their worries better. Talk about it regularly and build anxiety management strategies into the daily routine.

BOREDOM

Every teacher at some point has heard a student complain, "This is boring!" Indeed, boredom is common in an educational setting (Goetz & Hall, 2014; Vogel-Walcutt, Fiorella, Carper, & Schatz, 2012). Boredom is associated with a lack of arousal and interest in one's environment. It reduces learning motivation, impedes learning, and sometimes leads to dropping out of school. Some students are disinterested because they have so-called trait boredom. This type of boredom is difficult to mitigate since its source is located within the student. More often boredom is related to environmental factors, such as a teacher's instruction. This means that boredom can be prevented or mitigated by changing the method of instruction or other factors in the classroom. In the classroom, boredom arises when students do not see the value of a task ("What's the point?") or the tasks are not clearly defined. Boredom also emerges if students lack the skills to complete a task or a teacher does not show interest in the task. Furthermore, repetitive tasks or tasks that are frequently interrupted also may evoke boredom (Goetz & Hall, 2014; Vogel-Walcutt et al., 2012).

How do we know when students are bored? While there is the telltale complaint of, "This is boring," students may not always give the teacher a direct indication that they are bored. Restlessness, slouched posture, decreased eye gaze, and off-task behavior are signs that boredom is growing. Paying attention to behavioral patterns can help you mitigate boredom before you lose student interest entirely. For instance, you may start noticing that after 15 minutes of sitting on the carpet, your students are antsy and are no longer looking at the board. In another situation, you may notice that the front half of the class is carefully watching your science experiment while students in the back are fiddling with their pencils. Keep in mind that students have to hear, see, and understand the material in order to sustain engagement.

How to Mitigate Boredom

Several recommendations can help you mitigate boredom in the classroom (Vogel-Walcutt et al., 2012):

- *Make learning meaningful.* As you introduce new material, think about the ways that it might be relevant to your students. Provide concrete examples of how to apply things students are learning to real life. Additionally, ask students to make connections between the learning material and things they have seen or experienced in their own lives.
- *Make sure students are equipped for learning.* Use pre-assessments and your knowledge of your students to plan lessons that are at an appropriate difficulty level. Activate prior knowledge and review foundational skills early in the lesson. If some students require more remediation, have more advanced students review the basics. If the lesson will be long, consider how you can incorporate active practice or pair work to sustain arousal.
- *Mix it up.* Doing the same thing over and over again can make students bored. Promote excitement and novelty by introducing different ways of practicing, moving on to new tasks, challenging students to do something more quickly, encouraging and testing predictions, or introducing elements of surprise.
- *Solicit and incorporate feedback.* Students of all levels are able to share some level of input on what they like and do not like in learning. Do they like learning in their seats or on the floor? Do they like it when you use the SmartBoard or when they work on their own papers? Try to seek feedback on things that can be adjusted and avoid seeking feedback on things that cannot – this will likely only fuel frustration.
- *Set the frame.* Have clear goals for your lessons and inform your students about those goals at the beginning of the lesson. Giving an overview of the goals helps students direct their attention to information that is meaningful and activate their relevant prior knowledge.

- ***Offer challenges***. Easy tasks can be boring to students. Find ways to challenge them.

CURIOSITY

Curiosity is a desire to learn for the sake of learning, not because of external benefits such as receiving a good grade or avoiding shame from poor performance (Markey & Loewenstein, 2014). It arises when students experience a knowledge gap – a feeling that they are missing an important piece of information necessary to comprehend something. This gap, however, should not be very large, as students have to perceive that they are capable of closing that gap. Curiosity facilitates learning: Students who experience curiosity have a better ability to focus their attention on the task, retain knowledge and skills, and seek information. Given the benefit of curiosity for learning, you can use the following strategies to foster it in the classroom (Markey & Loewenstein, 2014).

- ***Make students feel comfortable to show their knowledge gap***. Create a learning environment where students feel comfortable taking risks and demonstrating knowledge gaps. You can model this by saying, "I am curious how many days it will take before these seeds will sprout. I do not have an answer, but we can find out." Students can focus on their knowledge gap when they are not afraid to make a mistake or to show that they do not know something.
- ***Show enthusiasm***. Your enthusiasm for the subject matter and your own curiosity can foster curiosity in your students. Opening statements like, "I am curious," "I want to know," and "I wonder" can help students adopt a curiosity mindset.
- ***Create opportunities for surprise***. Surprise can stimulate curiosity. Surprise arises when students' expectations are challenged. For example, they may expect a large piece of wood would sink but a little metal bolt would not. They feel surprised when they learn otherwise. This is a great opportunity to pique their curiosity about why some large objects may float and small ones sink.
- ***Answer questions***. Curiosity can be reinforced when teachers answer students' questions or encourage them to answer those questions. Doing this helps students make a positive association between being curious and closing their information gaps. Asking students to make predictions also fosters their curiosity. Even if their answer is incorrect, they may feel surprised, which can stimulate their curiosity.

- *Use a Know-Want-to-Know-Learned graphic organizer.* Using a Know-Want-to-Know-Learned graphic organizer helps students explicitly identify their knowledge gaps and stimulate their desire to fill them.

Chapter Summary

- Emotions are an important part of learning. They affect attention, information processing, memory, motivation, and engagement.
- Emotions arise from academic material, perceptions of competency and ability to complete tasks, interactions with peers and teachers, and social comparisons.
- Anxiety is the most common negative emotion in the classroom and contributes to many negative outcomes. Anxiety arises from negative appraisals, poor sense of competence, and parental expectations.
- Boredom reduces motivation and impedes learning. Being aware of signs of boredom will allow you to adapt your instruction.
- Curiosity arises from the awareness that one does not know something and motivation to close this knowledge gap. It promotes exploration and attention.

Self-Reflective Activities

Think back to when you were an elementary school student. Recall one situation when you experienced negative emotions. Describe that situation in detail. Who was involved in that situation? What specifically did you feel? Why do you think you remember that situation?

Now, recall one situation when you experienced positive emotions. Describe that situation in detail. Who was involved in that situation? What specifically did you feel? Why do you think you remember that situation?

Describe both experiences in your self-reflection journal.

Small Group Activities

Activity 1. Emotion-Eliciting Situations in the Classroom

Identify classroom situations that can potentially evoke anxiety in students. Consider how learning tasks, peer relationships, and the teacher's behavior can cause anxiety.

Identify classroom situations that can potentially evoke anger in students. Consider how learning tasks, peer relationships, and the teacher's behavior can cause anger.

Activity 2. Role-Play

Develop a brief lesson plan about butterflies to teach to second-grade students. Deliver your lesson as a group. Make your lesson as engaging as possible but also developmentally appropriate. Use strategies to evoke curiosity and amusement in your audience. Other students in the class can offer feedback about effective or ineffective strategies to engage them.

Self-Care Tool Kit

My Special Place Meditation

Often, we need a break from what's going on in the present (or when we're thinking about the past or worrying about the future). One way to do this is to use a special place meditation. Your special place is a place you can retreat to in your mind to find some peace and comfort in the moment. The following is a practice exercise to help you find your special place.

Begin by sitting comfortably in a chair, feet on the floor, and hands in your lap. Lower or close your eyes and begin to focus on your breath. Take several long, slow, and deep breaths in and out, bringing yourself into the present. Now begin to find your special place. Retreat into your mind and imagine a place where you would feel comfortable and safe. This may be a place that you already know or a place you need to make up. It might be somewhere in your home, somewhere outside, or a place you would like to vacation.

Once you have settled on your special place, begin to imagine yourself there. Where would you be sitting? Imagine what it feels like. Is there grass or sand beneath you or possibly the soft, comfortable cloth of a sofa? Try to imagine what it feels like as you sit comfortably in your special place. What does the air feel like on your skin? Notice how your body settles into place as you begin to relax in comfort.

What can you smell around you? What are your senses telling you about this place? Let your senses tell you about this space – the smells, the sights, the textures, and maybe even the taste. In this space, what emotions do you feel? Happy, content, or nostalgic? Whatever you feel here, begin to fill yourself up with that feeling, letting it seep into your mind and throughout your body, reveling in how you feel right now. Let yourself feel comfortable, light, full of contentment. Start coming back into the present moment, wiggling your fingers and toes and bringing your attention to the seat beneath you. Take a long breath in and a slow breath out. You are here.

REFERENCES

Day, S. L., Connor, C. M., & McClelland, M. M. (2015). Children's behavioral regulation and literacy: The impact of the first grade classroom environment. *Journal of School Psychology, 53*(5), 409–428. https://doi.org/10.1016/j.jsp.2015.07.004

Flook, L., Repetti, R. L., & Ullman, J. B. (2005). Classroom social experiences as predictors of academic performance. *Developmental Psychology, 41*(2), 319–327. https://doi.org/10.1037/0012-1649.41.2.319

Fredrickson, B. L. (2013). Positive emotions broaden and build. *Advances in Experimental Social Psychology, 47,* 1–53. https://doi.org/10.1016/B978-0-12-407236-7.00001-2

Furrer, C., Skinner, E., & Pitzer, J. (2014). The influence of teacher and peer relationships on students' classroom engagement and everyday motivational resilience. *Teachers College Record, 116,* 101–123.

Goetz, T., & Hall, N. C. (2014). Academic boredom. In R. Pekrun & L. Linnenbrink-Garcia (Eds.), *Educational psychology handbook series: International handbook of emotions in education* (pp. 311–330). Routledge/Taylor & Francis Group.

Goetz, T., Pekrun, R., Hall, N., & Haag, L. (2006). Academic emotions from a social-cognitive perspective: Antecedents and domain specificity of students' affect in the context of Latin instruction. *British Journal of Educational Psychology, 76*(2), 289–308. https://doi.org/10.1348/000709905X42860

Gumora, G., & Arsenio, W. F. (2002). Emotionality, emotion regulation, and school performance in middle school children. *Journal of School Psychology, 40*(5), 395–413. https://doi.org/10.1016/S0022-4405(02)00108-5

Immordino-Yang, M. H. (2016). *The Norton series on the social neuroscience of education - Emotions, learning, and the brain: Exploring the educational implications of affective neuroscience.* W. W. Norton & Company.

Lobman, C. (2014). "I feel nervous . . . very nervous": Addressing test anxiety in inner city schools through play and performance. *Urban Education, 49*(3), 329–359. https://doi.org/10.1177/0042085913478621

Lohbeck, A., Nitkowski, D., & Petermann, F. (2016). A control-value theory approach: Relationships between academic self-concept, interest, and test anxiety in elementary school children. *Child & Youth Care Forum, 45*, 887–904. https://doi.org/10.1007/s10566-016-9362-1

Mainhard, T., Oudman, S., Hornstra, L., Bosker, R. J., & Goetz, T. (2018). Student emotions in class: The relative importance of teachers and their interpersonal relations with students. *Learning and Instruction, 53*, 109–119. https://doi.org/10.1016/j.learninstruc.2017.07.011

Markey, A., & Loewenstein, G. (2014). Curiosity. In R. Pekrun & L. Linnenbrink-Garcia (Eds.), *Educational psychology handbook series – International handbook of emotions in education* (pp. 228–245). Routledge/Taylor & Francis Group.

McDonald, A. S. (2001). The prevalence and effects of test anxiety in school children. *Educational Psychology, 21*(1), 89–101. https://doi.org/10.1080/01443410020019867

Mouratidis, A., Vansteenkiste, M., Michou, A., & Lens, W. (2013). Perceived structure and achievement goals as predictors of students' self-regulated learning and affect and the mediating role of competence need satisfaction. *Learning and Individual Differences, 23*, 179–186. https://doi.org/10.1016/j.lindif.2012.09.001

Pekrun, R., & Stephens, E. J. (2012). Academic emotions. In K. R. Harris, S. Graham, T. Urdan, S. Graham, J. M. Royer, & M. Zeidner (Eds.), *APA handbooks in psychology - APA educational psychology handbook, Vol. 2: Individual differences and cultural and contextual factors* (pp. 3–31). American Psychological Association. https://doi.org/10.1037/13274-001

Ringeisen, T., & Raufelder, D. (2015). The interplay of parental support, parental pressure and test anxiety – Gender differences in adolescents. *Journal of Adolescence, 45*, 67–79. https://doi.org/10.1016/j.adolescence.2015.08.018

Steinbeis, N., & Singer, T. (2013). The effects of social comparison on social emotions and behavior during childhood: The ontogeny of envy and Schadenfreude predicts developmental changes in equity-related decisions. *Journal of Experimental Child Psychology, 115*(1), 198–209. https://doi.org/10.1016/j.jecp.2012.11.009

Vogel-Walcutt, J. J., Fiorella, L., Carper, T., & Schatz, S. (2012). The definition, assessment, and mitigation of state boredom within educational settings: A comprehensive review. *Educational Psychology Review, 24*(1), 89–111. https://doi.org/10.1007/s10648-011-9182-7

CHAPTER 9

How to Understand and Respond to Children's Emotions

Children experience a myriad of emotions. They feel happy when others care about them and joy when playing with friends. They may experience anger when they do not get what they want or when a friend was treated unfairly. They can also become anxious when speaking in front of the class or when their parents do not pick them up on time after school. An event that seems trivial to adults may evoke a strong emotional reaction in children. Furthermore, children will remember that event for a long time – emotional memories are long-lasting. Children also have different ways to express their emotions. Some children show their emotions openly, while others may have little emotional expression. Lack of external expression does not mean that children do not have any emotions. Quite the opposite, they may experience very intense emotions.

Emotions drive our behaviors. Therefore, understanding children's emotions will help you to understand why they do what they do. Furthermore, showing children that you understand their emotions is important for building relationships in the classroom. Understanding children's emotions is also important for managing potential emotionally intense outbursts in the classroom. Children rarely display aggression without signs of being emotionally upset and displaying emotional escalation. The ability to recognize emotional cues allows teachers to intervene effectively and preemptively before children's behaviors become problematic. This is important because it becomes increasingly difficult to calm a child as behavior escalates. Additionally, children who repeatedly get to this point in a crisis cycle are "practicing" negative behaviors, making it more likely for them to repeat such behaviors.

A teacher's misinterpretation of disruptive behavior and its underlying emotion(s) can inadvertently escalate a conflict, ultimately leading the teacher to feel emotionally drained (Chang & Davis, 2009). Unfortunately, sometimes teachers think that a child is purposefully refusing or not complying. As a result, the teacher emotionally escalates with the child and engages in angry redirection, inadvertent shaming, and punishing behaviors. Therefore, it is important to accurately identify both the external expression of emotions and the underlying needs and internal experience of the child in order to respond effectively.

PLACING A CHILD'S EMOTIONAL BEHAVIOR IN CONTEXT

In order to understand children's emotions, you first need to "read" their nonverbal emotional cues, such as facial expression, posture, and arousal levels. Accurate interpretation of emotions also requires attention to the child's voice volume and tone and the child's level of engagement with others. For example, children who feel sad often avoid group activities, and those who feel angry tend to speak louder and faster. You also need to pay attention to how feelings are manifested. While emotional expressions are universal across cultures, there are culture-specific emotion display rules. As you learned earlier, some cultures promote open emotional expression while others promote a more reserved display of emotions.

"Reading" of nonverbal behavior is important in order to understand a child's feelings, but it is not enough. Sometimes the outward behavior may not match a child's inner experience. For example, in children with trauma, aggression may be a manifestation of their anxiety. Shame can lead to false bravado, while "acting out" behaviors might stem from feelings of fear or powerlessness, being out of control, or having a need for boundaries. Given that, understanding children's emotions may not be simple and straightforward. That is why you need to place children's emotional behavior in context.

Distal and proximal factors interact and create emotion-eliciting situations for children. Increased awareness of such factors will help you more accurately recognize and understand children's emotional experiences and find a way to respond to them. For example, a teacher raising her voice may elicit fear from a child to whom a raised voice was a prelude to physical discipline or shaming in his family. Keep in mind that emotions might be elicited through the activation of memories of previous relational transactions. A student receiving critical feedback from a teacher may be reminded of her father telling her that she never does anything right. Awareness of a connection between current and past relational experiences is important for understanding children's emotions.

Earlier, you learned how emotional schemas influence our emotional experiences. Emotional schemas determine not only how children interpret emotion-eliciting events but also their attention to specific elements of events. An attachment-related working model represents an early schema that can significantly impact a child's experiences. An insecurely attached child often seeks signs of potential rejection in interactions with the teacher. That is why when the teacher is helping other children in the classroom, this child may become visibly upset and even start acting up. Without contextual knowledge (i.e., the child's insecure attachment), the child's behavior may come as a surprise. Furthermore, the teacher may erroneously assume that the child became upset because of a disagreement with his peer. In this case, the teacher would likely try to separate the two children instead of giving attention to the child. It is easy to predict that this action will not solve the problem.

EMOTIONS SIGNAL A CHILD'S NEEDS

Children's emotional behavior is more accurately understood when considering their needs. All children have needs for safety, mastery, autonomy, competency, power, and relatedness (Glasser, 1998; Ryan & Deci, 2017). Understanding a child's experience in this context broadens the available strategies for responding to the child's emotions. Understanding an association between children's needs and emotions can inform effective responding and prevent problem behaviors.

Anger often signals a need for power (Keltner, Oatley, & Jenkins, 2018). Imagine a strong-willed child in the classroom who likes to be a leader; however, he does not have this opportunity because of behavioral problems. This child might respond with anger if you put limits on him. In this case, his anger signals to you that his need for power is being blocked. However, if you recognize that this child has a need for power, you can provide him with an opportunity to take a leadership role. In this case, his need for power would be met, thus minimizing opportunities for angry reactions. Anxiety, on the other hand, signals a need for orientation and control (Epstein, 1990). Children need to make sense of their experiences, know what is going on around them, and control their environment. That is why when a teacher makes changes in the classroom frequently (e.g., in the schedule or small group composition), it might cause anxiety in children because their environment becomes unpredictable.

AWARENESS OF YOUR OWN EMOTIONAL EXPERIENCES AND REACTIONS

As a teacher, you need to be aware of how your own experiences may impact your perception of students' emotions. Failure to attend to your own triggers and experiences may hinder accurate interpretation of another's experience. Awareness of your own emotional experiences will reduce bias and increase openness to a broad range of factors that might influence your emotional reactions. For instance, a teacher who experienced a contentious parental separation growing up may assume that a student is appearing sad because his parents are in the process of divorcing. However, this interpretation might be inaccurate, and the child is actually sad because his friends did not invite him to join a soccer game. Awareness of your own personal history is important for an accurate understanding of children's emotions. Furthermore, you need to separate your emotions from those of your students. You may become very upset when learning that one of your students has very little food at home or no warm clothes. While your emotional reactions are understandable, they can be overwhelming and cause distress. Experiencing distress while empathizing with others' unfortunate life circumstances may contribute to emotional burnout and make you ineffective in responding to your students' needs. That is why teachers' ability to regulate their emotions is critical in this regard.

EMPATHETIC ATTUNEMENT

"It is a deep comfort to children to discover that their feelings are a normal part of the human experience. There is no better way to convey that than to understand them" (Ginott, 2003, p. 21). Understanding children's emotions requires empathetic attunement. Empathetic attunement means being aware of and responsive to a child's emotional experience. A teacher's empathy allows students to feel that they are seen, heard, and deeply understood (Jordan & Schwartz, 2018). It further creates an emotional connection between teacher and child. It is particularly important when children experience intense emotions. Interactions with a warm and caring teacher provide a corrective emotional experience for children. Empathetic attunement also allows you to validate children's emotions. For example, statements like, "You will be fine," or "Everything will be OK," invalidate the child's emotional experience and do not make him or her heard. You need to show children that you understand their emotions.

Attunement is a two-part process that begins with empathy (Erskine, 2015). Empathy is sensing a child's experience, like seeing the world through his or her eyes. However, attunement goes beyond understanding how a child feels and includes communication of your understanding to the child. This is a delicate matter, as you have to keep in mind the child's need for security. That is why you need to be respectful of and sensitive to a child's vulnerabilities. For example, after an emotional outburst, a child might feel ashamed. Make sure that your interactions with the child do not exacerbate this feeling. Attunement involves empathetic awareness of a child's relational needs, including the need to feel validated, affirmed, and important to others (Erskine, 2015). These needs can be met when you show your understanding of the child's experiences and help him or her openly express his or her feelings without fear of being rejected or punished.

Empathetic attunement can be promoted by using several strategies. First, it includes matching a child's emotional experience. Anxious and timid children need a soft look and quiet voice; with energetic children, you need to show energy as well. Consider a child who was pushed down by another child and starts yelling, "Hey, you pushed me!" In talking with that child, using a tone that matches the child's angry experience is likely to be validating and provide a message that the child's experience is understood. In contrast, a neutral response may be experienced as invalidating.

Second, attuned responding includes the ability to verbally convey to a child his or her emotional experience. For example, you might move next to a girl standing alone at recess and say, "It looks like you are feeling sad. I saw that you were trying to join the girls playing with blocks, and they didn't invite you to play with them." This reflection shows the child that she is understood. It also creates a relational transaction in which the child can use the adult to manage her emotional experience. Use a gentle and curious attitude if you are not sure of the child's emotional experience. You might say, "I saw you put your head down when we started talking about Picture Day. It looks like you feel a bit sad. Am I right?" This conveys that you are interested while leaving space for the child to provide clarification. Avoid peppering a child with many questions, as it can make the child feel overwhelmed. As a result, the child may retreat inward and reduce his or her communication with you. Additionally, speculating extensively about what a child feels (especially when the child is anxious) may introduce new worries. Remember to address emotional issues privately when possible in order to reduce feelings of embarrassment or shame.

Empathic responding is rooted in a nondefensive stance that avoids blaming others for their behaviors or problems they created. It includes openness to acknowledge the teacher's contribution to emotional situations in the classroom. Perhaps the lesson was a little longer than planned and children had difficulty staying engaged, or perhaps the new seating design in the classroom is contributing to more chatting among students. Empathic responding can be derailed when teachers feel wronged by a child, an experience that is often rooted in their own beliefs and values. For some, it may interact with a common value that "children should respect their elders;" for others, noncompliance may be perceived as a threat to the goals of being an efficacious teacher. You need to be able to recognize when you experience an intense emotional reaction to a child's behavior and engage in reflection that allows for a more empathic stance.

EMOTIONAL COACHING

Emotional coaching is an effective strategy to practice empathetic attunements (Gottman, Katz, & Hooven, 1997). Imagine a situation where you assign your students to work on their journals. You see one student start to write and then erase his work over and over. After a few minutes, he gets up and stomps to the trash can, where he rips his paper before going back to his desk and putting his head down. You can provide a child with emotional coaching using the following steps:

- Identify the child's feelings. (How does the child feel?)
- Allow the child to experience the feeling (unless it is intensely negative or scary).

- Reflect on how you feel. Is there a need to regulate yourself before responding to the child?
- Think about what could possibly make the child feel this way.
- Label the child's feelings and make a connection between those feelings and a potential cause: "You are upset because you really wanted to do well on this task, but it was hard for you."
- Get affirmation from the child that you understand him or her correctly: "Did I understand you correctly?"
- Validate the child's feelings: "Most kids would feel that way if that happened to them."
- Problem solve with the child's feelings: "You can keep practicing, and it will get easier."

WHAT TO DO WHEN THE EMOTIONAL CONNECTION IS BROKEN

It is not uncommon for a teacher to feel emotionally disconnected from students. In the end, teachers are human beings with their own relational and emotional needs, and students can elicit feelings of frustration, annoyance, and displeasure. This disconnection may be a result of fatigue or arise when working with children with behavioral problems. The lack of an emotional connection makes it difficult to be attuned to a child and, in some cases, may even lead a teacher to avoid interactions with that child. Three strategies can help you to reconnect emotionally with your students: notice, pause, and reconnect (Jordan & Schwartz, 2018). First, teachers have to notice signs of emotional disconnection. These can be feelings of anger, annoyance, or boredom. If you notice these feelings associated with a child or children, pause and reflect on what is happening to you internally. For example, you may be uncomfortable or feel unequipped to deal with the situation. It is possible that the child's behavior may have triggered something related to your own personal experience beyond the classroom, like feelings of rejection, being undervalued or unappreciated, or powerlessness. It is important for you to remain present with the child while reflecting on uncomfortable feelings you experience.

Keep in mind that sometimes children may not be ready or desire to make a connection with you, as they may want to protect themselves against being hurt (Jordan & Schwartz, 2018). A child's emotional security should take priority, so give him or her space. Reconnection with a child may be difficult if you already have a strained relationship with him or her. In this situation, think of positive moments associated with the child or remind yourself that your goal is to have a good teacher-student relationship to help the student succeed academically.

It is also important for you to reflect on what may have led you to disconnect emotionally from the child. Some teachers may have difficulty connecting with students because of their own childhood or relational experiences (Jordan & Schwartz, 2018). It is important to think about potential triggers that might lead you to disconnect from another person. In addition, it is helpful to reflect on how you disconnect from others. Some people may disconnect by ignoring or even blaming others. Setting time aside to reflect on your relationship with a child can help you better understand that child's emotional experiences and your reactions toward him or her. One way to do this is through weekly journaling where you can reflect on one or more children with whom you are struggling. Finally, you should also practice showing empathy toward yourself. Your emotional health ultimately affects your effectiveness as a teacher and the emotional climate in the classroom.

Chapter Summary

- Children feel a variety of emotions, and these emotions drive their behaviors. Understanding children's emotions allows a teacher to respond effectively and can prevent emotional and behavioral escalation.
- Emotional behaviors arise from proximal and distal experiences. What the child feels is determined in part by his or her relational history. Children also have needs for power, mastery, and competence, which influence their emotions and reactions.
- Teacher reactions to student emotions are important. How you react is likely to be influenced by who you are: your history, personal life, and ability to keep yourself from being overwhelmed by others' experiences, needs, and emotions.
- Teachers can support children's emotions by empathic attunement, which involves recognizing and responding to the child's emotions and being able to convey to the child that you understand his or her experiences. Emotional coaching is a way to do this.
- Building and maintaining relationships with students is challenging when students evoke unpleasant feelings for you or remind you of struggles or challenges in your own life. It is important

to be aware of and open to these experiences so that you can reflect on what is causing them and utilize strategies to rebuild the connection.

Self-Reflective Activities

Think about your school experiences and when you felt emotionally connected with your teacher(s). Which teachers' behaviors made you feel emotionally connected? If you do not recall such an experience, reflect on situations when you felt emotionally disconnected from your teachers. Write your reflections in your journal.

Small Group Activities

Activity 1. How Does This Girl Feel?

Using the internet, find the painting "Disgrace" by Charles Burton Barber (1845–1894). In your group, discuss the character's emotions using the following questions:

- What emotions is this girl experiencing?
- What events preceded this situation? Use your imagination to come up with a scenario.
- What do you think might happen after this scene?
- Will she feel other emotions?
- How do you think those emotions might manifest?
- How do you feel about this girl?
- What do you want to do?

Activity 2. Vignettes

Read the following vignette and discuss how Darren might feel.

> **Darren**
>
> Ms. Lopez's third-grade class is sitting on the carpet doing a language arts lesson. Ms. Lopez writes two words on the board and asks if any student can create a sentence with those words. Darren is the first student to raise his hand, and he eagerly waves his arm in the air, bouncing in his seat. When Ms. Lopez calls on him, Darren looks up and says "Hmm . . ." Ms. Lopez quickly says, "Let's see who else might know!" and calls on another child.

Consider the following contextual information and discuss if it changes how you think about Darren's feelings.

1. Darren's mom just gave birth to another child.
2. Kids on the playground teased Darren at recess earlier in the day because he got an answer wrong during the science lesson.
3. Ms. Lopez stopped at Darren's table and corrected him while he was completing his warm-up activity before the lesson.

Discuss the best ways of responding to Darren in each situation.

CINDY

Read the following scenario and discuss how Cindy might feel.

> Mrs. Simm's second-grade class is getting ready to go to P.E. The children begin to line up at the door, and Cindy races to be first. Scott steps in front of Cindy and tells her he is the line leader today. Cindy's face turns red, and her eyes fill up with tears.

Consider the following contextual information and reflect if it changes how you think about Cindy's feelings.

1. Cindy was at the end of the line for the last P.E. class, and they ran out of jump ropes, her favorite gym activity.
2. Cindy missed her turn to be line leader last week because she left early for a doctor's appointment.
3. Scott cut in front of Cindy getting on the bus this morning.
4. Cindy did poorly on her developmental reading assessment earlier in the day.

Discuss the best ways of responding to Cindy in each situation.
Discuss and summarize in your group what you have learned from these activities.

Activity 3. Compare and Contrast

Compare and contrast the following two vignettes. Discuss how the teacher's behavior in each vignette could affect student emotions. Make predictions about the students' behavior and performance after the events described in the vignettes.

Mrs. Smith

Mrs. Smith's class is in the midst of language arts when everyone is startled by a loud noise as something crashes into the window. Mrs. Smith drops the book she is holding and exclaims, "Oh my, what was that!?" Her students jump from their seats and run to the window to see what has happened. Mrs. Smith stands by the board and futilely pleads with her students to sit down, even as some of them begin to climb up the bookshelf in hopes of a better view. "It was probably just a bird," Mrs. Smith says, feeling more irritated as she watches the clock creep closer to the end of the block. She thinks with dread of the upcoming state reading assessment that she fears many of her students will not pass and then finds herself yelling, "Sit down now!"

While several students comply, a handful remain at the window and start yelling, "There's a dead bird. I see a dead bird; the bird crashed and died!"

Mrs. Smith says louder now that everyone is to "get in your seats, right now!"

It takes another five minutes before everyone is seated, and as Mrs. Smith tries to start up the lesson again, a student blurts out, "Is that bird really dead?" Children murmur to one another, as one becomes a bit tearful.

"I'm sure the bird is fine," Mrs. Smith says. "You all just need to focus on reading; we only have ten minutes left." Despite her repeated redirection, her students continue talking and appear dysregulated. As the block ends and she walks her class to lunch, she finds herself feeling defeated and exhausted.

Mrs. Jones

Across the courtyard, Mrs. Jones's class was also startled by a loud noise. Mrs. Jones jumps, briefly startled, and then calmly walks to the window to investigate. As she does, she tells her students, "Well that was startling. It can be a bit scary when we hear a noise we aren't expecting. Sometimes animals get confused by the glass and try to go through it. I think that's what happened. Everything is ok. Read the first question on your sheet and I will look." As one student starts to get up, Mrs. Jones gently touches his shoulder on her way by and kindly but firmly whispers, "I've got it; you stay here. When we do the questions, I want you to be ready to answer number one."

The students are alert but remain seated. As Mrs. Jones briefly looks outside; she updates the students. "It was a bird, everything is ok. You know, we're actually going to learn about how different animals use their senses to fly and catch their prey in science this year! I can't wait to tell you more about it." As she returns to the front of the room, she smiles assuredly and reminds the students, "Ok, we are working on . . ." and the students look thoughtfully at the board. Mrs. Jones feels calm and in control of her lesson.

Activity 4. Mirror Me!

Part 1. Pair up with a peer. Have one person say a simple phrase (e.g., "Dinner is ready!" or "We are going to work on a math problem") with an angry voice, an anxious voice, and then a happy voice. The other person imitates exactly what the first person said. Change roles and repeat.

Part 2. Pair up with a peer. Find a space where you can do small movements. Face each other. Have one person make a movement (e.g., doing a circle with one hand and then the other). The other person imitates that movement. Then the second person shows a different movement, and the first person imitates. Continue taking turns repeating the other person's movements. The goal is to achieve a seamless transition between the movements. Discuss your experiences.

Self-Care Tool Kit

Loving-Kindness Meditation (modified from Kabat-Zinn, 2018)

Loving-kindness meditation is a means to build feelings of self-love, acceptance, and compassion for others. Practicing this type of meditation can increase positive emotions and foster a sense of caring directed toward you and others.

Start by finding a quiet and, ideally, private space. Allow yourself to find a comfortable position, sitting or lying down. Notice your breath. Take several breaths, in and out, feeling the air move through your mouth and nose. Notice the air moving through your body without trying to change your breath, just noticing. You may notice different thoughts entering your mind, just notice them and allow them to pass, bringing your attention back to your body and your breath.

Let your mind move toward a figure in your life who loves you or loved you unconditionally. Allow yourself to generate an image of this figure in your mind. As you think about this figure, allow yourself to feel the love and kindness shown to you by them. Envision their love and kindness as a glowing, warm light moving toward you, like warm sunshine gently meeting your skin. Feel this love wash over you, warming you. Envision this warm feeling saturating your being. Allow yourself to experience the warmth and comfort of their love for you, exactly as you are. Feel the peace of being accepted just as you are, without conditions or judgments. Let your heart be immersed in this love. Feel it surround you like a soft, warm blanket. Feel your breath continue to flow, in and out, as you remain enveloped in this warm cocoon of loving kindness.

Allow yourself to focus on the peaceful, warm feelings. Allow yourself to feel grateful for you, exactly as you are. If you find critical or judgmental thoughts moving through your mind, envision them leaving your body as you exhale, and as you inhale, focus on bringing the warm, kind light inward. Surround yourself with kind messages, which perhaps you repeat in your mind with each inhale. Find the words that feel meaningful and important to you.

> May I be happy.
> May I be safe.
> May I be healthy, peaceful, and strong.
> May I give and receive appreciation today.

As you begin to complete your meditation, bring your attention back to your body. Feel the ground underneath you. Begin to wiggle your fingers and toes. Envision what the room around you looked like before you closed your eyes. When you feel ready, open your eyes. Offer yourself thanks for taking time to attend to your own feelings and needs.

As you move through your day, you can return to the warm feelings you experienced during this exercise. Envision the love around you and focus on the sensation of being enveloped in warmth.

REFERENCES

Chang, M.-L., & Davis, H. A. (2009). Understanding the role of teacher appraisals in shaping the dynamics of their relationships with students: Deconstructing teachers' judgments of disruptive behavior/students. In P. A. Schutz & M. Zembylas (Eds.), *Advances in teacher emotions research: The impact on teachers lives* (pp. 95–127). Springer.

Epstein, S. (1990). Cognitive-experiential self-theory. In L. A. Pervin (Ed.), *Handbook of personality: Theory and research* (pp. 165–192). Guilford Press.

Erskine, R. G. (2015). *Relational patterns, therapeutic presence: Concepts and practice of integrative psychotherapy*. Routledge.

Ginott, H. (2003). *Between parent and child: The bestselling classic that revolutionized parent-child communication*. Three Rivers Press.

Glasser, W. (1998). *Choice theory*. Harper and Row.

Gottman, J. M., Katz, L. F., & Hooven, C. (1997). *Meta-emotion: How families communicate emotionally*. Lawrence Erlbaum Associates, Inc.

Jordan, J. V., & Schwartz, H. L. (2018). Radical empathy in teaching. *New Directions for Teaching and Learning, 53*, 25–35. https://doi.org/10.1002/tl.20278

Kabat-Zinn, J. (2018, November 8). This loving-kindness meditation is a radical act of love. *Meditation*. Retrieved from www.mindful.org/this-loving-kindness-meditation-is-a-radical-act-of-love/

Keltner, D., Oatley, K., & Jenkins, J. M. (2018). *Understanding emotions* (4th ed.). Wiley-Blackwell.

Ryan, R. M., & Deci, E. L. (2017). *Self-determination theory: Basic psychological needs in motivation, development, and wellness*. Guilford Press.

CHAPTER 10

Dealing With Difficult Emotions in the Classroom

> *First-grade students are completing an art project when the time comes to go to lunch. David continues cutting and gluing while the students around him are cleaning up. You give the class a second verbal instruction to cease their work. David continues gluing with increased vigor, avoiding eye contact with you. You approach David and ask him to finish the work and join the others who are lining up for lunch. David turns his face to you and yells, "I hate you!" Then he throws his materials on the floor and runs toward the door screaming.*

How would you feel if you were David's teacher? What would you do? How would this episode affect the other children in the classroom? When children have episodes of emotional dysregulation (like in the opening scenario), it can be frightening, frustrating, and exhausting for teachers. That is why it is important for you to understand why and how children become dysregulated and, most importantly, how to help them.

In children, dysregulated behavior can range from hostile and aggressive behavior to withdrawal and emotional shutdown. Regardless of the behavioral manifestation, emotionally dysregulated children often feel overwhelmed by their emotions and do not know what to do to feel better. Some children show their emotional distress by directing it outward into their environment. This might include breaking or throwing materials, physical aggression toward others, and screaming or using hostile words. While it is difficult and scary to watch, these behaviors often result from children's distress and attempt to protect themselves. However, behaviors stemming from emotional dysregulation are not always loud or hostile. They can take the form of an avoidant response in which children attempt to remove themselves from a situation. While the children may look calm, internally they feel very distressed. Yet in other children, emotion dysregulation manifests as an emotional shutdown. This is the "freeze" part of the "flight, fight, or freeze" stress response. Children who freeze may appear physically startled or even vacant. Children with a history of trauma may freeze without conscious awareness. Their bodies have learned to protect them from harmful experiences by taking their conscious experience "offline."

You may be wondering why emotional dysregulation takes so many forms. It certainly would be easier if the signs were always clear and if they were consistent across children. The causes and manifestations of emotional dysregulation are influenced by several factors. One is a child's temperament. As you learned in Chapter 6, every child is born with a natural "set point" for irritability, anger, emotional control, and anxiety. Some children are more easygoing and less reactive from very early on, while some are irritable and easily upset. Children's life experiences may also influence how they express their emotions. For instance, a child who lives in a household where emotions are not shown outwardly may try to manage their emotions independently. Another child who has previously been harmed or witnessed violence may lash out physically as a means of self-protection.

UNDERSTANDING THE EMOTIONS OF CHILDREN WITH INSECURE ATTACHMENT

Children with different attachment styles have different emotional experiences and behaviors. Securely attached children believe that others are supportive and helpful. They easily connect in a positive way with peers and teachers and often respond appropriately in emotionally laden situations (Kennedy & Kennedy, 2004). They cope better with stress and seek comfort from their teacher when necessary. Children with insecure attachment, on the other hand, have difficulty handling stressful situations. Some do not seek support from others when distressed, tend to overregulate their emotions, and may look distant or isolated (Kennedy & Kennedy, 2004). Others may respond to stress with intense emotions. These children seek high levels of attention from adults. In the classroom, they present as irritable, impatient, and difficult to console. They may cling to the teacher and have difficulty engaging in classroom routines. Finally, children with disorganized attachment, a particular kind of insecure attachment, do not have a consistent set of strategies when under stress and vacillate between different means of responding. When perceiving a threat, they may at times withdraw while at other times use aggressive behavior as a means of defending themselves. Teachers may perceive these children as unpredictable and difficult to connect with (Kennedy & Kennedy, 2004).

Importantly, children can develop secure relationships with their teachers despite having an insecure attachment with their primary caregivers (Kennedy & Kennedy, 2004). You have an important opportunity to provide emotionally corrective experiences to these children and maximize their opportunities for learning. Teachers can help overregulated children express their emotions by modeling and giving indirect suggestions. For example, you may say to the whole class, "When we are anxious, we can talk to someone we trust about our anxiety."

In response to an extreme display of emotion, the teacher can offer validation, suggest a self-soothing strategy, and define the appropriate behavior. This might sound like, "I see that you are very upset. But I cannot stand close to you when you kick; that's not safe for us. Let's walk to the corner together and take some deep breaths to calm down." Similarly, a screaming child might be told, "I can tell that you are very angry and need my help. Your voice sounds very loud and in the classroom; we use an indoor voice that sounds like *this*. Use your indoor voice to tell me, 'Mrs. Smith, I need help,' and I'd be happy to help you."

Additionally, teachers can help insecurely attached children rely on their presence by creating routines. For instance, the teacher might set up a "check-in" plan where the child stops at the teacher's desk after unpacking each morning to talk for a couple of minutes about anything of interest. A child who is asking for help excessively might benefit from a visual checklist reminder of what to do when stuck (e.g., I tried it, I asked two friends for help, and I raised my hand and waited patiently). Such a child might also benefit from being given a certain number of "help" tickets to use throughout the day. He or she can apply unused tickets at the end of the day toward a relational reward, such as a special lunch with the teacher.

In responding to insecurely attached children, it is most important for teachers to handle their own negative emotions and not abandon the children. This does not mean that children can behave in any way they wish. Instead, teachers can help them by accepting their emotions while teaching them to self-soothe, seek help, and connect with others. Ideally, these strategies should be taught before a child is in an acute crisis. If such a crisis occurs, the teacher might say, "I see that you're very angry; it made you really upset that he took your toy. Hitting isn't safe. You can use your angry fists to squeeze this ball or yell as loud as you like into that pillow." In this way, the child hears that his or her emotions are acceptable, sees that you remain connected despite disapproval of the behavior, and is introduced to a better way to handle difficult emotions. In contrast, minimizing the event ("It's fine, we have other toys right here"), shaming the reaction ("Don't get crazy," "You're being ridiculous."), or focusing on consequences alone ("You just lost recess!") are likely to invalidate the child's feelings and undermine trust.

Keep in mind that it can be hard to respond adaptively in the moment. If you later recognize that a situation was handled poorly, it is worthwhile to make a purposeful repair with the child. Take the child aside, talk about the event without shaming and blaming, and use it as an opportunity to help the child understand his or her emotions, as well as yours. When you acknowledge your own emotions and mistakes, it will show the child that you care about the relationship and want to maintain a connection with him or her.

EMOTIONS AND EMOTION REGULATION IN CHILDREN WITH TRAUMA

You may encounter children in your classroom who have experienced traumatic or other significant adverse experiences. These children will need your special attention. Trauma can be a singular event, such as an illness, injury, accident, or exposure to a natural disaster. Trauma can also stem from chronic experiences of physical or emotional threats within a relational context. This type of trauma threatens a child's foundational sense of security and trust in relationships with other people (Perry, 2009). Traumatic experiences lead to the disruption of children's physical, emotional, social, and cognitive development, and, subsequently, their functioning in the classroom (Tobin, 2016). Importantly, children who have experienced trauma may have difficulty accurately "reading" emotional cues in other people and understanding their own emotions.

A common reaction after experiencing a traumatic event is a change in arousal level (Perry, 2009; Tobin, 2016). A child may startle more easily, be overly attentive to what is happening in the environment, and have trouble keeping his or her mind focused. These behaviors make sense because they are intended to detect potential danger and could protect the child from potential harm. But if the body continues to be vigilant when danger is not present, the effort is no longer helpful. Prolonged arousal becomes exhausting and prevents the child from effectively attending to other things in the environment, like what is being taught or what his or her friends are saying to him or her.

Trauma has a powerful impact on a child's ability to learn and thrive in school. In the classroom, children who have experienced trauma may be more nervous and fearful than other children (Tobin, 2016). They may also complain about headaches, stomachaches, or nausea. Traumatized children may have further difficulties with concentration, appear more withdrawn, act more childishly, or be more or less active than usual. Children who experience trauma may also be more reactive or upset when redirected by a teacher. These children often receive lower grades, are more likely to repeat a grade, and have higher rates of dropping out of school.

Unfortunately, the behaviors associated with trauma often leave children vulnerable to being retraumatized and impede their ability to access healing interventions and relationships. Interpretations of their behavior as "bad" or "devious" elicit punitive or rejecting responses from adults. Traumatized children's uncertainty and distrust can make it hard for others to connect with them. For these reasons, it is helpful to remember that problematic behavior stems from an injury, rather than a willful act of disrespect.

Sometimes children with a history of trauma respond to specific trauma-related triggers. These triggers are experiences or things in the environment that activate intrusive traumatic memories or even lead children to feel that they are reexperiencing the trauma, called a flashback. These triggers can be sights, smells, discussions, or other stimuli that serve as reminders of a traumatic experience. For instance, a child who experienced a house fire may show trauma symptoms at the next fire drill. He or she may become agitated, fearful, or even start acting up. A child once bitten by a dog may become upset when seeing a dog near the playground or dog fur on another child's clothing. Other connections may not be so obvious. A classroom visitor may be wearing the same fragrance as an assault perpetrator, prompting intrusive memories, flashbacks, or fear. Unknown to you, it may be the anniversary of a significant loss or when a traumatic event happened.

It may seem daunting to think about how to support a traumatized child. While therapy is helpful, research also shows that teachers and other important adults are critical to helping a traumatized child develop adaptive behaviors and reestablish healthy ways of engaging with the environment. The Sanctuary Model (Bloom, 2013) highlights some of the areas where traumatized children lack skills or need additional support in order to recover and reengage in everyday tasks. This model uses the acronym SELF to describe how to help children with trauma. The first principle, Safety (S), highlights the importance of feeling safe as the foundation for all other healing. This includes physical, psychological, and relational safety. Traumatized children also need help with Emotion (E) regulation. They benefit from being explicitly taught how to manage their emotions. Loss (L) relates to the need to address grief and loss associated with trauma. This involves acknowledging the loss while also creating space for happiness and joy. Finally, Future (F) refers to the need to see possibilities for oneself in the future.

Here are some ways that you can help to support the healthy development of a child who has experienced trauma (Bloom, 2013; Ludy-Dobson & Perry, 2010; Tobin, 2016).

- ***Help the child to develop trust through his or her relationship with you.*** As you strive for this, be prepared that a child with relational trauma is likely to initially reject your efforts. They are used to feeling shamed, blamed, hurt, and rejected. Continue to offer positive, genuine feedback to the child. Make a point to repair your relationship with the child after episodes of dysregulation or misbehavior.
- ***Create a sense of relational and psychological safety.*** This can be done by being predictable, having clear expectations, utilizing routines, maintaining structure, and effectively modulating your own emotions. A "safe space" should be available when the classroom is not safe. For instance, another child acting out may be a trigger for a traumatized child, and it may be appropriate to allow the traumatized child to relocate to the "safe space."
- ***Help to develop a sense of autonomy and competence.*** Children with trauma histories often feel that the world is happening *to* them and that they have no means to influence it. Help them to develop a sense of autonomy and self-efficacy by including them in classroom activities. Promote the child's sense of competency. Children with trauma experiences often have negative thoughts about themselves and the world. Find ways for the child to excel by assigning tasks that they can master (watering plants, running errands, etc.).
- ***Give frequent positive feedback.*** Keep in mind that traumatized children have a disrupted reward system and are not able to effectively work toward rewards. That is why it is important to give them

frequent positive feedback and to help them anticipate pleasurable activities.
- **Promote play and encourage exploration.** Children with chronic trauma often miss developmentally appropriate play and exploration because they are so vigilant to danger that they are not able to immerse themselves in age-appropriate experiences. Create play opportunities and give explicit encouragement to explore.
- **Help to self-regulate.** The brain networks involved in stress responding are disorganized or poorly regulated in children with trauma. Traumatized children benefit from patterned, repetitive, and somatosensory activities. These activities may include drumming, tapping, moving, and singing with dancing. Engaging in these activities helps to organize a child's internal rhythms and can have a calming effect. These activities are also good tools for developing self-awareness and body-mind integration.

TANTRUM IN THE CLASSROOM

In some children, emotion dysregulation may result in temper tantrums. Children have temper tantrums when they lose emotional control (Roy et al., 2013). Observing and trying to calm down a child in a tantrum state is exhausting and anxiety provoking for teachers. It is also anxiety provoking for the other children in the classroom. Furthermore, it derails the learning process by not only taking time away from academic tasks but also causing emotional overarousal in the other students and the teacher. It takes a while to bring emotional arousal back to a level conducive to learning. Most children do not have tantrums, but some do. Why is that? Usually, it is because they are more emotionally reactive than other children, meaning they react faster and more intensely to situations that may not bother others (Roy et al., 2013). They also have deficits in emotion regulation.

Temper tantrums involve two processes: anger and distress. Anger peaks early on in the tantrum, while distress behaviors, like crying and seeking comfort, slowly increase as the child progresses in the tantrum state (Potegal, Kosorok, & Davidson, 2003). Temper tantrums may also take different forms. Children with depression tend to direct hostility internally through self-disparaging statements or self-injurious behavior. Those with disruptive behavior disorders have more frequent tantrums and direct their aggression toward others. These children also have the most difficulty recovering after a tantrum (Belden, Thomson, & Luby, 2008).

What Can Cause a Temper Tantrum?

Temper tantrums may have different causes. Some children cannot handle frustration appropriately and react with intense anger, leading to a tantrum. For these children, learning how to deal with frustration is important. For example, when seeing that a child's frustration is building, a teacher may provide assistance and reassurance. Another cause for a tantrum is when a child is being overstimulated – for example, by too much noise or activity in the classroom. This is a common antecedent for a tantrum in children with autism. Therefore, managing the classroom stimulation level can be a preventative measure. Some children develop tantrums as a result of distress related to fear of rejection or even harm. These children may engage in tantrums in order to feel connected to another person or to elicit soothing. Other children use a tantrum as a tool to access something desired, like attention or control. They make a connection (often without awareness) between acting out and getting something they want. That is why adults have to be careful not to reinforce a tantrum by giving children access to desired objects, activities, or people after a tantrum.

Phases of a Tantrum

A tantrum usually goes through several phases. It generally starts with a *trigger*. What triggers a tantrum varies depending on the child. It might be being told "no," an impending transition, a change in the schedule, or another child's behavior. Additionally, something that has happened earlier in the day, a distal factor, can make the child more vulnerable to becoming distressed. If the child cannot self-soothe or receive support from others after a trigger, they enter the *agitation* phase. The child may whine, argue, or raise his or her voice. The child's face may flush, or he or she may sweat. Internally, the child is distressed, and his or her body prepares for "fight or flight." As the child becomes more upset, he or she moves into the *acceleration* phase. During this period, tantrum behaviors become more intense, and children lose their ability to control themselves. They show more intense behaviors, like screaming, throwing, or hitting. Eventually, the tantrum reaches its *peak*, the most intense part of the tantrum. Once a tantrum has peaked, the child enters the *de-escalation phase*, using a softer voice, pausing aggressive behavior, slowing movements, or retreating or hiding. De-escalation is a vulnerable time when a child can be easily agitated again. While a child might appear to be calming externally, the internal process of calming generally takes longer. It may be tempting to start making repairs or to process what has happened at this point, but it is best to ensure plenty of time has passed before engaging in this process. In the final phase, the *recovery phase*, the child returns to his or her usual state of behavior.

Emotions During a Tantrum and How to Respond to Them

Let's look at a child's emotional experiences at each phase of a tantrum and how to help the child (Mullen, 1983). Early on, when a child is first upset, you may notice mild irritation, complaining, or withdrawal. This is a good time to check in individually to see how the child is feeling or what is bothering him or her. It is important to help the child to feel heard and understood. Even if the issue seems trivial from your perspective, avoid being dismissive or telling the child that there is no problem. Gently address any misunderstandings on the child's part. For instance, a child who thinks there is no recess today could be informed that there will be recess but not at the regular time. If indeed there is no recess, you can help the child by validating and labeling his or her experience. Match the child's level of affect and say, "You are really upset that there is no recess today! It is unfair to you that you can't go outside and play!" Being heard is a powerful experience, even when there is nothing to be done to change the circumstance.

Despite your best efforts, these strategies may not impede the tantrum. If the child continues to become more upset, he or she likely feels out of control. The child might feel defeated in trying to manage his or her behaviors and not able to do so. When this happens, you can help by taking control (Mullen, 1983). This is often counter to what adults may try to do, which is to find a way to appease the child or using threats of punishment. Do not engage the child in reflection of his or her behavior at that point, as it is likely to increase the child's distress. To take control, you should set limits and clear expectations using simple and repetitive language. You should also emphasize safety by firmly but warmly indicating that it is your job as the teacher to help children be in control of their bodies and words.

As the tantrum escalates further, the child may be verbally aggressive ("I will kill you!") or physically aggressive (hitting, kicking, throwing) (Mullen, 1983). These behaviors are intended to make others feel anxious or afraid. However, it is the child's attempt to gain control over the situation by acting as if he or she has power and can make him or herself feel better. This is when it is important for you to regulate your own emotions and not to take the child's negative behaviors and threats personally. It is helpful to separate yourself from personal attacks as much as you are able to do so. If a child is acting in an unsafe manner, "first, then" language can be helpful in reestablishing safety. This might sound like, "First I need to see a calm body, then I will talk with you," or "First you need to go to the cool down space, then you can have the markers." Provide a way out or a way for the child to "save face." You can help to soothe agitation by providing solutions to end the tantrum. For instance, "I know you were upset about being late for recess. If we can help you get safe, you'll still have ten minutes outside. Let's go!"

As the child's anger dissipates, there is likely to be more pronounced sadness (Mullen, 1983). The child may hide under a desk or put his or her head down. He or she may verbalize wanting to be left alone. Avoid the urge to give commands, assign a task, insist the child talk about the behavior, or institute punishments. At this point, the child is likely feeling exhausted and guilty. You can let the child know that you will check on him or her in a bit and that you are available if the child needs anything. Do not be surprised if your offer is not welcomed – the child may attempt to preserve himself or herself from embarrassment by remaining alone. This is the time to allow the child to continue to calm down and to allow yourself time to recover as well. If there is something you know that can soothe the child (stuffed animal, Play-Doh, sensory toy, etc.), you might place it in his or her proximity but avoid any lengthy verbal engagement. Similarly, while the child may appear to be calming, it is wise to avoid providing any materials that the child might use to harm himself or herself, others, or property until there has been a longer period of calm. As the tantrum nears its end, try to remember that the child is likely increasingly feeling embarrassment or shame.

When the episode has passed, find a time to talk with the child. It is helpful to offer the child a chance to share his or her experience and for you to convey that you understand how the child felt. This is also a good time to help the child separate emotions from behavior. Emphasize to the child that his or her feelings are normal and acceptable. At the same time, discuss that there are different ways to deal with difficult feelings. Help the child to think about ways to solve the problem differently, things he or she can do to feel better, or ways to let an adult know he or she needs help. In this discussion, try to avoid shaming or blaming the child because it is likely to lead the child to be defensive or even hostile. As with teaching the child to separate emotions and behavior, you need to help the child separate your relationship from the incident. The child can still be a valuable and good person who has done an unacceptable action. Let the child know that you still care for him or her and that while the behavior was unacceptable, you will work together to find new ways for the child to manage his or her feelings and behaviors.

Don't rush the recovery phase. In the wake of a tantrum, both the child and adult need time and space to recover. Wait until you feel you can engage with the child in a calm and collected manner. Remember that a child can look outwardly calm but still be emotionally activated. Avoid introducing too many demands or pushing reparative activities too quickly after a tantrum. Children experience strong emotions, including shame and remorse, even when they are back in control of their bodies, and these strong emotions can reactivate a tantrum. Instead, engage the child in a quiet activity, such as reading a book with a peer model, coloring, resting his or her head quietly at a desk, or sitting with a preferred adult.

If you suspect tantrums have become a habit that allows the child to escape difficult or nonpreferred activities, you can reintroduce these tasks at a later time. Try to emphasize the importance of learning and resist the temptation to present it as punishment. When the child is calm, it may also be an opportunity to explore how he or she feels about the task or if the child did not understand something. When indicating that the child will need to complete missed work, keep it simple. For instance, "It's my job to help you learn, and when you got upset, you missed some important stuff!"

TEACHER EMOTIONS WHEN RESPONDING TO AN EMOTIONALLY DYSREGULATED CHILD

> As teachers we have a room, a group, equipment, materials, a curriculum, instructional methods, and grades, but most of all, we have ourselves. What happens to us emotionally in the process of teaching emotionally

> disturbed kids is the critical factor in determining our effectiveness.
>
> (Fritz Redl cited in Long, 1996, p. 44)

It is very important for you to be aware of your own emotions and thoughts when you respond to an emotionally dysregulated child. Are you anxious? Angry? Have you already assigned blame in your mind for the situation? Everyone has some level of bias in how they interpret any situation and being mindful of your thoughts and emotional state before intervening can help to keep the situation from escalating.

Some things can be ignored, and some are best addressed quickly and directly. Begin to develop a sense of what is best ignored and what should be attended to promptly. Remember, anything that threatens safety requires immediate intervention and cannot be ignored. At the same time, it is easy to assume the worst is going to happen when a child has a history of problem behaviors. This assumption may lead you to be overly emotionally activated and to respond more forcefully than necessary. Nonetheless, if something is a consistent trigger for a child, it may be helpful to intervene proactively when the trigger occurs.

If a child's dysregulated behaviors become a pattern or are increasing in frequency, do not hesitate to enlist other resources. It can be helpful to talk with other teachers or specialists to generate new ways of understanding and responding. In these conversations, you may be inclined to defend your own efforts ("I'm already doing that!"). Managing the behavior of children with emotional outbursts is tiresome and can chip away the feelings of effectiveness and satisfaction. Be open to different ways to work with children with emotion dysregulation.

Chapter Summary

- Children's emotional dysregulation elicits many reactions from their teachers. Understanding the range of difficult behaviors and what can cause them can empower you and make it feel more manageable when you encounter them.
- Children's attachment style affects their emotional expression, emotional reactivity, and ability to cope. Fortunately, teachers can develop strong relationships with these children and provide corrective experiences. Recognizing and responding effectively to attachment-driven emotional behavior can help the child to regulate their emotions more effectively.

- Trauma experiences have significant impacts on children's ability to focus and connect with others in the classroom. They may be distracted or dysregulated by trauma triggers. Remember the SELF Model (Bloom, 2013) to support traumatized children. Establish *S*afety, foster *E*motion regulation skills, acknowledge the *L*oss, and help the child to see possibilities for the *F*uture.
- Tantrums are disruptive episodes that affect the child, as well as the child's classmates and the teacher. Recognizing and responding early can prevent a tantrum from escalating. Once a tantrum has passed, both you and the child will benefit from time to recover before processing the event. At each phase of the tantrum, the child will feel different emotions, including frustration, anger, guilt, remorse, and shame. Awareness of these emotions can guide effective intervention.
- Big feelings in children elicit big feelings in the adults around them. Being mindful of your own thoughts and feelings in a difficult situation will allow you to intervene most effectively. Try to openly and nonjudgmentally acknowledge your own reactions and do not hesitate to seek support for managing difficult behaviors.

Self-Reflective Activities

Rate your level of emotional comfort dealing with the situations that follow from 1 – not comfortable at all to 5 – very comfortable.

A child is walking around the classroom and looks upset. As he walks by a table where two children are doing math problems with manipulatives, he pushes all the pieces to the floor.

1 _____ 2 _____ 3 _____ 4 _____ 5

Not comfortable at all   Very comfortable

A child yells in the face of another child, and when asked to stop, the first child yells, "Nobody likes you anyway!"

1 _____ 2 _____ 3 _____ 4 _____ 5

Not comfortable at all   Very comfortable

The overhead announcement system indicates that it is too cold for outdoor recess, and several students mumble, "Hey, that's not fair," and "No, it's not THAT cold!"

1 _____ 2 _____ 3 _____ 4 _____ 5

Not comfortable at all   Very comfortable

Your class has recently returned from recess, and one student is dashing back and forth from his desk to the door while you attempt to start a lesson. You ask that student to take her seat. She suddenly turns her face to you and yells, "I hate you! You are mean!"

1 _____ 2 _____ 3 _____ 4 _____ 5

Not comfortable at all   Very comfortable

It is the week before school vacation, and it seems impossible to manage your class. Several students are running around, while some students are rolling on the floor. You try different strategies, but nothing works. One of your colleagues enters the classroom to borrow a book.

1 _____ 2 _____ 3 _____ 4 _____ 5

Not comfortable at all   Very comfortable

The whole class goes to the carpet for a lesson, but one student remains at his desk with his head down. You approach him and touch his shoulder. He shrugs your hand off and starts crying.

1 _____ 2 _____ 3 _____ 4 _____ 5

Not comfortable at all   Very comfortable

Reflect on your level of comfort dealing with each situation in your self-reflection journal. Why are some situations more comfortable than others? What factors might affect your level of comfort (e.g., personal experiences, beliefs, self-esteem)?

Small Group Activities

Activity 1. Triggers

Read each of the following situations about children who have experienced trauma. For each one, consider relational interactions, learning content, school events, and physical stimuli that may act as a trigger for a trauma reaction.

1. Last month, there was a tornado while Joey was visiting his grandmother's home in a neighboring state. The family was able to huddle together in a lower-floor bathroom before it reached the home. Unfortunately, the ceiling collapsed, and it was several hours before the family could escape from the property, and Joey's father suffered a broken leg.
2. Erin's mother lost her job, and within a month, the family was abruptly evicted from their apartment. They relocated to a shelter, taking only small bags of personal possessions. While there, Erin's tablet was stolen, and she got lice several times. On several occasions, there were physical fights among the residents.
3. Carmen's family has been living in the United States since she was an infant, but they have not been able to establish citizenship. Carmen returned to her apartment complex one afternoon, and several government vehicles and policemen were around. She ran frantically to their unit, but her father had already been placed in custody by ICE agents. The next time she spoke to her father, he was in Mexico and not permitted to return to the United States.
4. When Alice was young, her mother was in a relationship with a man who was physically abusive. Many nights she sat behind her door listening to her mother trying to stifle crying. This man often arrived at their home intoxicated, and his behavior was unpredictable. He often screamed about her mother's cooking or complained that the house was not clean.
5. Steven's father has always been in charge of discipline at their home. When Steven's grades do not meet his father's expectations or when a teacher reports that Steven is not paying attention well, Steven dreads his father's punishment. He knows that his father will be after him with the broom handle or a belt. He hopes that he won't have to explain another black eye to his teacher.

Activity 2. Vignettes

Ms. King

Read the following scenario and discuss Ms. King's missteps at each stage of the tantrum.

> Declan is a second-grade student in Ms. King's class. He requires a lot of attention and often gets upset when things are not going his way. Ms. King is growing tired of trying to modify the environment to meet his demands.

> Today, Declan and another child go to get math blocks, and Declan demands that the other child give him the green set he just selected. The other child says they are his and takes them to his desk. Ms. King looks up from across the room and thinks, "Good, someone should put that kid in his place."
>
> Declan's hands form fists, and his face turns red. Ms. King continues what she is doing, and a minute later, Declan dumps the bucket of cubes on the floor.
>
> "Completely unacceptable!" Ms. King thinks and she shouts across the room, "Declan, you are in second grade, stop acting like a two-year-old."
>
> Other kids chuckle, and one says loudly, "He's such a baby."
>
> Declan shouts, "I am not a baby" and begins pushing other materials off the counter.
>
> Ms. King stands up, hands on her hips, and says, "Pick that up now, or there will be no recess for you."
>
> Declan only becomes more enraged, and yells, "If you take my recess, I'll kill you!" Declan continues yelling and throwing things, requiring Mrs. King to evacuate her class to another room. Ultimately, Declan is removed to the principal's office.
>
> Ms. King thinks, "Good, let someone else deal with it." When he returns, she ignores him for the rest of the day.

Mrs. Manfred

Read the following scenario. Discuss what Mrs. Manfred did well at each stage of the tantrum.

> Isaiah is a student in Mrs. Manfred's second-grade class. Mrs. Manfred has learned that when Isaiah gets angry, he escalates in a hurry, so she tries to intervene quickly when something might be upsetting. Today, Mrs. Manfred sees Isaiah and another student bump into one another as they change stations. Mrs. Manfred stops her small group lesson and immediately moves to the area. She hears Isaiah say to the other student, "Hey, you pushed me!"
>
> Mrs. Manfred places her hand on Isaiah's shoulder and gently says, "What's happening over here?"
>
> Isaiah glares at the other child and shouts, "He pushed me, on purpose! He always pushes me."

Mrs. Manfred tells the other student to go to his seat. She kneels to meet Isaiah at eye level and puts her hand on his shoulder. She says, "I can see that you are very angry. Most kids get angry when they think someone pushed them on purpose. I think Alex bumped you by accident."

Isaiah stomps his foot and says, "You always take his side! He did it on purpose."

Mrs. Manfred responds, "I can see that you're still really upset. I'm sorry you got bumped. It looks like you need some time to cool down, and we can talk more afterward. Do you want to sit at your desk or the calm down corner?" Isaiah ignores her but walks to his seat. Mrs. Manfred decides to let him be and that she will talk to him at the next break.

Self-Care Tool Kit

Grounding

Grounding is a particular type of coping strategy that is designed to "ground" you in or connect you with the present moment. Grounding is a helpful coping strategy for people who have experienced trauma. The goal of this activity is to limit intrusive thoughts about the trauma and to redirect attention to the outside world. This technique also works well when you are under significant stress. When you feel like you cannot control your mind, "ground" yourself in reality using the following directions:

- Breathe deeply – look around and name five objects you see
- Name five sounds you hear – breathe slowly and deeply
- Name five things you can physically feel – breathe slowly and deeply
- Name five colors you see in the room – breathe slowly and deeply

This coping strategy can also be used to calm down emotionally dysregulated children, as it brings their brain activity from hyperaroused to a normal state.

REFERENCES

Belden, A. C., Thomson, N. R., & Luby, J. L. (2008). Temper tantrums in healthy versus depressed and disruptive preschoolers: Defining tantrum behaviors associated with clinical problems. *The Journal of Pediatrics, 152*(1), 117–122. https://doi.org/10.1016/j.jpeds.2007.06.030

Bloom, S. (2013). The sanctuary model. In J. D. Ford & C. A. Courtois (Eds.), *Treating complex traumatic stress disorders in children and adolescents: Scientific foundations and therapeutic models* (pp. 277–294). Guilford Press.

Kennedy, J. H., & Kennedy, C. E. (2004). Attachment theory: Implications for school psychology. *Psychology in the Schools, 41*(2), 247–259. https://doi.org/10.1002/pits.10153

Long, N. (1996). The conflict cycle paradigm on how troubled students get teachers out of control. In N. Long, W. C. Morse, & R. G. Newman (Eds.), *Conflict in the classroom: The education of at-risk and troubled students* (pp. 244–265). Pro-Ed.

Ludy-Dobson, C. R., & Perry, B. D. (2010). The role of healthy relational interactions in buffering the impact of childhood trauma. In E. Gil (Ed.), *Working with children to heal interpersonal trauma: The power of play* (pp. 26–43). Guilford Press.

Mullen, J. K. (1983). Understanding and managing the temper tantrum. *Child Care Quarterly, 12*(1), 59–70. https://doi.org/10.1007/BF01258080

Perry, B. D. (2009). Examining child maltreatment through a neurodevelopmental lens: Clinical applications of the neurosequential model of therapeutics. *Journal of Loss and Trauma, 14*(4), 240–255. https://doi.org/10.1080/15325020903004350

Potegal, M., Kosorok, M. R., & Davidson, R. J. (2003). Temper tantrums in young children: Tantrum duration and temporal organization. *Journal of Developmental and Behavioral Pediatrics, 24*(3), 148–154. https://doi.org/10.1097/00004703-200306000-00003

Roy, A. K., Klein, R. G., Angelosante, A., Bar-Haim, Y., Leibenluft, E., Hulvershorn, L. . . . Spindel, C. (2013). Clinical features of young children referred for impairing temper outbursts. *Journal of Child and Adolescent Psychopharmacology, 23*(9), 588–596. https://doi.org/10.1089/cap.2013.0005

Tobin, M. (2016). *Childhood trauma: Developmental pathways and implications for the classroom*. Australian Council for Educational Research. Retrieved from http://research.acer.edu.au/learning_processes/20

CHAPTER 11

Creating an Emotionally Positive Classroom

A positive emotional classroom environment involves healthy student-teacher relationships, positive classroom management, peer support, and student agency (Reyes, Brackett, Rivers, White, & Salovey, 2012). Students in classrooms characterized by a positive emotional climate have better grades and are more engaged in learning (Reyes et al., 2012). As a teacher, you will have a powerful role in setting the emotional tone for the classroom and determining the kind of relationship you will have with your students.

Good relationships are an essential part of a positive classroom environment. Close, caring teacher-student relationships and high-quality peer relationships are important for school engagement, learning, and performance (Furrer, Skinner, & Pitzer, 2014). Students who do not have positive relationships with teachers and peers become emotionally disconnected from school. High-quality relationships in the classroom are characterized by kindness, mutual satisfaction, respect, and support. Learning is an emotional endeavor, and students must feel that their teachers are responsive to their emotional needs. The relational transactions that take place between teacher and student offer an important opportunity to meet students' emotional needs. In emotionally positive classrooms, teachers provide both emotional and organizational support to their students. Emotional support refers to the teacher's ability to create a warm, safe, and responsive classroom environment, while organizational support entails setting clear goals and expectations and effective classroom management (Bailey, Denham, Curby, & Bassett, 2016).

WHY POSITIVE TEACHER-STUDENT RELATIONSHIPS ARE IMPORTANT

Students who experience positive relationships with their teachers are more engaged academically and have better social skills (Sabol & Pianta, 2012). Positive relationships also serve as a protective factor for students at risk for behavioral and socioemotional problems. When students perceive their teachers as being emotionally supportive, they experience less anxiety, fewer behavioral problems, and can better regulate their stress (Ahnert, Harwardt-Heinecke, Kappler, Eckstein-Madry, & Milatz, 2012; Sabol & Pianta, 2012). In contrast, strained student-teacher relationships decrease students' ability to manage stress effectively. Additionally, students who have conflictual relationships with their teachers are more likely to have conflictual relationships with their peers. They are also disengaged in the classroom and display negative behaviors (Ahnert et al., 2012).

Teachers have the power to reshape students' relational models by being warm, sensitive, and responsive to students' needs. Students who experience negative caregiving practices at home may be set on a more positive developmental path if they have a positive relationship with their teacher (Sabol & Pianta, 2012). The relationship between teachers and students is especially important for students who are at risk for learning or behavioral problems and those from multi-stressed families. When working with challenging students, it is important to remember that you play an important role in their lives. For some students, a relationship with you will be one of the most significant relationships they have outside of their families.

Teacher-student relationships, especially in early childhood education, set the stage for children's relationships with future teachers (Sabol & Pianta, 2012). As such, it is crucial that early childhood educators be able to establish warm and sensitive relationships with their students to help them make positive connections with their teachers in the future. Positive student-teacher relationships are also a protective factor for teachers' own well-being (Spilt, Koomen, & Thijs, 2011). One study found that teachers who experience enjoyment in their relationships with students also have lower levels of emotional exhaustion (Taxer, Becker-Kurz, & Frenzel, 2019).

DIMENSIONS OF TEACHER-STUDENT RELATIONSHIPS

Student-teacher relationships are characterized by three dimensions: closeness, conflict, and dependency (Ahnert et al., 2012). Closeness is the level of warmth and open communication a teacher has with a student. Teachers with high levels of closeness are viewed by their students as approachable and supportive (Ahnert et al., 2012). Closeness also encompasses the level of sensitivity and emotional support teachers provide to their students. This dimension helps students regulate their emotions and decreases overall stress in the classroom. The conflict dimension is a teacher's tendency to perceive students as angry or unpredictable (Ahnert et al., 2012). In this case, teachers feel emotionally exhausted and view the relationship as negative (Morris-Rothschild & Brassard, 2006). The last dimension, dependency, is characterized by the teacher's perception of how dependent or overly reliant a student is on the teacher. Students who have a high dependency may ask for help unnecessarily or follow the teacher in a clingy manner. Teachers working with dependent students report more difficulty in their relationships (Ahnert et al., 2012). Conflict and dependency in relationships with teachers are related to students' problems with school adjustment, decreased engagement in the classroom, and increased negative attitudes toward school (Ahnert et al., 2012).

STUDENT NEEDS AND RELATIONSHIPS

High-quality relationships in the classroom are those that satisfy students' fundamental needs for relatedness, competence, and autonomy (Furrer et al., 2014). *Relatedness* is the need for connection with others and belonging to a larger group; *competence* is the need to feel effective in task performance and social interactions; *autonomy* is the need to be the source of action.

> In the classroom, teachers and peers are social partners who can meet (or undermine) a student's needs via three pathways: (1) relatedness *is promoted by* warmth *or undermined by* rejection; (2) competence *is promoted by* structure *or undermined by* chaos; *and* (3) autonomy *is promoted by* autonomy support *or undermined by* coercion.
>
> (Furrer et al., 2014, p. 104)

Need for Relatedness

A teacher's involvement and warmth are essential for making students feel that they belong in school (Furrer et al., 2014). When students feel cared for, they have more positive feelings about school, want to perform well, and have positive relationships with others. Establishing a caring relationship helps to promote good behavior, as students are motivated to comply with classroom rules. Students need to feel that you genuinely care about them. While you likely care for all of your students, they may not always realize it. Show them that you care by being curious about their lives and giving them opportunities to share things with you about themselves (Boynton & Boynton, 2005). Talk with students directly about things you notice, like a team jersey, a picture of a pet, or a special snack. Learn about their backgrounds, personal preferences, and past learning experiences. Try to find opportunities to connect individually with each of your students and show them that you truly enjoy your interactions with them.

Good relationships with peers are also important to satisfy students' need for relatedness (Furrer et al., 2014). You can help your students to connect with one another by assigning group work, creating opportunities for them to get to know one another, and engaging them in cooperative learning tasks. Students feel understood and cared for by their peers when they have opportunities to talk and listen to each other, share their experiences, and provide emotional support.

Need for Competence

Teachers foster competence when they are consistent and predictable. This promotes a sense of safety in which children feel comfortable and able to engage more effectively in learning. It also helps them develop an internal locus of control, where they are able to associate their own actions with predictable outcomes. Students with an internal locus control understand that the world does not happen *to them*; instead, they understand how their own actions influence outcomes. This consistency and predictability are particularly important for students with disrupted relationships with caregivers because these students may have difficulty predicting outcomes due to inconsistencies in past encounters.

Need for Autonomy

Providing students with choices is one way to satisfy their need for autonomy. While much is dictated by the schedule of the day or the demands of the curriculum, teachers can find creative opportunities for making choices. Even small choices, like offering two different colored markers for a child to select from, can convey the message that the child's preferences matter. Keep in mind that giving too many choices can be overwhelming, especially for young children. To make choices more manageable, you can offer a forced choice ("Should we read this book or this one?") or a choice from a small array ("Pick one of these marbles to start"). Autonomy in peer relationships can be achieved when students collaborate with each other, negotiate different perspectives, or explore and challenge their points of view (Furrer et al., 2014).

HOW TO INFUSE POSITIVE EMOTIONS INTO THE CLASSROOM

One way to cultivate a positive emotional climate is by creating and capitalizing on moments of enjoyment in the classroom. When these moments of joy occur, teachers build personal resources that help prevent emotional exhaustion and develop positive student-teacher relationships (Taxer et al., 2019). A positive emotional climate is promoted when teachers show enthusiasm about what they are teaching. Furthermore, research informs us that creating a positive mood at the beginning of the lesson helps students learn (Becker, Goetz, Morger, & Ranellucci, 2014). This can be done by engaging students in a brief activity like sharing good news, introducing the lesson with a joke, or asking students to recall positive elements of their earlier class. To maintain a positive early tone, it is also advisable to postpone unfavorable feedback about your students' performance until the end of class.

Have High Expectations and Confidence in Your Students

Teachers should hold high expectations for their students and make efforts to help students academically. Holding high expectations sends the message that you believe in your students' abilities and want them to be successful. Teachers' expectations become a "self-fulfilling prophecy" in which students behave and perform consistently with what is believed about them (Boynton & Boynton, 2005). If your students do not think you expect much from them, they are likely to disengage and underperform.

One way you can convey your confidence in student abilities is by soliciting student participation in lessons (Boynton & Boynton, 2005).

It is important that you involve all of the students in the classroom. Teachers may feel hesitant calling on low-performing students because they do not expect them to have an answer. If the struggling student does not answer right away, teachers may try to limit embarrassment by quickly asking another student to answer. Teachers tend to wait longer for students they have confidence in but move on more quickly from students whom they believe do not have an answer. You can combat this in a number of ways (Boynton & Boynton, 2005). Be purposeful about calling on all students even when you have a sense that a student may not answer correctly. Place students' names on a piece of paper or Popsicle sticks and pull out a name randomly each time you ask a question. This will send a clear message that everyone is expected to be involved. Provide some additional time for students to consider their answers. You might also offer a hint, ask them a question within the question to build understanding, or work through the problem together in the moment.

Convey your confidence in your students' abilities by explicitly stating that you believe they can achieve the lesson goals (Boynton & Boynton, 2005). Provide evidence of instances where something has initially been difficult, but through perseverance and practice, students have achieved mastery. For example, before a test, you might say, "I know that each of you can do well on this. I have seen you reading the problems carefully, checking your work, and taking your time." When students know that you believe in them, they are inspired to work to your standards and meet your expectations (Boynton & Boynton, 2005). Do not rescue your students from challenges; instead, provide support and model how to handle them and seek assistance.

Make Students Proud of Their Achievements

Pride is a positive emotion we feel when we attribute our success to our effort. Making students proud of their achievements not only contributes to a positive emotional climate in the classroom but also fosters students' motivation to learn. You can use several strategies to help students feel proud (Boynton & Boynton, 2005). Let your students know that you are proud of their accomplishments and behavior. You might comment on their kind actions, patience, taking responsibility, teamwork, and effort. Show your pride in student work by placing examples of their work where it will be visible to others, such as on bulletin boards, in hallways, and in public spaces. Make this explicit by letting students know that you want others to see their work. As you walk by another teacher, comment loudly how well your students are walking in line or what a great report you just received from the music teacher. You can build pride into routines by regularly recognizing things that you notice happening. Consider developing an end-of-day or end-of-week "Pride" ritual where you highlight something that made you feel proud of your students.

Discipline With Care

Teachers have goals for their relationships with students and goals related to behavioral control and discipline, which can be in conflict with one another (Aultman, Williams-Johnson, & Schutz, 2009). Relational goals require closeness and care, while goals related to behavioral control and discipline require distancing. These two dimensions are informed by teachers' identities as caring professionals but also by the professional task of managing students' behavior and promoting academic learning. It can be difficult for teachers to know how to respond when these goals do not clearly align. You want your students to have a positive relationship with you and may feel compelled to respond in a way that maintains this closeness. At the same time, avoiding behavioral management in order to get along with your students will not make for a productive learning environment. Harsh discipline can undermine a child's sense of safety and importance within the classroom environment. In contrast, students who are disciplined in ways that convey respect are better able to maintain positive relationships with adults (Boynton & Boynton, 2005). Teachers often express concern that a strong response is necessary to maintain order within the classroom. Notably, while such responses may promote compliance, the shame of the experience may contribute to student withdrawal and may increase fear within the classroom. Such emotions are not conducive to learning or exploration, and learning may likely be sacrificed in an attempt to instill control.

When a student misbehaves or breaks a rule, focus on separating your feelings from your response to the student. Review what happened in a private or semiprivate location when you and the child are both calm enough to talk about it. During the conversation, allow the child to offer his or her perspective and validate the child's emotional experience (Boynton & Boynton, 2005). You might say something like, "I could tell you felt *really* mad when those kids wouldn't let you play with them.

I feel mad too when I am left out." This would be a good time to help the student generate alternative behaviors. Emphasize that while all feelings are OK, not all actions are acceptable. Explain why the student's behavior violated a rule. For instance, "In our school, we expect all students to be safe and keep others safe," or, "In our school, we expect students to be respectful." Ideally, a consequence would be a restorative solution in which the student in some way makes amends, such as cleaning up a mess he or she made or helping a child he or she hurt. As you discuss the response to the child's actions, it is appropriate to let the child know he or she is capable of acting differently. Convey that while a consequence is necessary, you continue to care about the child.

After a behavioral incident, it is helpful to review your belief in the child's ability to succeed (Boynton & Boynton, 2005). This might be when a child returns from a trip to the office or the morning after a difficult day. You can reinforce this by purposefully noticing when a child is doing something that he or she recently struggled with. As you do this, remember that some children may not have an experienced adult who believes in them. The child may not respond as you expect and may reject your comments or ignore them. Remain steadfast in your approach, and the child will begin to learn that you truly care and believe in his or her ability.

WHAT CAN UNDERMINE POSITIVE RELATIONSHIPS IN THE CLASSROOM?

Positive relationships in the classroom can be undermined when students do not feel welcomed and valued (Furrer et al., 2014). For example, this may happen when teachers do not have time to interact informally with students but focus only on academics or when teachers disregard students' input and do not listen to their perspectives. A teacher's impatience and irritated voice can communicate to students that they are not welcomed. Additionally, teachers who are not available when students struggle contribute to a negative relational climate in the classroom. This can also be said about inconsistent teachers and teachers who do not give clear instructions. These teachers may create a chaotic classroom environment. Coercive or controlling interactions by teachers also undermine relationships. Such interactions may entail guilt-inducing criticism and promoting compliance through authoritarian reasons ("Do it because I said so"). These types of interactions undermine students' sense of autonomy and ownership in learning (Furrer et al., 2014). Negative relationships with peers, including hostility or rejection, can also have negative consequences. They may make students feel lonely and sad or may evoke fear and anxiety.

A negative relational cycle between student and teacher can contribute to a negative emotional climate in the classroom. When a student acts out, a teacher may react negatively to that behavior. The teacher may then view the student in a more negative light and become more vigilant to potential misbehavior. This increased scrutiny increases the probability that the student will feel judged and then act out again. Indeed, a student's angry or aggressive behavior at the beginning of the year often leads to increased teacher–student conflicts throughout the year (Sabol & Pianta, 2012).

Similarly, power struggles between students and teachers may undermine their relationships and the emotional climate in the classroom. Power struggles can have a negative impact on relationships and academic outcomes, as students may feel confused or worried about their performance and the evaluation by their teacher (Ahnert et al., 2012). This also extends to punitive situations where a power imbalance is present. For example, a student asks why he is being punished, and the teacher's response is, "Because I am the adult and I said so!" In this situation, the teacher exercises power but does not provide constructive and helpful feedback about what the child did wrong.

A teacher's conflict management style may be directly related to the teacher's own attachment history. Teachers with a history of insecure attachment may have more difficulty regulating their emotions during a conflict with a student, which may lead them to either avoid conflict or use less constructive conflict resolution strategies (Morris-Rothschild & Brassard, 2006). A teacher with attachment problems of his or her own might experience great stress when addressing a student–teacher conflict. This would make it more difficult to establish a positive teacher–student relationship or to repair the relationship after a conflict (Morris-Rothschild & Brassard, 2006). Therefore, teachers need to be aware of their own relational history to be effective in managing difficult interpersonal episodes in the classroom.

Chapter Summary

- Emotionally positive classrooms are important for learning. You can build an emotionally positive classroom through fostering relationships and emotional and organizational support.

- Student-teacher relationships are especially important for students who lack other supportive relationships.
- Holding high expectations is important. Expect participation from all students and let your students know that you believe they can do difficult things. Help your students to feel proud of what they accomplish.
- You need to balance maintaining positive relationships with your students with the need for behavioral management in the classroom. As you discipline, do it with respect and care, teach appropriate responding, and remember it is about the behavior not the student as a whole.
- There are many things that can interfere with positive relationships. Take care to balance focus on academics and on your students as people. Consider student input and avoid power struggles. Be mindful of how your own experiences and attachment may influence your response.

Self-Reflective Activities

My Relationships

Consider the following scenario: Over the past few months, every time you make plans with a particular friend, the friend cancels at the last minute or shows up very late. Think for a moment about how you would handle this. Would you be inclined to talk to the friend about it directly? Would you make excuses just not to meet with the friend anymore? Would you get angry and confront the person the next time it happens? Now briefly consider other conflicts you have experienced. Take some time to write in your self-reflection journal about how you tend to respond to conflict. Specifically, think about the following:

- How comfortable do you feel talking to others when there is a problem in the relationship?
- Do you have a particular style in responding to conflict?
- Are there differences in how you handle conflict within some relationships as compared to others? Where do you think these differences stem from?
- What would need to be different for you to discuss these things more openly?
- How will you handle relational difficulties with your students? What challenges might you face?

Small Group Activities

Activity 1. Interests and Hobbies

Share your interests and hobbies with your group. When learning about your peers' interests and hobbies, show encouragement. Reflect on how you felt when sharing your interests and hobbies and when receiving encouragement from your peers.

Activity 2. Creating a Story

Use positive emotion words to create a short story. Use the following list of positive emotions: happiness, gratitude, curiosity, love, joy, and pride. Present your story to the large group. Observe and reflect on the nonverbal behavior of your audience. What emotions did you notice? How did they manifest?

Activity 3. Letter to Your Future Students

In your group, write a letter to your future students. What would you like to tell them? What kinds of relationships would you like to have with them? How do you envision their relationships? What can you promise them as a teacher? Present your letter as a group to the whole class. Reflect on how you felt while writing this letter.

Self-Care Tool Kit

Savoring the Future

Imagine positive events or things that will happen in the near future. Make your vision as detailed as possible. If you like, you may draw a picture of those events. Take ten minutes a day to engage in this activity to increase your positive emotions.

REFERENCES

Ahnert, L., Harwardt-Heinecke, E., Kappler, G., Eckstein-Madry, T., & Milatz, A. (2012). Student-teacher relationships and classroom climate in first grade: How do they relate to students' stress regulation. *Attachment and Human Development*, *14*(3), 246–263. https://doi.org/10.1080/14616734.2012.673277

Aultman, L. P., Williams-Johnson, M. R., & Schutz, P. A. (2009). Boundary dilemmas in teacher-student relationships: Struggling with "the line." *Teaching and Teacher Education*, *25*(5), 636–646. https://doi.org/10.1016/j.tate.2008.10.002

Bailey, C. S., Denham, S. A., Curby, T. W., & Bassett, H. H. (2016). Emotional and organizational supports for preschoolers' emotion regulation: Relations with school adjustment. *Emotion*, *16*(2), 263–279. https://doi.org/10.1037/a0039772

Becker, E. S., Goetz, T., Morger, V., & Ranellucci, J. (2014). The importance of teachers' emotions and instructional behavior for their students' emotions – An experience sampling analysis. *Teaching and Teacher Education*, *43*, 12–26. https://doi.org/10.1016/j.tate.2014.05.002

Boynton, M., & Boynton, C. (2005). *The educator's guide to preventing and solving discipline problems*. Association for Supervision and Curriculum Development.

Furrer, C., Skinner, E., & Pitzer, J. (2014). The influence of teacher and peer relationships on students' classroom engagement and everyday motivational resilience. *Teachers College Record*, *116*, 101–123.

Morris-Rothschild, B. K., & Brassard, M. R. (2006). Teachers' conflict management styles: The role of attachment styles and classroom management efficacy. *Journal of School Psychology*, *44*(2006), 105–121. https://doi.org/10.1016/j.jsp.2006.01.004

Reyes, M. R., Brackett, M. A., Rivers, S. E., White, M., & Salovey, P. (2012). Classroom emotional climate, student engagement, and academic achievement. *Journal of Educational Psychology*, *104*(3), 700–712. https://doi.org/10.1037/a0027268

Sabol, T. J., & Pianta, R. C. (2012). Recent trends in research on teacher-child relationships. *Attachment and Human Development*, *14*(3), 213–231. https://doi.org/10.1080/14616734.2012.672262

Spilt, J. T., Koomen, H. M., & Thijs, J. T. (2011). Teacher wellbeing: The importance of teacher-student relationships. *Educational Psychology Review*, *23*, 457–477. https://doi.org/10.1007/s10648-011-9170-y

Taxer, J. L., Becker-Kurz, B., & Frenzel, A. C. (2019). Do quality teacher-student relationships protect teachers from emotional exhaustion? The mediating role of enjoyment and anger. *Social Psychology of Education*, *22*(2019), 209–226. https://doi.org/10.1007/s11218-018-9468-4

CHAPTER 12

How to Foster Children's Emotional Competencies

To be successful in school, children need more than the ability to read, write, and do math. They need to be emotionally competent to have good relationships with teachers and peers and to be successful academically. Research informs us that emotional competence is important for school readiness and early learning (Denham, Bassett, Way et al., 2012). Early education teachers play an essential role in promoting emotional skills in children (Denham, Bassett, & Zinsser, 2012). They can support children's emotional competencies by modeling, responding to children's emotions, and the direct teaching of emotional competencies (Morris, Denham, Bassett, & Curby, 2013). In this chapter, you will learn how to help children develop emotional competencies, including emotional awareness, emotion regulation, expression of emotions, and understanding emotions in others.

TEACHING CHILDREN EMOTIONAL AWARENESS SKILLS

Emotional awareness is important because emotions lead to action. For example, when a child feels sad and accurately recognizes his or her emotion, he or she will likely seek support. However, if the emotion is inaccurately understood, then the behavioral response can be maladaptive. For instance, a child may feel upset, but without good awareness, he or she may respond with aggression to relieve his or her feeling of discomfort. Children with better emotional awareness know how to respond appropriately in emotion-eliciting situations (Saarni, Campos,

Camras, & Witherington, 2006). These children are also more attuned to their own needs and can regulate their emotions better. Furthermore, emotional awareness is a part of a child's emerging knowledge of self.

As you already know, emotions are often associated with internal experiences. For instance, when we feel anxious, our heart races, and we might feel a knot in our stomach. When we are happy, it might feel like having energy and desire to engage with people and activities, while sadness might be associated with a lack of energy. Increasing children's emotional self-awareness involves cueing them to their own internal experiences through using reflective language. Reflective language provides a description of the child's emotion. For instance, you might say, "Johnny, you look frustrated. Do you need some help?" When you label a child's emotion, you make a connection between his or her inner experience and a word. The next time the child experiences a similar emotion, he or she will have a better understanding of his or her emotions. You can also comment on a physical manifestation of an emotion and its cause: "I see a lot of frowny faces. Many of you look disappointed because you really wanted to go outside today, but we need to stay indoors." Keep in mind that it is important to label not only negative but also positive emotions. For example, "Angela, I see your face smiling, and you are standing so tall, you look very proud of what you made." This reflection reinforces a student's positive experience and makes it more accessible to him or her. Furthermore, students will likely remember this positive experience. You can also promote emotional awareness by asking students to consider where in their bodies they feel certain emotions. For instance, you can provide a body outline and ask them to indicate or draw their emotion where it is felt.

It is important for students to understand the degree of intensity of their emotions, as it can inform them about what to do with the emotion. For example, being a little bit anxious is OK, but a significant level of anxiety requires some intervention. You can teach emotional intensity using a "Feelings Thermometer." Provide an outline of a thermometer marked "1" at the bottom and "5" near the top. Explain that the same type of feeling can be small or big: The child might feel happiness at a "1" when presented their favorite snack, a "3" during a playdate, and a "5" on his or her birthday. Provide another emotion and ask the child to detail situations that provoke different intensities of the emotion. Encourage the child to detail what the emotion looks and sounds like at different levels.

HOW TO FOSTER EMOTION REGULATION IN STUDENTS

Children face many situations in the classroom that require emotion regulation skills. For example, some students might become frustrated when having difficulty with an academic task; others may feel angry after a conflict on the playground during recess. Students might feel anxious when you give them feedback about their performance or on the day of a test. When these emotions are strong and not well regulated, they can distract students from learning. Research informs us that children with good emotion regulation skills have better grades, better relationships with teachers and peers, and are more engaged in learning (Eisenberg, Eggum, Sallquist, & Edwards, 2010; E. L. Davis & Levine, 2013; Valiente, Lemery-Chalfant, & Swanson, 2010). In addition, emotion regulation is necessary for cooperative learning, as it helps children negotiate their perspectives and resolve disagreements among each other (Järvenoja & Järvelä, 2009). Furthermore, children with good emotion regulation skills are more attentive to social situations and respond more effectively. Those who do not have good emotional regulation skills may quickly become emotionally overaroused and as a result miss important social cues (Saarni et al., 2006). Difficulty with regulating emotions is associated with emotional and behavioral problems and peer rejection. Emotional dysregulation often leads to aggressive behavior (Röll, Koglin, & Petermann, 2012).

To learn how to regulate their emotions, children need nurturing and supportive adults (Izard, Stark, Trentacosta, & Schultz, 2008). That is why teacher-child relationships are central to students' ability to regulate their emotions (Bailey, Denham, Curby, & Bassett, 2016). Warm and responsive teachers help children regulate their emotions. Children also need to develop a belief that they can change the experience of negative emotions, that negative emotions are not permanent, and that they will pass.

Students learn by watching others. They observe how their teacher interacts with others and responds to emotionally charged situations. For example, a teacher can be kind and patient toward others or react with irritation or even anger. If a teacher repeatedly engages in the same behavior, it is likely that students will imitate their teacher. To be a good model, it is essential that your behavior be consistent with what you want your students to do. For instance, when talking to your students about settling peer conflicts in a respectful and calm manner, it would be ill-advised to raise your voice at a student for violating classroom rules. Your students will be learning from what you say and do, and it is important to "practice what you preach."

Reappraisal of the situation is another important emotion regulation skill (Gross, 2015). Recall that appraisals are the meaning that we assign to a situation. An inaccurate appraisal might lead to strong negative reactions. For instance, if a child erroneously appraises a situation as threatening, he or she might react with aggression to defend him or herself. Another example is a child who misinterprets his or her peer bumping into him or her in the hallway as intentional. This appraisal is likely to elicit anger. Reframing "bumping" behavior as accidental will yield a less negative emotional reaction. You can support reappraisal by gently providing additional information or a different perspective.

Teachers can anticipate students' emotions and preemptively label them as a means of supporting emotion regulation. For instance, prior to a school assembly, teachers might talk with their class about how the fun music might make the students feel excited and want to jump and run. Then they can generate strategies for managing and expressing their emotions appropriately. It is important for children to learn the difference between *experiencing* emotions and *acting* upon their emotions. For instance, it is OK to be angry, but it is not OK to hit someone; or it is OK to be sad, but it is not OK to say mean words to your friends.

TEACHING STUDENT EMOTION REGULATION SELF-TALK

Positive self-talk is an important emotion regulation tool. For instance, children with anxiety often have negative self-talk such as, "I can't do it," "I will make a mistake," or "Others will laugh at me." You can teach students to become aware of when they are having negative self-talk and to practice using positive statements. The following positive self-talk statements can help to reduce anxiety:

> "I know what to do."
> "I'll keep trying."
> "I can ask for help when I need it."
> "Even if I make a mistake, it's OK because everyone makes mistakes."

Other students might have difficulty inhibiting their aggressive or disruptive behavior resulting from being angry or upset. These students can benefit from positive statements, such as the following:

> "I can stay cool even though I am upset."
> "I know I am upset, but I can take a deep breath and calm down."
> "Even if I am very angry, I will keep my body and words safe."

Emotion regulation self-talk encourages the belief that children have control over their emotional experiences and can adopt a growth mindset.

STRATEGIES TO REDUCE EMOTIONAL AROUSAL

Children who have difficulty downregulating their emotional arousal often have difficulty inhibiting actions prompted by their emotions. They tend to act impulsively on what they feel (Izard et al., 2011). For example, a very upset child might start kicking others. Not surprisingly, this can create behavioral problems in the classroom and distract children from learning. That is why children need to learn strategies to bring their arousal down. This can be done through relaxation and mindfulness activities.

These activities should be practiced with the whole class during nonstressful situations. It is helpful to make a regular routine of practicing them and to teach that they can be used when children feel "big" emotions to help them calm down. Later, when children are in a distressed or dysregulated state, they will know how to use these strategies. In such moments, you can also provide a model and visual reminders of how to use the strategies.

Deep Breathing

Deep breathing is a simple and effective way to assist children in calming their bodies. With young children, it is helpful to teach this skill using visualization. When teaching a deep inhale, encourage students to picture their bellies filling up like a balloon or to breathe in as if they are smelling a flower. When teaching a controlled exhale, ask them to imagine that they are blowing out birthday candles or trying to roll a ball across the table with their breath. As an alternative, you can have them pretend to be holding a cup of hot chocolate and take a deep smell on the inhale and then slowly and gently blow on it to cool it off on the exhale. Children may benefit from practicing with pinwheels to see how their breath moves the air. While children are engaged in deep breathing, teachers can ask students to focus their attention on a particular object or sound, such as the sound of chimes or a bell.

Visualization

Visualization is another strategy for children to use to calm down. Help them to imagine a place where they feel calm and safe, which can be real or imagined (e.g., floating on a cloud). As they imagine this place, encourage them to imagine in detail different sights, sounds, smells, and other physical sensations that occur in their calm place. Explain to them that they can "visit" this comforting place when they are upset in order to calm down and find solutions to their problems.

TEACHING CHILDREN TO EXPRESS THEIR EMOTIONS

The healthy expression of emotions facilitates children's relationships with teachers and peers. It also helps them to meet their needs. Imagine a child who is frustrated and starts ripping his papers. This is not the best way for him to express his emotions. Verbalizing, "I am very frustrated/upset/angry that I cannot get this right" is a more adaptive way to tell others how he feels. Using this response, the child will likely receive help from a teacher or a peer.

Children need to learn how to modulate their emotional expression according to social standards (Cole & Hall, 2008). Keep in mind that rules for emotional expression in a child's family may be different from those in the classroom. For example, in some families, it is appropriate to yell when excited; however, this behavior is inappropriate in the classroom. This is why it is important to explicitly teach, model, and remind all students of the emotion display rules in the classroom. For example, you may say that it is OK to yell on the playground when you get excited. In the classroom, however, voices need to be quieter. When students have trouble displaying emotions in acceptable ways, private re-teaching is helpful to reduce embarrassment.

While some children might be very emotionally expressive, others may have difficulty showing their emotions. There are many reasons why children may not openly show their emotions. Some may not have the means to express their emotions, as they have a poor emotional vocabulary. Others may be reluctant to express their emotions because of a fear of negative reactions from others, including losing friendship or love. The tendency to suppress emotional expression may also originate in the family where parents lack emotional expression themselves or emotional expression is not accepted.

Regardless of the reason, expressive suppression is not healthy and may lead to emotional and behavioral problems. Very anxious children often suppress their emotions, which further exacerbates their anxiety. Keep in mind that these children may look composed and not cause any problems in the classroom. Watch and survey how your class responds to emotion-eliciting situations. Who laughs loudly and openly and who only smiles faintly? Which students grumble loudly, and which ones hardly seem to show any reaction when the group is upset? You can then begin to watch for more subtle emotional cues in these more constrained children. Perhaps they fidget slightly, assume a distant look, or make less eye contact with you when they are suppressing their emotions. Recognizing these cues will allow you to check in with these students and encourage them to begin to share how they are feeling.

Children need to learn various healthy ways to express their emotions. This may include expressing emotions through words, expressive arts, and movement.

STRATEGIES TO TEACH EMOTIONAL VOCABULARY

A rich emotional vocabulary is important for children to understand their own emotions and the emotions of other people. One study showed that children who use emotion words more frequently demonstrate better emotional understanding (Ornaghi & Grazzani, 2013). Children with a good emotion vocabulary have easier access to emotion words in emotion-eliciting situations. This makes them more aware of their own and others' emotions and helps them understand nuances of emotions in various situations. Children with a good emotional vocabulary also experience fewer negative emotions and can better regulate their emotions (Lindquist, MacCormack, & Shablack, 2015; Saarni et al., 2006). The following are some strategies to teach emotional vocabulary.

You can label children's emotions as described earlier. You also can also systematically introduce an emotion word of the day or week. Try to teach a family of emotion words. For example, in addition to using the word "happy," you can use other words such as joy, excitement, delight, and pleasure. This helps children develop an emotional vocabulary bank that extends common emotion words. You can provide students with emotion charts or pictures to help their emotion vocabulary grow and to associate emotion words with facial expressions. As children begin to use their emotional vocabulary to describe their experiences, you should praise their efforts in order to encourage its continued use.

Storybooks are excellent tools to teach emotional language. When reading a story, focus on the characters' feelings by using the following questions:

- How does the character feel?
- Why does he or she feel this way?
- What does he or she need?
- How do *you* feel while listening to this story?

Children can also use drawings to depict a character's feelings or engage in dramatic activities to reenact the character's feelings.

Language games can be used to foster emotional vocabulary after reading a story. To play this game, read a sentence from a story that contains an emotion word and then ask students to say what that emotion word reminded them of (Grazzani & Ornaghi, 2011). As an example, if a sentence contained the word "angry," you can say, "If I say the word 'angry,' what does that remind you of?" Model for students how to craft their responses beginning with, "I am angry when . . ." Engage students in conversation and encourage using the target emotion word as much as possible.

TEACHING STUDENTS TO UNDERSTAND OTHERS' EMOTIONS

Understanding others' emotions is important for maintaining positive relationships with others. Children who can understand emotional cues in others are more successful in social interactions and more popular among peers (Saarni et al., 2006). Importantly, they also have a better ability to concentrate and sustain attention in the classroom (Trentacosta, Izard, Mostow, & Fine, 2006). These students are perceived more positively by their peers, which leads to more positive social relationships.

Accurately reading the emotional cues of others is also important for empathy. If a child, for some reason, cannot detect signs of distress in others, then he or she cannot show compassion and assist a person in need. Keep in mind that children who were abused or have witnessed violence may have difficulty understanding the emotions of other people. As a result, they are less successful in social situations (Saarni et al., 2006).

Understanding others' emotions requires several skills. First, students need to read nonverbal cues, including facial expressions, body language, and tone of voice. It is easier for children to understand positive emotions than negative ones. Second, they need to use contextual cues. When contextual information is given, children can be more accurate in detecting the emotional expressions of others (Gross & Ballif, 1991). For example, when looking at a picture of a girl who seems down, children need contextual information to discern what she is feeling. If the girl could not go outside because of rain, she feels *sad*. However, if she received a gift she did not like, she feels *disappointed*. It is also important to discuss contextual information that includes a rationale for *why* a person might be experiencing a particular emotion. For example, a teacher might remark, "He is sad because he really wanted to go on that field trip with the class but could not." The ability to infer emotions emerges relatively early. Preschoolers can correctly infer emotional responses in others if they have knowledge about the situation (Saarni et al., 2006). Children in early elementary school can take into account another's personality or life circumstances to understand his or her emotions.

Children need to understand that someone can experience more than one emotion at a time. For example, Anne feels happy to go on vacation with her parents, but she is also sad that she will not see her friends for a while. Furthermore, they need to learn that different people may feel differently about the same situation. For instance, Jane may feel excited about the first day of school, but Johnny might feel nervous. Finally, we need to teach children to understand the emotional consequences their actions have on others. For example, if a child does not keep his promise, his friend will be disappointed. Similarly, if one does not follow the rules of a game, others might be upset or even angry.

Understanding others' emotions requires affective perspective taking (Carlo, 2006). You can use situations in the classroom to teach this skill. For example, when two children have a conflict, you can teach them to look at the situation from the perspective of the other person: "How did

Julio feel when you said mean things to him?" or, "How did Anna feel when you did not invite her to play?" Mimicking the facial expressions of other people can help to understand how they feel (Davis, Winkielman, & Coulson, 2017). That is why when reading a story describing characters' emotions you can ask children to show those emotions. For example, "Little Bear felt sad when he got lost in the woods. Show how Little Bear looked when he felt sad."

Chapter Summary

- Emotional competence is important for school success. Teachers can promote emotional skills in the classroom.
- Teachers can help students be aware of how they are feeling by noticing the child's emotions and commenting on them. Labeling emotions helps children associate feeling states with emotion words. Teachers can also help children learn that the same emotion can be felt at different intensities.
- Teachers can help students regulate emotions. This can be achieved through developing trusting student-teacher relationships, teacher modeling, helping students to reappraise situations in more adaptive ways, and pre-teaching adaptive emotion expression. Teachers can also instruct students in deep breathing, positive self-talk, and visualization.
- In order for children to recognize and modulate their emotions, it is important that they develop a strong emotional vocabulary. You can teach emotion words by labeling emotions, direct teaching emotional vocabulary, and using book characters to highlight emotional experiences.
- Children need to learn about other people's feelings in order to have satisfactory relationships with others. Help children to understand how emotions arise in different contexts and take affective perspectives of others. Children should also be explicitly taught that people can feel more than one emotion at a time.

Self-Reflective Activities

Gather paper and crayons. Reflect on how you feel right now. Focus on your sensations and your internal feelings. Express your feelings using lines, shapes, and colors. Reflect on how you feel while doing this activity. Does it change how you feel? Is it easy or difficult to express your feelings through drawing?

Small Group Activities

Activity 1. Emotion Words in a Story

In small groups, write a family of emotion words for anger, sadness, and anxiety. For example, a family of emotion words for happy includes joyful, delightful, glad, cheerful, and merry.

Create a short story and use a given emotion word (e.g., anxiety) and its family throughout the story. Read the story to the whole group and act out the given emotions (one group member reads the story and others show the emotion).

Activity 2. Modulation of Emotions

Choose an emotion to express. Select one group member to serve as the activity leader. The remainder of the group will be actors who will express the emotion using their faces and bodies. During the activity, the group leader will direct the intensity of the actors' emotional expression by the position of his or her hand (raising it or lowering it down). Group members modulate their emotional expression to be more intense when the leader's hand is higher and show less intense emotional expression the lower the hand goes. Repeat the activity using several emotions, rotating roles with each emotion.

Activity 3. Creative Ways to Express Emotions

Generate ideas of how you could teach your students to express their emotions using art and movement. Keep in mind developmental appropriateness as you consider potential ideas. Think about when it would be appropriate to use those activities during the school day and how you might connect these to other academic tasks.

Activity 4. Deep Breathing Practice

Group members take turns guiding the rest of the group in the following activities:

- **Bubble breathing:** Imagine that you are trying to blow the biggest bubble. Take a slow breath and then slowly breathe out to not break the bubble as it grows.
- **Hot chocolate breath:** Pretend to breathe in the smell of hot chocolate through your nose and then slowly breathe on the hot chocolate through your mouth to cool it down.
- **Belly buddies:** Lay down on the floor or sit in your chairs while holding a stuffed animal on your belly. Watch your animal when you breathe in and see what it does (it goes up). Watch your animal when you breathe out (it goes back down). You may play calming music in the background while you narrate this.
- **Breathing like a bird:** Stand and make sure that you have plenty of room around you. Stretch both of your arms out. When you inhale, bring your arms up by your ears, like birds about to take off. And when you exhale, bring your arms down by your sides like you are flapping your wings. Repeat this several times so you can get a feel for the rhythm of breathing.

Activity 5. Guided Imagery Practice

Group members take turns guiding the rest of the group in the following activities (read the narratives slowly with a soft voice):

- **Floating on a cloud:** Find a comfortable position, closing your eyes or resting your head on the table. Imagine that your body is very, very light, as light as air. (Pause). You are nestled in a big, white, fluffy cloud. Feel the softness of it against your legs and arms, like a blanket. You look around as you gently float through the sky. (Pause). Feel your breath slow as you enjoy the peace of the sky and feel held within your cloud. (Pause). You feel the air move over your skin as your cloud slowly descends downward, enjoying the comfort of the cloud as you float your back toward your classroom. (Pause). Take a few deep breaths as you feel your feet underneath you and reopen your eyes.
- **Sitting in a field:** Find a comfortable position, closing your eyes or resting your head on the table. Imagine that you are sitting in a field. You feel the cool, freshly mowed grass beneath you, and can smell the grass in the outdoor air. (Pause). You hear birds chirping as they call to one another. You take a big breath in and breathe out loudly through your mouth, enjoying the field around you. You

look around and see wildflowers growing nearby. (Pause). They look so beautiful with their purple, pink, yellow, and blue colors. As a gentle breeze blows, you inhale their beautiful scent and watch the petals flutter against the bright blue sky. (Pause). You look up to see the sky is gently fading from blue to orange, red, and purple as the sun begins to set. You tilt your head back, feeling the last of the sun on your face, warming up your body. Take a few deep breaths as you feel your feet underneath you and reopen your eyes.

Self-Care Toolbox

Progressive Muscle Relaxation

Progressive muscle relaxation is a type of active meditation that helps to release tension. By intentionally contracting and releasing your muscles, you will build your awareness of tension and develop an ability to intentionally relax your body. This helps to manage stress and anxiety.

To begin, sit comfortably in a chair or lay down on the floor, and close your eyes if you feel comfortable doing so. Bring your awareness to your breath. Feel the air move in through your nose, through your chest, and into your belly as it moves through your body. Allow the ground to hold you as you sink deeper into the surface below you. Continue breathing gently in and out. This breathing rhythm will guide you as you tense and relax your muscles.

First, bring your awareness to your toes. As you inhale, squeeze your toes, like you're scrunching up your socks or the carpet beneath your feet. Hold your feet like this, counting 3–2–1, before releasing your breath. Feel the tension leave your feet as you exhale. Continuing up the leg, tense your calf muscles on your inhale for 3–2–1. Exhale and release, feeling your calves relax. Now notice your thigh muscles and inhale to tense for 3–2–1. Exhale to release and allow your legs to feel heavy against the surface below. Moving to your backside, on your inhale, tense for 3–2–1. Exhale and relax your muscles below you. Take a couple of moments here and notice any sensation you may feel in your lower body; you may feel heaviness or lightness or nothing at all. Notice what effect intentionally holding tension and releasing it in your lower body has had.

On your next inhale, tense your abdominals, drawing your belly button toward your spine and holding for 3–2–1. Exhale letting your abdomen relax. Moving up to your chest, inhale and tense your chest muscles for 3–2–1. Exhale to let it all go. Move your attention now to your upper back and shoulder blades. On your inhale, draw your shoulder blades toward one another and hold for 3–2–1. Exhale relax them back to their normal position. Bring your attention to the tops of your shoulders. Inhale to bring your shoulders up toward your ears and hold for 3–2–1. Exhale relax them back down. Moving down your arms, inhale and flex your biceps or upper arms for 3–2–1. Exhale to let it go. Bring your attention to your palms and fingers. Inhale, squeeze your fingers toward your palms, making a fist for 3–2–1. Exhale let it go. Take a moment to notice your torso and arms now – what sensations do you notice? These sensations are possible clues to where you may hold your tension throughout the day. Stay here for a moment, noticing how you feel without judgment.

As you're ready, bring your awareness to your jaw. On your inhale, press your top teeth and bottom teeth together for 3–2–1 and exhale release your bottom teeth from your top teeth and allow them to stay there. Now on your inhale, bring your tongue to the roof of your mouth and press for 3–2–1, exhale to release your tongue to the bottom of your mouth. Notice your eyes and inhale to squeeze your eyelids shut for 3–2–1, exhale and let it go. Finally, bring your attention to your forehead. On your inhale, scrunch your forehead up like you're frustrated for 3–2–1, exhale and let it go.

Allow your breath to come back to a normal rhythm and relax into the surface below you. Again, notice any sensation or lack of sensation you may be experiencing as you breathe in and out. Give yourself permission to stay here for a while, breathing gently and noticing where your breath goes. When you are ready, begin to bring your awareness back, wiggling your fingers and toes and deepening your breath. Gently flutter your eyes open as you come back to the space.

REFERENCES

Bailey, C. S., Denham, S. A., Curby, T. W., & Bassett, H. H. (2016). Emotional and organizational supports for preschoolers' emotion regulation: Relations with school adjustment. *Emotion, 16*(2), 263–279. http://dx.doi.org/10.1037/a0039772

Carlo, G. (2006). Care-based and altruistically based morality. In M. Killen & J. G. Smetana (Eds.), *Handbook of moral development* (pp. 551–579). Lawrence Erlbaum Associates Publishers.

Cole, P. M., & Hall, S. E. (2008). Emotion dysregulation as a risk factor for psychopathology. In T. P. Beauchaine & S. P. Hinshaw (Eds.), *Child and adolescent psychopathology* (pp. 265–298). John Wiley & Sons Inc.

Davis, E. L., & Levine, L. J. (2013). Emotion regulation strategies that promote learning: Reappraisal enhances children's memory for educational information. *Child Development, 84*(1), 361–374. https://doi.org/10.1111/j.1467-8624.2012.01836.x

Davis, J. D., Winkielman, P., & Coulson, S. (2017). Sensorimotor simulation and emotion processing: Impairing facial action increases semantic retrieval demands. *Cognitive, Affective & Behavioral Neuroscience, 17*(3), 652–664. https://doi.org/10.3758/s13415-017-0503-2

Denham, S. A., Bassett, H. H., Way, E., Mincic, M., Zinsser, K., & Graling, K. (2012). Preschoolers' emotion knowledge: self-regulatory foundations, and predictions of early school success. *Cognition & Emotion, 26*(4), 667–679. https://doi.org/10.1080/02699931.2011.602049

Denham, S. A., Bassett, H. H., & Zinsser, K. (2012). Early childhood teachers as socializers of young children's emotional competence. *Early Childhood Education Journal, 40*, 137–143. https://doi.org/10.1007/s10643-012-0504-2

Eisenberg, N., Eggum, N. D., Sallquist, J., & Edwards, A. (2010). Relations of self-regulatory/control capacities to maladjustment, social competence, and emotionality. In R. H. Hoyle (Ed.), *Handbook of personality and self-regulation* (pp. 21–46). Wiley-Blackwell.

Grazzani, I., & Ornaghi, V. (2011). Emotional state talk and emotion understanding: A training study with preschool children. *Journal of Child Language, 38*, 1124–1139. https://doi.org/10.1017/S0305000910000772

Gross, A. L., & Ballif, B. (1991). Children's understanding of emotion from facial expressions and situations: A review. *Developmental Review, 11*(4), 368–398. https://doi.org/10.1016/0273-2297(91)90019-K

Gross, J. J. (2015). Emotion regulation: Current status and future prospects. *Psychological Inquiry, 26*(1), 1–26. https://doi.org/10.1080/1047840X.2014.94078

Izard, C. E., Stark, K., Trentacosta, C., & Schultz, D. (2008). Beyond emotion regulation: Emotion utilization and adaptive functioning. *Child Development Perspectives, 2*(3), 156–163. https://doi.org/10.1111/j.1750-8606.2008.00058.x

Izard, C. E., Woodburn, E. M., Finlon, K. J., Krauthamer-Ewing, E. S., Grossman, S. R., & Seidenfeld, A. (2011). Emotion knowledge, emotion utilization, and emotion regulation. *Emotion Review, 3*(1), 44–52. http://dx.doi.org/10.1177/1754073910380972

Järvenoja, H., & Järvelä, S. (2009). Emotion control in collaborative learning situations: Do students regulate emotions evoked by social challenges. *British Journal of Educational Psychology, 79*(3), 463–481. https://doi.org/10.1348/000709909X402811

Lindquist, K. A., MacCormack, J. K., & Shablack, H. (2015). The role of language in emotion: Predictions from psychological constructionism. *Frontiers in Psychology*, *6*, 444. https://doi.org/10.3389/fpsyg.2015.00444

Morris, C. A. S., Denham, S. A., Bassett, H. H., & Curby, T. W. (2013). Relations among teachers' emotion socialization beliefs and practices and preschoolers' emotional competence. *Early Education & Development*, *24*(7), 979–999. https://doi.org/10.1080/10409289.2013.825186

Ornaghi, V., & Grazzani, I. (2013). The relationship between emotional-state language and emotion understanding: A study with school-age children. *Cognition and Emotion*, *27*(2), 356–366. https://doi.org/10.1080/02699931.2012.711745

Röll, J., Koglin, U., & Petermann, F. (2012). Emotion regulation and childhood aggression: Longitudinal associations. *Child Psychiatry and Human Development*, *43*(6), 909–923. https://doi.org/10.1007/s10578-012-0303-4

Saarni, C., Campos, J. J., Camras, L. A., & Witherington, D. (2006). Emotional development: Action, communication, and understanding. In N. Eisenberg, W. Damon, & R. M. Lerner (Eds.), *Handbook of child psychology: Social, emotional, and personality development* (pp. 226–299). John Wiley & Sons, Inc.

Trentacosta, C. J., Izard, C. E., Mostow, A. J., & Fine, S. E. (2006). Children's emotional competence and attentional competence in early elementary school. *School Psychology Quarterly*, *21*(2), 148–170. https://doi.org/10.1521/scpq.2006.21.2.148

Valiente, C., Lemery-Chalfant, K., & Swanson, J. (2010). Prediction of kindergartners' academic achievement from their effortful control and emotionality: Evidence for direct and moderated relations. *Journal of Educational Psychology*, *102*(3), 550–560. https://doi.org/10.1037/a0018992

CHAPTER 13

Teacher Emotions in the Classroom

Teaching is an inherently emotional practice because it calls for passionate and emotional beings (Hargreaves, 2004). "Creating and sustaining a dynamic, engaging lesson . . . requires hard emotional work, investment, or labor. So too does remaining calm and unruffled when confronted by threatening student behavior" (Hargreaves, 2004, p. 814). Not only does the act of teaching require emotional investment but also interactions between students and teachers are characterized by deep emotionality (Meyer, 2009). Teachers may experience anxiety when students are taking statewide tests, anger when they cannot achieve their instructional goals, or sadness when they have to say goodbye to their students. Teachers may also feel excitement when they begin a new school year, pride when students do well on their assessments, or love toward their students. Furthermore, emotions guide teachers' instructional behavior. Teachers who experience more positive emotions use a broader repertoire of instructional strategies and make learning material more accessible for students to learn (Frenzel, Goetz, Stephens, & Jacob, 2009). On the other hand, experiencing negative emotions might limit teachers' instructional behavior to fewer choices or strategies.

Teachers hold different beliefs about emotions, which are shaped by their personal histories, professional experiences, and culture at large. These beliefs influence how teachers interpret emotions in the classroom and how they manage their own emotions along with those of their students (Cross & Hong, 2012). For instance, a teacher who believes negative emotions should be avoided may be dismissive of a student who begins to cry. Another teacher who sees emotions as a signal about a child's needs may be more inclined to approach the crying

DOI: 10.4324/9781003219774-13

child and provide support. That is why it is important for teachers to explore "their values and beliefs and recognize in what ways emotions 'color' their decisions and practices" (Zembylas, 2011, p. 39). Teachers may also have different ideas about what constitutes a good education compared to those held by the school administration and parents. Facing incongruous goals can be anxiety provoking and lead to confusion and dissatisfaction (Kelchtermans, 2011).

SOURCES OF TEACHER EMOTIONS IN THE CLASSROOM

As you learned earlier, emotions are often evoked as a result of our appraisal of a situation. Teachers have expectations about their students' performance and behavior in the classroom, which further affect their appraisals (Frenzel et al., 2009). For example, some teachers believe that students have to follow instructions exactly while some allow flexibility and creativity. Some teachers envision their classroom as a place with a lot of energy and interactions among students and can tolerate a lot of noise in the classroom. Yet others believe that the ideal classroom is a quiet place where students do not mingle much with each other but focus on tasks. Teachers appraise their students' performance and behavior against their visions. They experience positive emotions when students' performance and behavior meet their expectations and feel negative emotions when their vision conflicts with the classroom reality.

Let's take a closer look at potential sources of teacher emotions.

Students' Performance

One source of teacher emotion is related to student performance. Teachers are invested in their students' academic performance because it, in part, reflects their professional competence (Kelchtermans, Ballet, & Piot, 2009). You will have certain standards of performance set by your school or regional district, alongside state and federal guidelines. High-stakes testing is a particularly visible measure of student performance. Results of these measures are critically examined by colleagues, administrators, and parents. Furthermore, testing results are often shared and reviewed in large meetings. Consider a situation in which a neighboring classroom was considered "proficient" on an assessment while your own class performed in the "needs improvement" range. It is understandable that testing can be anxiety provoking for teachers. Teachers may feel especially anxious if they have a group of students who perform below grade level throughout the school year.

Student Classroom Behavior

Student classroom behavior is another source of teacher emotions. When students are noncompliant or inattentive, teachers often become frustrated, angry, and even confused (Skoglund & Åmot, 2020; Sutton & Wheatley, 2003). Problematic behaviors impede teachers' instructional goals, as a teacher might spend a significant amount of instructional time trying to discipline students. It is no surprise that managing students' problem behavior not only elicits negative emotions in teachers but also often leads to emotional exhaustion. Keep in mind that your emotions depend on how you appraise students' behavior. Imagine a student who asks you what to do on an assignment right after you finished giving instructions. This situation may or may not be emotionally provoking. If you doubt your instructional skills, then you might interpret the student's behavior as a confirmation of your insufficient skills. In this case, you will likely feel anxiety. In a case where you think you delivered the instructions well but appraise that the student missed it because he or she was chatting with a peer, you may feel angry. Finally, if you think that the student did not hear your instructions well because of the noisy air conditioner, you may not experience negative emotions at all.

Changes in the Educational Setting

Changes and reforms in the educational setting can evoke teacher emotions, as they can create an environment of ambiguity and uncertainty (Reio, 2005). These changes may require teachers to adjust to different leadership styles, policies, and student demographics, which can contribute to a teacher's emotional vulnerability (Kelchtermans et al., 2009; Van Veen & Sleegers, 2009). For example, a teacher may feel confused and frustrated when a new principal changes the curriculum that he or she has been using for years. Policy decisions made by school administrators and the school board are an important source of teachers' emotions and vulnerability, especially when these decisions do not take into account teachers' perspectives. At the same time, having a competent administrator who can implement positive changes for the school is reassuring to teachers and may mitigate potential negative experiences (Cross & Hong, 2012).

Relational Context

Teachers experience positive emotions when they are recognized by their school community, parents, and the broader community (Chen, 2016). They also experience positive emotions when former students visit them (Sutton & Wheatley, 2003). Supportive relationships with colleagues are a source of positive emotional experiences. At the same time, colleagues can evoke negative emotions when they are perceived as uncooperative or competitive. Parents perceived as uncaring or irresponsible can also elicit negative emotions in teachers (Sutton, 2007).

Teacher Self-Efficacy

Emotions can arise in relation to teachers' sense of self-efficacy. When teachers see themselves as effective and act according to their beliefs and values, they experience positive emotions (Nias, 1996). Similarly, teachers experience positive emotions when they feel professionally successful and experience personal and professional growth (Zembylas, 2002; Hargreaves, 2000). On the other hand, the self-perception of being an ineffective teacher may lead to anger. Beginning teachers are especially vulnerable to anxiety resulting from a feeling of being overwhelmed and underprepared (Chang, 2009).

ANGER AND GUILT IN TEACHERS

Anger can be a particularly difficult emotion for teachers to deal with. As you learned earlier, we feel angry when we experience a barrier to achieving our goals. Emotional display rules often dictate that it is unprofessional for teachers to show their anger in the classroom. That is why teachers often use the word "frustrated" when, in reality, they feel angry (Sutton & Wheatley, 2003). It is not uncommon for teachers to hide or suppress their anger. This strategy may be helpful in the short term; however, it does not mitigate the experience of anger. In other words, even if you don't show your anger, you will continue to feel angry.

Several situations can potentially lead to a teacher feeling anger. One situation is when a teacher perceives a student as being disrespectful

(Martin, 2018). This perception is related to the teacher's beliefs regarding how students should or should not behave toward authority figures. Another situation is when students do not follow instructions, which may obstruct teachers' instructional goals. Anger can also arise when teachers experience stress from being pressed for time, and they have to hurry to move students from one setting or activity to another (Skoglund & Åmot, 2020). Finally, anger may occur when teachers feel they are being asked to complete a lot of paperwork or are mandated to teach a certain way by local educational authorities (Martin, 2018).

Guilt is another difficult emotion for teachers to deal with. Guilt is a self-conscious emotion that arises when we believe our behavior does not meet our own or others' standards. Teachers experience guilt when they believe they let down or upset their students or colleagues (Farouk, 2012). For example, they may feel guilty when they do not have enough time to attend to students who need additional support. Another guilt-evoking situation is when teachers lose their temper and make students upset. These behaviors violate the ideal view teachers have of themselves. Teachers who have very high and unrealistic expectations of themselves may be more susceptible to guilt.

Guilt is an unpleasant emotion. When it becomes chronic and unreasonable, it may lead to significant emotional problems, including depression. However, occasional guilt cannot and should not be eradicated from the teaching profession (Farouk, 2012). Teachers are human beings who care about their students and hold high standards for themselves. Therefore, they may occasionally perceive themselves as not fully meeting those standards and not providing the best instruction and care for their students. In this case, guilt may promote teachers' strivings for self-improvement.

EMOTIONAL LABOR AND BURNOUT

Think about the following questions: What emotions are appropriate and not appropriate for teachers to show to their students? Can teachers show their anxiety? Can they show their anger and frustration? These questions are related to emotion display rules. Emotion display rules are closely linked to teachers' ideas about professionalism (Zembylas, 2002). While they may not be easily recognized by teachers, these rules exert significant power over teachers' emotional experiences. For example, they can inhibit teachers' spontaneous expression of emotions and make them show "appropriate" emotions only. Furthermore, teachers may evaluate their own professional behavior in terms of how well they follow emotion display rules (Zembylas, 2002).

When teachers express emotions "appropriate" for their job despite having different internal experiences, it is called emotional labor (Wang, Hall, & Taxer, 2019). Emotional labor is a part of a teacher's work (Zembylas, 2002). Teachers usually openly express positive emotions but tend to suppress or hide their negative emotions (Taxer & Frenzel, 2015). In one study, teachers shared that they suppress or fake their emotions during about one-third of all lessons (Keller, Chang, Becker, Goetz, & Frenzel, 2014). They find anger to be a difficult emotion to express outwardly to their students. As one teacher reflected, "I easily become frustrated and discouraged, but I have learned that I can't reflect these feelings onto the students. I have learned to control my emotions – especially when we are having a bad day and the students misbehave" (Meyer, 2009, p. 85). Teachers may receive implicit and explicit messages from administrators and school systems about what emotions are acceptable to show in the classroom (Sutton & Wheatley, 2003). Emotional labor requires a lot of emotional energy and, as a result, may lead to emotional exhaustion and burnout (Wang et al., 2019).

When teachers have difficulty managing their stress, it may lead to emotional burnout, a state of physical and emotional exhaustion. When experiencing emotional burnout, teachers feel that their emotional resources are depleted (Keller et al., 2014). Emotional burnout diminishes teachers' job satisfaction, enjoyment, and enthusiasm. It also reduces teachers' ability to provide high-quality instruction and leads to decreased enjoyment (Keller et al., 2014). Teacher emotional burnout is a potential cause for teachers leaving their job.

Burnout does not happen overnight; instead, it builds over time. That is why it is important for you to recognize the early signs of burnout. These may include cynicism toward the profession, increased emotional exhaustion throughout the day or after work, and decreased self-efficacy: the feeling that you cannot handle day-to-day tasks (Carter, 2013). Additional signs may include feeling irritable and quick to anger, lacking the desire to attend social gatherings, sleep problems, change in appetite, and anxiety. Engaging in self-care is important to prevent emotional burnout.

TEACHER EMOTION REGULATION

Effective emotion regulation is important for teachers to stay emotionally healthy, be effective in their job, and have positive relationships with students and colleagues. Teachers who have difficulty regulating their emotions are at an increased risk for emotional burnout. Emotion regulation has implications for a teacher's ability to successfully deliver instruction and manage students' behavior and contributes to the overall emotional climate in the classroom (Garner, 2010). Teachers consider the regulation of their emotions as a daily task (Sutton, 2004). They believe that good emotion regulation is important for effective teaching and for being a positive role model for students. Managing negative emotions also helps teachers to stay focused. Effective emotion regulation allows teachers to more accurately consider the situation they are in, which leads to more informed responses.

Chapter Summary

- Teaching is an inherently emotional practice. Teachers hold diverse beliefs about their emotions and emotional expression, which are informed by their histories, experiences, and the broader culture.
- Teachers' emotions arise in relation to how a given situation fits with their hopes and goals. There are many emotion-evoking factors in the classroom: student performance, and behavior, changes in the educational setting, relational interactions, and sense of self-efficacy.
- Anger and guilt tend to be especially difficult emotions for teachers to manage. Anger is often viewed as an unacceptable emotion. Guilt is uncomfortable and arises when teachers feel they are not meeting their own or others' standards.
- It is important to be aware of emotion display rules. Teachers often alter their emotional expression to fit these rules, leading to emotional exhaustion. If emotional exhaustion isn't addressed, it can lead to burnout.
- Being able to regulate emotions effectively can protect teachers from burnout, help them to be more effective in their work, and improve their relationships with others.

Self-Reflective Activity

Reflect on the following situations in terms of the emotional impact they may have on you. What feelings might these situations bring up for you and why? Which situations would evoke the strongest emotional reaction from you, and which would be less emotionally provocative? Reflect on your goals, expectations, and personal experiences and how they might impact your emotional reaction to these situations.

1. A student trying to complete an assignment becomes frustrated and starts kicking things around her.
2. You worked very hard to plan a lesson; however, your students do not seem to grasp the material that you are teaching.
3. An administrator is coming in shortly to conduct a formal observation in your class, and the class cannot seem to settle down.
4. Parent-teacher conferences are this week, and you do not have time to get things ready.
5. The children in the recess soccer game are getting increasingly agitated and fighting over the rules.
6. A parent sends you an angry email demanding to know why no one is preventing her child from being picked on.
7. A group of students refuses to do what you ask them to do. Instead, they continue talking to each other.

Small Group Activities

Activity 1. Group Discussion

Discuss the following questions in your group:

- What can make a teacher anxious in the classroom? How could that impact his or her ability to teach? How could the teacher's anxiety affect students?
- What can make a teacher sad in the classroom? How could that impact his or her ability to teach? How could it affect students?
- What can make a teacher happy in the classroom? How could that impact his or her ability to teach? How could it affect students?

Activity 2. Vignettes

In small groups, read and discuss the following vignettes.

Noncompliance

You've just taught a writing lesson on paragraphs, and your students have returned to their seats to complete a graphic organizer using the ideas you generated as a group. Mrs. Graham, the PTA president, is the classroom volunteer today and is stuffing envelopes at a table in the corner.

Within a few minutes, you notice that Sean has not taken out a pencil or started his paper and is whispering and laughing with his neighbor Brendan. You send the boys a warning glance, and Brendan turns to his paper. To your dismay, Sean soon begins tapping Brendan's desk in an effort to get his attention again. You walk toward the boys and tell Sean he needs to move and do his work at the back table.

He looks up at you and says, "But he started it!"

You repeat your direction more firmly, and Mrs. Graham looks up, watching the situation.

Sean's face hardens and he says, "No, I don't have to, and you can't make me!"

- How would you feel in this situation?
- What might you be thinking in this situation?
- What would your first reaction be?
- What would you actually do?
- How would your feelings inform your action?
- What would you do to deal with your feelings?

Common Assessment

Your building has scheduled common planning time and you, and your grade-level teammates are getting ready to gather in a nearby classroom. You know the group will be reviewing the results of the most recent common math assessment at the meeting. As you walk into the room, you recall how hard your students worked on the unit and how you held several afterschool tutoring sessions for students who seemed to be struggling. The results of your exit tickets leading up to the test averaged around 80%. As you sit down at the table, you see the results for the grade level, and your group performed the lowest of the four classes with a 62% average. You notice that the first-year teacher next door had an 85% class average. The meeting facilitator sits down and begins to review the data with the group.

- How would you feel in this situation?
- What might you be thinking in this situation?
- What would your first reaction be?

- What would you actually do?
- How would your feelings inform your action?
- What would you do to deal with your feelings?

Activity 3. Reappraisal

Read the following situations and generate self-talk that would lead to negative emotions. Then reappraise the situation and generate self-talk that would lead to more positive emotions.

- Sally has not turned in her homework for the past two weeks.
- Johnny daydreams during class, does not pay attention to lessons, and does not complete his classwork.
- Other students repeatedly complain that Gloria engages in name-calling and cheats during games.
- Despite multiple reminders to raise his hand, Sam repeatedly calls out during lessons. When he is not calling out, he is talking to other students, playing with his supplies, and making noises by tapping his feet and drumming his pencils on his desk.

Self-Care Tool Kit

Body Scan Meditation

This is a type of meditation that brings your attention to different parts of your body. As you complete this, avoid labeling the sensations you feel as good or bad. Just notice them and move on to a different body part.

Sit in your chair in a comfortable position (you may also lie on your back). Your legs should be relaxed. If you're sitting, keep your legs uncrossed with both feet firmly planted on the floor and your arms relaxed by your sides or in your lap. You may have your eyes open or closed, whatever makes you most comfortable. If you choose to keep them open, angle them downwards or find a spot to focus on. Focus on your breathing, in and out, for about two minutes, until you begin to feel your body relax onto the floor or into your chair.

To begin the body scan, bring your attention to your feet. Notice any sensation or feeling, or lack of feeling, while you continue to breathe. Continue to focus on your feet for three to five breaths. Now bring your attention to your ankles. Notice any sensation or feeling, or lack of feeling, while you continue to breathe. Continue to do this as you move up to your knee, thigh, hip, and backside. Once you've completed the sequence in your lower body, you can continue to move upward, focusing on your torso, your lower back, stomach, upper back, and chest. Pay close attention to any parts of your body where you may feel discomfort, pain, or increased tension. If you feel any tension, try to release it.

Next, bring your attention to your shoulders and neck – people tend to hold a lot of tension there. Release your tension. Focus your attention on your face – your jaw, lips, eyes, and forehead. Release tension if you feel it.

Once you have completed the body scan, bring your attention to your full body. Notice how it feels. Begin to open your eyes, wiggle your fingers and toes, and stretch. Take a deep breath and say, "This is my body. I live here."

REFERENCES

Carter, S. B. (2013). The tell tale signs of burnout . . . Do you have them? *Psychology Today*. Retrieved from www.psychologytoday.com/us/blog/high-octane-women/201311/the-tell-tale-signs-burnout-do-you-have-them

Chang, M.-L. (2009). An appraisal perspective of teacher burnout: Examining the emotional work of teachers. *Educational Psychology Review*, *21*(3), 193–218. https://doi.org/10.1007/s10648–009–9106-y

Chen, J. (2016). Understanding teacher emotions: The development of a teacher emotion inventory. *Teaching and Teacher Education*, *55*, 68–77. https://doi.org/10.1016/j.tate.2016.01.001

Cross, D. I., & Hong, J. Y. (2012). An ecological examination of teachers' emotions in the school context. *Teaching and Teacher Education*, *28*(7), 957–967. https://doi.org/10.1016/j.tate.2012.05.001

Farouk, S. (2012). What can the self-conscious emotion of guilt tell us about primary school teachers' moral purpose and the relationships they have with their pupils? *Teachers and Teaching*, *18*(4), 491–507. https://doi.org/10.1080/13540602.2012.696049

Frenzel, A. C., Goetz, T., Stephens, E. J., & Jacob, B. (2009). Antecedents and effects of teachers' emotional experiences: An integrated perspective and empirical test. In P. A. Schutz & M. Zembylas (Eds.), *Advances in teacher emotion research* (pp. 129–151). Springer.

Garner, P. W. (2010). Emotional competence and it's influences on teaching and learning. *Educational Psychology Review*, *2010*(22), 297–321. https://doi.org/10.1007/s10648-010-9129-4

Hargreaves, A. (2000). Mixed emotions: Teachers' perceptions of their interactions with students. *Teaching and Teacher Education, 16*(8), 811–826. https://doi.org/10.1016/S0742-051X(00)00028-7

Hargreaves, A. (2004). Inclusive and exclusive educational change: Emotional responses of teachers and implications for leadership. *School Leadership & Management, 24*(3), 287–309. https://doi.org/10.1080/1363243042000266936

Kelchtermans, G. (2011). Vulnerability in teaching: The moral and political roots of a structural change. In C. Day & J. C.-K. Lee (Eds.), *New understandings of teacher's work* (pp. 65–82). Springer. https://doi.org/10.1007/978-94-007-0545-6

Kelchtermans, G., Ballet, K., & Piot, L. (2009). Surviving diversity in times of performativity: Understanding teachers' emotional experience of change. In P. Schutz & M. Zembylas (Eds.), *Advances in teacher emotion research* (pp. 215–232). Springer.

Keller, M. M., Chang, M. L., Becker, E. S., Goetz, T., & Frenzel, A. C. (2014). Teachers' emotional experiences and exhaustion as predictors of emotional labor in the classroom: An experience sampling study. *Frontiers in Psychology, 5*, 1442. https://doi.org/10.3389/fpsyg.2014.01442

Martin, R. C. (2018). Anger in the classroom: How a supposedly negative emotion can enhance learning. *New Directions for Teaching and Learning, 153*, 37–44. https://doi.org/10.1002/tl.20279

Meyer, D. K. (2009). Entering the emotional practices of teaching. In P. Schutz & M. Zembylas (Eds.), *Advances in teacher emotion research* (pp. 73–91). New York, NY: Springer.

Nias, J. (1996). Thinking about feeling: The emotions in teaching. *Cambridge Journal of Education, 26*(3), 293–306. https://doi.org/10.1080/0305764960260301

Reio, T. G. (2005). Emotions as a lens to explore teacher identity and change: A commentary. *Teaching and Teacher Education, 21*(8), 985–993. https://doi.org/10.1016/j.tate.2005.06.008

Skoglund, R. I., & Åmot, I. (2020). When anger arises in the interaction with children in kindergartens – The staff's reactions to children's resistance. *Scandinavian Journal of Educational Research*, 1–12. https://doi.org/10.1080/00313831.2020.1739138

Sutton, R. E. (2004). Emotional regulation goals and strategies of teachers. *Social Psychology of Education, 7*(4), 379–398. https://doi.org/10.1007/s11218-004-4229-y

Sutton, R. E. (2007). Teachers' anger, frustration and self-regulation. In P. A. Schutz & P. Reinhard (Eds.), *Emotions in education* (pp. 259–274). Academic Press. https://doi.org/10.1016/B978-012372545-5/50016-2

Sutton, R. E., & Wheatley, K. F. (2003). Teachers' emotions and teaching: A review of the literature and directions for future research. *Educational Psychology Review, 15*(4), 327–358. https://doi.org/10.1023/A:1026131715856

Taxer, J. L., & Frenzel, A. C. (2015). Facets of teachers' emotional lives: A quantitative investigation of teachers' genuine, faked, and hidden emotions. *Teaching and Teacher Education, 49*, 78–88. https://doi.org/10.1016/j.tate.2015.03.003

Van Veen, K., & Sleegers, P. (2009). Teachers' emotions in a context of reforms: To a deeper understanding of teachers and reforms. In P. Schutz & M. Zembylas (Eds.), *Advances in teacher emotion research* (pp. 233–251). New York, NY: Springer. https://doi.org/10.1007/978-1-4419-0564-2_12

Wang, H., Hall, N. C., & Taxer, J. L. (2019). Antecedents and consequences of teachers' emotional labor: A systematic review and meta-analytic investigation. *Educational Psychology Review*, 1–36. https://doi.org/10.1007/s10648-019-09475-3

Zembylas, M. (2002). "Structures of feeling" in curriculum and teaching: Theorizing the emotional rules. *Educational Theory, 52*(2), 187–208. https://doi.org/10.1111/j.1741-5446.2002.00187.x

Zembylas, M. (2011). Teaching and teacher emotions: A post-structural perspective. In C. Day & J. K. Lee (Eds.), *New understandings of teacher's work: Professional learning and development in schools and higher education* (Vol. 100, pp. 31–43). Springer. https://doi.org/10.1007/978-94-007-0545-6_3

CHAPTER 14

Teacher Identity and Emotional Well-Being

TEACHER PROFESSIONAL IDENTITY AND EMOTIONS

Why did you decide to be a teacher? What does it mean for you to be a "good teacher"? What professional goals do you have? Your answers to these questions are informed by your emerging professional identity. Teacher identity is "how teachers define themselves to themselves and others" (Lasky, 2005, p. 901). This includes how teachers understand themselves in the context of their job, reasons for becoming a teacher, their vision for best teaching practices, and relationships with their students. It also includes their understanding of how teachers should act in the classroom (Mayer, 2011). "Good teaching cannot be reduced to technique; good teaching comes from the identity and integrity of the teacher" (Palmer, 1997, p. 16). A teacher's identity and selfhood are the most decisive elements of teaching. Your identity and sense of who you are as a teacher give meaning to your work. Furthermore, they allow you to connect with your students. A positive sense of professional identity is important for your well-being and satisfaction with your job.

Teachers face many emotional and pedagogical obstacles through ever-changing policies, curriculums, and expectations, which may prompt questions about their professional identity (Day, 2011). A teacher's professional identity may be stable or unstable based on navigation of multiple contexts (Day, 2011). The instability of societal or personal expectations regarding their profession may contribute to instability in their professional identity.

New teachers enter the profession with specific visions and goals for themselves and their students. Their ability to achieve that vision and feel successful predicts their commitment and motivation to stay in the teaching profession through the first several years (Mayer, 2011). Teachers may envision themselves as helpers of children and conduits of knowledge. They may also see their mission as changing children's lives. However, new teachers are often confronted with a reality that may not coincide with their visions and expectations. They may experience the classroom as a political place governed by rigid standards and encounter students who struggle academically and behaviorally. These realities bring challenges associated with teachers adjusting their ideal professional identity to their everyday job (Mayer, 2011).

Teacher emotions are an essential part of teacher identity, as they impact teachers' beliefs, values, goals, and overall purpose for teaching (Mayer, 2011). In fact, teacher identities are constructed through emotional processes (Zembylas, 2005). Teachers build a history of experiences termed "genealogies of emotions in teaching" as they attempt various ways of managing emotional situations that arise in classroom contexts (Zembylas, 2005, p. 938). Teachers' emotions are the means by which they navigate and interpret events in the classroom and the culture of the schools in which they work (O'Connor, 2008).

Teachers bring their goals, values, and personal experiences into the classroom (Zembylas, 2005). In order to understand how and why teachers respond in emotional situations, it is important to understand how a teacher's identity interacts with classroom situations. Classroom experiences such as decision-making, emotional exchanges, and giving and receiving feedback evoke feelings that have a powerful influence on identity. For instance, concern for students not doing well academically often evokes anxiety and self-blame, which might undermine the teacher's sense of mastery and ultimately affect her identity. At the same time, pride and joy when seeing a child's progress contribute to a sense of success and a view of oneself as a competent teacher (Zembylas, 2005).

Caring for students is an essential part of a teacher's professional identity and is intimately connected to a teacher's instructional and classroom management strategies (O'Connor, 2008). Teachers' identities are connected to their ability to be empathetic in the classroom and how they act upon their emotions and respond to students' emotions (Cross & Hong, 2012). "The greatest satisfactions of elementary school teaching are found . . . not in pay, prestige or promotion but in . . . *psychic rewards* of teaching: the joys and satisfactions of caring for and working with young people." These rewards "are central to sustaining teachers' senses of self; their senses of value and worth in their work" (Hargreaves, 1994, p. 173).

Teachers' feelings underlie the way they approach their job. Learning and teaching always involve deep emotions, whether they are acknowledged or not. Teaching is an intensely relational job that creates multiple interactions in the classroom, some one-on-one and some with the whole group. These interactions then create a myriad of emotional experiences. "Reflecting on one's own emotions and seeing teaching as an emotionally complex engagement can enrich a teacher's experience, pedagogy, and students' motivation and response in class" (Nair, 2018, p. 45). While student learning is a product of the teacher, teaching is also a process that reflects how teachers convey learning material and forge relationships in the classroom (Nair, 2018). This process is deeply emotional since teachers demonstrate their passion in what they teach and display care for those they teach through their emotions. A teacher's emotional investment is an engine that propels students' motivation to learn.

TEACHER EMOTIONAL WELL-BEING

> *Classroom teaching . . . is perhaps the most complex, most challenging, and most demanding, subtle, nuanced, and frightening activity that our species has ever invented. In fact, when I compared the complexity of teaching with that of a much highly rewarded profession, doing medicine, I concluded that the only time medicine even approaches the complexity of an average day of classroom teaching is in an emergency room during a natural disaster.*
> (Shulman, 2004, p. 504)

Indeed, teaching is a very demanding job in many ways. Teachers must juggle many responsibilities simultaneously: delivering instruction, building relationships with students, responding to student needs, and managing personal emotional reactions. When teachers do not attend to their own emotional needs, they put their well-being at stake. That is why you need to cultivate your ability to stay emotionally healthy. The following are some recommendations on how to do so.

Be Aware of Your Goals and Values

One way to stay emotionally healthy is to have a clear awareness of your personal and professional goals and values. These goals and values implicitly influence your interpersonal transactions in the classroom (Mansfield & Beltman, 2014). Teachers who set clear and attainable goals are less emotionally reactive to a student's poor performance. In contrast, teachers who set unreasonable goals are more likely to become upset and frustrated. It is a good practice to reevaluate and adjust your goals in the context of your student population and the school's goals. You may write down your goals at the beginning of each year and revise them as you learn more about your students.

Keep in mind that students, families, and even colleagues may not share your goals. Therefore, the recognition of this potential incongruence may mitigate the frustration that results when these goals inevitably clash. For example, you may work very hard to help a struggling reader to reach grade level. You are likely to feel angry if this child's family does not read with him daily. It is healthy to acknowledge your potentially divergent values. Some families will not value education in the same way you do. Acknowledging your hopes for the student and the barriers to achieving them allows you to adjust your goals based on what can be accomplished without additional practice.

Develop Self-Efficacy

Self-efficacy is a protective factor against job strain, job stress, and burnout from teaching (Schwarzer & Hallum, 2008). When teachers believe in their ability to be effective in teaching and managing classroom behavior, they experience less emotional burnout (Skaalvik & Skaalvik, 2007). The best way to develop self-efficacy is to focus on experiences where you already have a level of mastery. There are going to be many difficult situations, and it will take time to feel proficient in many tasks. Acknowledge what you are doing well and do not dwell on the negative. You have to develop confidence in your repertoire of skills, feeling prepared to act and respond to emotional situations in the classroom. Listen for positive and encouraging feedback from parents, students, colleagues, and school leadership and internalize your successes.

Setting reasonable goals is another way to foster self-efficacy. What your district or state sets as a goal may not always be attainable and may leave you feeling ineffective. Consider setting your own smaller goals for your students. Remember, while all students have the ability to learn, it is important to recognize that broad life experiences outside of the classroom may make learning more challenging for some students.

Understanding this will prevent you from internalizing misbehavior or student failures as signs of your incompetence or students' ill will.

Maintain Separation Between Professional and Personal Identities

It is very important to maintain a separation between your professional identity and personal identity. If your identity is grounded solely in your professional work, it puts you at risk for interpreting your professional performance as a primary reflection of your self-worth. Therefore, in order to stay emotionally healthy, you need to cultivate hobbies and interests outside your profession and make time for them. It is also common in the teaching profession to bring work home, and you are strongly encouraged to avoid this. If you find yourself struggling to complete tasks during your work hours, consult with experienced teachers and find ways to streamline your work. Be aware of your beliefs: You do not need to be working on teaching all of the time to be a good teacher.

It can be helpful to develop transition routines to mark the delineation between work and home. For some, this is a commute home, singing along to a song, taking a brief walk, or calling a friend. If you find yourself stuck on a difficult event from the day, write it down or plan a time to revisit it with a mentor. These things are important to prevent affect spillover – when you keep thinking about negative work events in the evening (Sonnentag & Binnewies, 2013). When this happens, the next morning, you will still experience negative emotions. To prevent affect spillover, you need to disconnect mentally from job-related negative events during the evening and have a good night. This will help you feel refreshed and positive the next morning.

Focus on Positive Emotional Experiences

Our emotions depend on our attentional focus. If we focus only on negative things, we feel miserable. However, we have the power to switch our focus to positive experiences. Think about what you usually do: Do you dwell on negative aspects of a situation, or do you try to find something positive? If you mostly see negative things, you can retrain yourself. For example, after your lesson did not go well, and you did not reach your instructional goals, you should try to find positive elements. Perhaps some students asked good questions, or students who are usually off task were more attentive. The ability to focus on positive things is especially important when working with students who have trouble learning or regulating themselves. If you think their deficits are impeding your goals, this will likely lead to frustration, which will not help you or them. Try to find positive qualities in those students – maybe they are kind or good helpers. You can also evoke positive emotions by focusing on positive memories. For instance, recall classroom situations that made you feel joy.

Find Joy in Teaching

"A joyful teacher is first and foremost a joyful learner" (Nair, 2018, p. 53). Cultivating reflective self-awareness is the first step to finding joy in teaching. This includes understanding the life experiences that have shaped you as a person and as a teacher. These experiences may be very different from the experiences of your students. Remain open to learning about your students' experiences and how they may intersect with events in the classroom. Learning about your students will help you to be emotionally connected to them. You can enhance your joy from teaching when you become passionate about what you are teaching. Your passion will ultimately fuel your students' interest and engagement. Finally, while you have to plan your lessons well, leave room for improvisation. Consider teaching as an act of creativity that opens students' minds to new ways of thinking, feeling, and acting.

Understand Things You Can and Cannot Control

Sometimes we try to control more things than we actually can. It is important to identify what we can and cannot control since trying to control the uncontrollable is liable to end in dissatisfaction, anxiety, frustration, and feeling ineffective. You can control how well you prepare, your lesson design, and how you deliver a lesson. Unfortunately, you cannot fully control how your students will learn. Learning is a very complex process affected by many factors.

Perhaps you are delivering a fantastic lesson that is well-tailored to your students' abilities. Despite this, one of your students is preoccupied with thinking about his parents who have been fighting at home. Can you prevent him from worrying and make him focus on the lesson? Very likely not. Perhaps he will have his most difficult academic year as he struggles with his parents' ultimate divorce. It is important to remember that your effort and preparation will not always clearly connect to learning outcomes because things that you cannot control may affect learning. This includes family stressors, psychological difficulties, political and social stressors, and even biological factors, like cognitive ability, illness, or attention problems.

This is not to say that your efforts do not matter. Simply, it is important to know that sometimes you will do everything that you can to promote a positive outcome, and factors beyond your control may prevent you from reaching your goals for your students. You can influence student learning by being sensitive to emotional needs and by creating a positive classroom environment. You can continue to grow and learn as a teacher. Focus on what you can control and find ways to celebrate your hard work regardless of the outcomes.

Find a Sense of Purpose and Meaning

Finding a purpose and meaning are important routes to well-being (Ryff, 2014). For teachers, having a purpose and meaning in their work can mitigate emotional burnout (Loonstra, Brouwers, & Tomic, 2009). Think about the following questions: What led me to want to be a teacher? How have teachers affected my life? What meaning does teaching give to me? What do I enjoy most about teaching? Reflecting on these questions can help you find meaning in your work. You may find meaning in the big things, like changing a child's life or teaching him or her to read. It is also important to consider where you find meaning in the small moments of teaching, such as the satisfaction of seeing a student understand a concept or the pride you instill when you praise a student. Perhaps you find purpose in being a consistent figure in your students' lives or knowing that you are contributing to their education. It is important to reflect on these ideas when you are starting out and when things are going well so that you can call on them when you feel emotionally depleted and want to quit. Focusing on the purpose of your work will help you to revive your zest for teaching.

Strive to Build a Social Support System

Leaning on social support is essential for your well-being. "The relationships between teachers and their colleagues are among the most educationally significant aspects of teachers' lives and work. They provide a vital context for teacher development and for the ways that teachers teach" (Hargreaves, 1994, p. 165).

Try to find a colleague at your school who shares similar values or goals. Ask for a mentor or find other ways to connect with veteran teachers. One way to build a sense of community and solidarity is to have a place where teachers feel comfortable enough to talk with one another and recharge. It is also important to know when to seek social support. After a challenging day, seeking support by connecting with friends, family, or fellow educators can help to decrease your negative emotional experiences.

Be mindful of getting caught in repetitive negative social encounters with colleagues. When things are challenging, sometimes these interactions can become focused on criticizing others, making mean-spirited assessments of families, or promoting a sense of doom, anxiety, or hopelessness. Choose your work friends thoughtfully. Additionally, strive to have friends from work and friends outside of education. Noneducator friends can help to push you to talk about things outside of teaching and keep you engaged with other hobbies.

Create a Self-Care Routine

Self-care is a very important part of enhancing and maintaining your emotional well-being. Teachers have "the obligation to *receive* care as well as to give it – to open themselves up to receiving care from others, instead of being like moral martyrs and always giving the care themselves" (Hargreaves, 1994, p. 177). Creating a good self-care routine is an individual experience, as everyone recharges in different ways. General recommendations include getting good sleep, finding ways to replenish yourself, and being kind to yourself. Good sleep is important for effective emotion regulation, as it helps to reduce activity in the amygdala, the brain structure involved in emotional processing (Zaccaro, Conversano, Lai, & Gemignani, 2019). Sleep hygiene includes going to bed at a regular time, avoiding using screen media before bed, and engaging in relaxing activities. Additionally, dedicate your weekends to activities, hobbies, or being with people you enjoy. Be attentive to your needs. For example, if you are feeling emotionally low, choose outdoor activities, exercise, or social activities to help increase your energy levels. On the other hand, if you find yourself fatigued and emotionally drained, listening to your favorite music, reading a book you enjoy, or meditating are good uplifting choices. Lastly, be kind to yourself and treat yourself with the same care and compassion that you treat others. The practice of self-empathy is important for teacher well-being and resilience, as it allows you to restore your empathy and feel more ready to reengage with teaching (Jordan & Schwartz, 2018). Remember, you will be more efficient and effective when you care for yourself. Make it a priority to maintain these routines throughout the school year. The time when you feel least able to do them is probably when you need them most.

Chapter Summary

- Your teacher identity informs how you teach, what motivates you in the classroom, and how you respond to events in the classroom. It is important to understand that your emotions, goals, beliefs, values, and experiences all influence your identity as a teacher.
- Relationships with students and the caring elements of teaching have significant impacts on teacher experiences. At times, these can be the source of joy and a sense of success and at other times, these can elicit disappointment or make one question one's efficacy.
- Teaching is a demanding and complex profession. It is important to acknowledge the difficulty of this job and to prioritize maintaining your own well-being. Consider the following to maintain emotional health:
  - Be aware of your goals and values. Remember that others may have different ideas about what is important or what to prioritize.
  - Find ways to feel effective. There will be many things that don't go well, and you will need to be purposeful about focusing on your successes and what you are doing well.
  - Separate your personal and professional lives. As much as possible, leave school at school. Don't take work home, and don't allow negative events from the day to overtake your evening.
  - Be purposeful about finding the positive. Be purposeful about recalling happy or funny teaching moments.
  - You cannot control everything. Put in your best effort and remember that there are elements of learning well beyond your control.
  - Remember why you signed up for this! When things get hard, go back to the basics of what teaching means to you.
  - Lean on others. Maintain a good support network of educators and noneducators and lean on them when you need them.
  - Develop a self-care routine and stick to it. When you feel like you don't have time for it is when you need it most.

Self-Reflective Activity

Take a moment to write a letter to your future self as a teacher. In the future, what do you want to remind yourself of? Think of the reasons you entered the profession, as well as your beliefs and values. What inspired you to become a teacher? Thinking ahead, what makes you most excited about being a teacher? What do you hope to instill in your students? What do you want your students to remember about you when they leave school?

Small Group Activities

Activity 1. What I Can and Cannot Control

Read the following statement and discuss in your group the (1) things you can control in the classroom, (2) things you can influence in the classroom, and (3) things you cannot control or influence in the classroom.

- My lesson plans and how I teach my lessons
- How I decorate my classroom environment
- My emotional response to students/colleagues/school leadership
- Student behavior and engagement
- My attitude, thoughts, and beliefs regarding my students
- Giving help to students who may be struggling academically
- Educational policy
- My attitude, thoughts, and beliefs regarding teaching
- Overall school goals, community, and expectations
- Students' abilities
- My personal and professional goals
- The standards that govern the curriculum I teach
- Others' opinions or thoughts about me as a teacher
- What I choose to pay attention to and not give attention to

Activity 2. Letter to Ms. Lin

The following is a scenario involving a first-year teacher, Ms. Lin. As a group, write a letter to Ms. Lin and encourage her. Provide her with tools to increase her own well-being, as well as ways to help shape her thinking so that she can feel more confident in her abilities. Think about what you would need to hear in this situation. What information have you learned in this book that would be helpful for Ms. Lin? Additionally, think of one way you can promote teacher well-being at school. What activities or supports could you advocate that your school put into place to help decrease teacher burnout?

> Ms. Lin is a first-year teacher who has just gotten back the results of the state tests for her students. She is shocked to see that approximately one-third of her class did not meet standards for proficiency on the reading assessment. Ms. Lin had envisioned herself as a helper for struggling students and someone who would promote learning in an underserved community. She feels an overwhelming sense of shame and wonders if she has made things worse for her students. She begins to contemplate whether she should have pursued a teaching career after all. As she goes on to start the afternoon reading lesson, she sees the class looking distracted and acting silly. She sighs and feels exhausted, wondering whether this lesson will even matter.

Activity 3. Emotionally Intelligent Classroom

For this activity, you will need poster paper, Post-its, and writing utensils.

Create a group poster titled "An Emotionally Intelligent Classroom." Focus on the emotional elements of the classroom environment that foster learning and relationships. Reflect on what makes an emotionally intelligent classroom and write each idea on a Post-it. Consider what an emotionally intelligent classroom would look like, sound like, and feel like. These could be single words ("trust") or phrases ("being aware of my own attachment"). Then, take some time to consider explicitly the perspective of your students. What would they say makes an emotionally intelligent classroom? When you've generated all of your ideas, consider how to arrange them on the poster. Did certain themes emerge? What ideas go together? After you have finished, reflect on how you felt working on this project.

REFERENCES

Cross, D. I., & Hong, J. Y. (2012). An ecological examination of teachers' emotions in the school context. *Teaching and Teacher Education, 28*(7), 957–967. https://doi.org/10.1016/j.tate.2012.05.001

Day, C. (2011). Uncertain professional identities: Managing the emotional contexts of teaching. In C. Day & J. C.-K. Lee (Eds.), *New understandings of teacher's work* (pp. 45–64). Springer. https://doi.org/10.1007/978-94-007-0545-6

Hargreaves, A. (1994). *Changing teachers, changing times: Teachers' work and culture in the postmodern age*. Teachers College Press.

Jordan, J. V., & Schwartz, H. L. (2018). Radical empathy in teaching. *New Directions for Teaching and Learning, 2018*(153), 25–35.

Lasky, S. (2005). A sociocultural approach to understanding teacher identity, agency and professional vulnerability in a context of secondary school reform. *Teaching and Teacher Education, 21*, 899–916. https://doi.org/10.1016/j.tate.2005.06.003

Loonstra, B., Brouwers, A., & Tomic, W. (2009). Feelings of existential fulfilment and burnout among secondary school teachers. *Teaching and Teacher Education, 25*(5), 752–757. https://doi.org/10.1016/j.tate.2009.01.002

Mansfield, C. F., & Beltman, S. (2014). Teacher motivation from a goal content perspective: Beginning teachers' goals for teaching. *International Journal of Educational Research, 65*, 54–64. https://doi.org/10.1016/j.ijer.2013.09.010

Mayer, D. (2011). "But that's the thing: Who else is going to teach besides the idealist?" Learning to teach in emotional contexts. In C. Day & J. C.-K. Lee (Eds.), *New understandings of teacher's work* (pp. 137–150). Springer. https://doi.org/10.1007/978-94-007-0545-6

Nair, I. (2018). Joy of being a teacher. *Teaching and Learning, 2018*(153), 45–54. https://doi.org/10.1002/tl.20280

O'Connor, K. E. (2008). "You choose to care": Teachers, emotions and professional identity. *Teaching and Teacher Education, 24*(1), 117–126. https://doi.org/10.1016/j.tate.2006.11.008

Palmer, P. J. (1997). The heart of a teacher identity and integrity in teaching. *Change: The Magazine of Higher Learning, 29*(6), 14–21. https://doi.org/10.1080/00091389709602343

Ryff, C. D. (2014). Psychological well-being revisited: Advances in the science and practice of eudaimonia. *Psychotherapy and Psychosomatics, 83*, 10–28. https://doi.org/10.1159/000353263

Schwarzer, R., & Hallum, S. (2008). Perceived teacher self-efficacy as a predictor of job stress and burnout: Mediation analyses. *Applied Psychology, 57*, 152–171. https://doi.org/10.1111/j.1464-0597.2008.00359.x

Shulman, L. S. (2004). *The wisdom of practice: Essays on teaching, learning, and learning to teach*. Jossey-Bass.

Skaalvik, E. M., & Skaalvik, S. (2007). Dimensions of teacher self-efficacy and relations with strain factors, perceived collective teacher efficacy, and teacher burnout. *Journal of Educational Psychology, 99*(3), 611–625. https://doi.org/10.1037/0022-0663.99.3.611

Sonnentag, S., & Binnewies, C. (2013). Daily affect spillover from work to home: Detachment from work and sleep as moderators. *Journal of Vocational Behavior, 83*, 198–208. https://doi.org/10.1016/j.jvb.2013.03.008

Zaccaro, A., Conversano, C., Lai, E., & Gemignani, A. (2019). Relationship between emotions, sleep and well-being. In A. Pingitore, F. Mastorci, &

C. Vassalle (Eds.), *Adolescent health and wellbeing* (pp. 153–166). Springer. https://doi.org/10.3934/Neuroscience.2018.1.1

Zembylas, M. (2005). Discursive practices, genealogies, and emotional rules: A poststructuralist view on emotion and identity in teaching. *Teaching and Teacher Education, 21*(8), 935–948. https://doi.org/10.1016/j.tate.2005.06.005

Index

achievement emotions 89
acting out behaviors 102
ADHD *see* attention deficit hyperactivity disorder (ADHD)
affective forecasting 3
African Americans, emotion regulation in 79
aggression 23–24, 35; *see also* anger
anger 23–24; attributional bias 23; in children 103–104; and tantrum 121; in teachers 164–165
anxiety 11, 21–23, 51, 91–92; and avoidance 13, 92; classroom 92–94; provoking situations 22–23; reducing 8; test 91
appraisals 11, 14–16, 148
Arab cultures 79–80
Asian Americans, emotion regulation in 79
Asian countries, cultural values in 73
attachment 58–60; disorganized 60, 116; insecured 59, 103, 116–118; secured 59
attentional deployment strategy 49
attention deficit hyperactivity disorder (ADHD) 65
attributional bias 23
autistic children 65, 122

basic emotions 61
basking 41
behavioral activation 63
beliefs, and emotions 18, 28
body scan meditation 170
boredom 12, 94–96

centering practice 18–19
children: challenges for immigrant 80–81; emotion socialization in 4; with insecure attachment 116–118; practicing negative behaviors 102; with special needs 65–66; with trauma, emotion regulation in 118–121; *see also* emotional competencies, in children; emotional development, in children
children's emotions, understanding and responding to: contextual knowledge of 102–103; emotional coaching 106–107; emotional disconnection 107–108; empathetic attunement 104–106; signaling child's needs 103–104; teacher's emotional experiences and reactions 104
Chinese schools 78
classroom: anxiety in 92–94; as complex social context 1; emotion-eliciting situations in 6, 43–44, 97–98; mixed emotions 43–44; *see also* positive emotions, in classroom; students' emotions, in classroom; teachers' emotions, in classroom
cognitive change strategy 50
collectivistic cultures 74–75
contextual cues to emotions 153
cultural orientations 74–75
cultural values 73, 75
culture(s): cultural orientations 74–75; emotional life of immigrant children

80–81 ideal affect 76; parenting and child emotional development 77; socialization in schools 77–78
curiosity 13, 96–97

deep breathing 8, 93, 149–150, 155–156
depression 25; in children 121; and guilt 165; in parents 64
developmental language disorders 65
discipline 139–140
disorganized attachment 60, 116
distress, and tantrum 121

East Asian cultures 14, 72, 78; balanced view of emotions 75; emotional calmness 76
emotional acceptance 44
emotional arousal 15, 65, 149–150
emotional awareness 43–45, 52, 145–146
emotional burnout 104, 166–167
emotional coaching 106–107
emotional competencies, in children: emotional awareness skills 145–146; emotional vocabulary 151–152; emotion regulation 147–149; reducing emotional arousal 149–150; self-talk 148–149; teaching children to express emotions 150–151; understanding others' emotions 152–154
emotional cues 101–102, 153
emotional development, in children: attachments 58–60; children with special needs 65–66; cultural models of parenting and 77; in early childhood 60–62; socialization in families 64–65; and temperament 62–63
emotional disassembly 62
emotional disconnection 107–108
emotional dysregulation: in children with trauma 118–121; and tantrum 121–125; teachers' response to child with 125–126; understanding insecure attachment of children 116–118
emotional exhaustion 45
emotional expressions 44, 45–47, 102, 150–151
emotional intelligence 3–4, 184
emotional labor 165–166
emotional schemas 61, 103
emotional skills 60, 66

emotional vocabulary 44, 46, 154; in early childhood 60–61; strategies to teach 151–152
emotional well-being, of teachersdeveloping self-efficacy 164, 177–178; finding joy in teaching 179; goals and values awareness 176–177; positive emotional experiences 178; purpose and meaning 180; self-care routine 181–182; separating professional and personal identities 178
emotion regulation 47–48, 75; *attentional deployment* strategy 49–50; in children with trauma 118–121; *cognitive change* strategy 50; in different cultural groups 78–80; *response modulation* strategy 50–51; *situation modification* strategy 49; *situation selection* strategy 49; in students 147–149; of teachers 167
emotions: accepting 55; achievement 89; and appraisals 11, 14–16, 17–18; basic 61; and beliefs 5–6, 18, 28; in classroom 6; contagious nature 90; contextual 13–14; creative ways to express 155; disassembled 62; display rules 165; eliciting situations 97–98, 102–103, 145, 151; explosive displays of 47; expressive 10; functional 11–12, 25, 46, 47; informative 12–13; leading to actions 13; and learning 89–90; linked to learning 89–90; mixed 43–44; modulation of 155; multidimensional 10–11; secondary 45; self-critical 25; traumatic children 118–121; understanding others 152–154; *see also* children's emotions, understanding and responding to; negative emotions; positive emotions; positive emotions, in classroom; students' emotions, in classroom; teachers' emotions, in classroom
emotion socialization: in children 4; in families 64–65; and schools 77–78
emotion words 75, 155
empathetic attunement 104–106
empathy 36, 62, 105, 106
experiential suppression 50–51
expressive suppression 151

facial expressions 6, 10–11, 153; books with 76; of emotions 10–11, 12, 46; mirroring 37
emotions socialization in families 64–65
feelings 11; *see also* emotions
flight/fight/freeze stress response 116

gratitude 35–36
grounding 131
guilt 25–27, 164–165

hope 34
humor 38–39

ideal affect cultural models 76
immigration, as stressors for children 80–81
individualistic cultures 74–75
insecure attachment 59, 103, 116–118
interests 34

joy 34

laughter 38–39
learning, and emotions 89–90
loneliness 80
love 37–38
loving-kindness meditation 112–113

meditation 93, 98
metatheories of emotions 64
mindfulness 84
mindful walking 30–31
mixed emotions, in classroom 43–44
moral reasoning, emotion-based 62

negative emotions 1, 11, 46, 88; anger 23–24; anxiety 21–23; avoiding 44; sadness 24–25; shame and guilt 25–27
negative self-talk 92

Om/Aum meditation 84–85

peer relationships 90–91, 133
positive affirmations 68–69
positive emotional experiences 178
positive emotions 1, 88; gratitude 35–36; humor and laughter 38–39; love 37–38; pride 34–35
positive emotions, in classroom: autonomy 136–137; competence 136; dimensions of teacher-student relationships 134–135; discipline with care 139–140; high expectations and confidence in students 137–138; importance of teacher-student relationships 134; infusing 137; making students proud for achievements 138–139; relatedness 135–136; student needs and relationships 135–137;
positivity resonance 37
preschool years, emotional regulation during 61–62
pride 34–35, 76, 138
progressive muscle relaxation 157–158
psychological needs 12

racial discrimination 79
reappraisals of emotions 50, 148, 170
response inhibition 48
response modulation strategy 50–51

sadness 24–25, 80
Sanctuary Model 120
savoring 41
schools/schooling 81; appropriate emotions 14; in Chinese culture 79; in Japan 78; socialization of emotions in 77–78; in United States 73–74
secondary emotions 45
secure attachment 59
self-critical emotions 25
self-efficacy 4, 164, 177–178
self-talk 148–149
shame 25–27, 79–80
situation modification strategy 49
situation selection strategy 49
socialization of emtoions 4, 64–65, 77–78
special needs children 65–66
stress: reduction techniques 8, 93
students' emotions, in classroom: anxiety 91–94; behavior 163; boredom 94–96; curiosity 96–97; emotional contagion 90; emotional disconnection of teachers 107–108; emotions linked to learning 89–90; peer relationships 90–91; performance 162–163; sources of emotions 89–91; teachers high expectations/confidence in 137–138; teachers' instruction and behavior 90

student-teacher relationships: dimensions of 134–135; emotional/organizational support in 133; importance of 134; negative 141; power struggles in 141

tantrums: causes of 122; and emotion dysregulation 121–122; phases of 122–123; responding to 123–125

teacher(s): anger 164–165; developing self-efficacy 164, 177–178; emotional disconnection from students 107–108; emotional experiences and reactions 104; emotion regulation of 167; empathy towards students 105; finding joy in teaching 179; goals and values awareness 176–177; identity and emotions 174–176 positive emotional experiences 164, 178; purpose and meaning 180; response to emotionally dysregulated child 125–126; self-care routine for 181–182; self-efficacy 164, 177–178; separating professional and personal identities 178; *see also* emotional well-being, of teachers; student-teacher relationships; teachers' emotions, in classroom

teachers' emotions, in classroom: anger and guilt 164–165; changes in educational setting 163–164; emotional burnout 48, 166–167; emotional labor 165–166; emotion regulation 167;

temperament 62–63, 116

temper tantrums *see* tantrums

trauma-related triggers 119

traumatized children: emotion/emotion regulation in 118–121; supporting 120–121

United States: cultural values in 73; meaning of shame 27

value appraisal 89

visualization 93, 150

worry 93; *see also* sadness

Printed in the United States
by Baker & Taylor Publisher Services